The New Europe
An Economic Geography of the EEC

G. N. Minshull

HOLMES & MEIER PUBLISHERS, INC.
NEW YORK

First published in the United States of America 1978 by
HOLMES & MEIER PUBLISHERS, INC.
30 Irving Place, New York, N.Y. 10003

Library of Congress Cataloging in Publication Data

Minshull, G. N.
  The New Europe, An Economic Geography of the EEC.
  Bibliography: P.
  Includes Index.
  1. European Economic Community Countries.
  1. Title.
  HC241.2.M49   1978   382′.9142   78-6581

ISBN 0-8419-0391-3

Printed in Great Britain

Contents

Preface and Acknowledgements

This book places into a geographical context the significant changes which have taken place in Western Europe since 1945. Great Britain's relationship with Europe is described and placed into the context of European integration. Geographical themes are examined within the framework of the origins, evolution, organisation and policies of the European Community. The economic geography of the nine Common Market countries is analysed thematically, and nine regions are chosen to illustrate the concept of the 'Core and Periphery'. The Community core is identified, and its essential unity demonstrated in relation to the ideas embodied in the Schumann declaration, 'Always prescribed by Geography, always prevented by History'.

My thanks are due to the European Communities Information Services in Brussels and London. Most of the information in the maps and tables is compiled from the statistics, data, reports and monographs issued by the European Community. Many other sources have been valuable, particularly *The Economist*, *The Times* and *The Guardian*, and *The Europa Year Book*. Books and learned journals which have been used are identified and acknowledged in the bibliography. Much of the material used has been compiled during periods of travel and field-study in Europe. I would like to thank the various embassies and information bureaux of the EEC for providing information, and also the following companies and institutions for permission to reproduce photographs in this book: Aerofilms Ltd. (pp. 40, 99, 108, 125, 131, 209, 258); The Belgian National Tourist Office (pp. 36, 42, 72, 112); Adam Opel AG (p. 169); British Steel Corporation (p. 62, top and bottom); Terence Soames (Cardiff) Ltd. (p. 71); The Irish Tourist Board (p. 103); The Royal Danish Embassy (pp. 107, 110, 128); The Italian State Tourist Centre (pp. 111, 220, 233); The Royal Netherlands Embassy (pp. 135, 200, 205, 206, 208).

I am indebted to all those people who have given advice, in particular Professor Allan Patmore, Michael Bradshaw and Roger Stone. Finally, I would like to thank my wife and family for their patience, assistance and understanding over a number of years.

G. N. Minshull
1978

1

The nation state and the EEC

The theme of this book is the change in the economic fortunes of Western Europe from the nineteenth century to the present day, and the internal and external pressures which are altering its whole economic and political structure. Essentially it relates to the growth and enlargement of the 'European Economic Community', often known as 'The Common Market'. (fig. 1.1.)

The principal characteristics of Western Europe may be summarised thus: countries with a relatively small land area and great physical diversity; many nation states separated by historic precedent and language barriers; wealthy countries with relatively dense populations; an industrialised and urbanised way of life; a well-watered environment with adequate fertile land and a temperate climate which supports a commercial system of agriculture.

Western Europe produced great trading nations from very early times. The early city states of Venice and Genoa were founded upon trade with the Mediterranean and the East. As early as the eleventh and twelfth century the Netherlands and Belgium were the centres for the trading activities of the Hanseatic League, and Bruges, Ghent and Amsterdam were famous trading ports. The British Empire was built initially around a nucleus of trading posts, and seapower was a major factor in its expansion. Overseas trade has become an essential part of life in Western Europe and great difficulties arise if any particular raw material is in short supply. An example is the supply and price of oil from the Middle East, which, when threatened in the Suez crisis of 1956, caused a petrol shortage, and which since 1973 has been a major cause of economic crisis. A prolonged strike in a key industry in the United Kingdom affects exports adversely and causes a balance of payments crisis. The United Kingdom exports a third of its car production, two-fifths of its engineering and metal products, and a third of its chemical manufactures.

The nineteenth and early twentieth century

Western Europe: the site of the 'Industrial Revolution'

Industrial growth began in Western Europe from the late eighteenth century onwards. The use of coal and steam power together with iron and steel products forged the basic industrial sinews with which these countries were able to act as world powers. In Great Britain the creation of canals and then railway transport

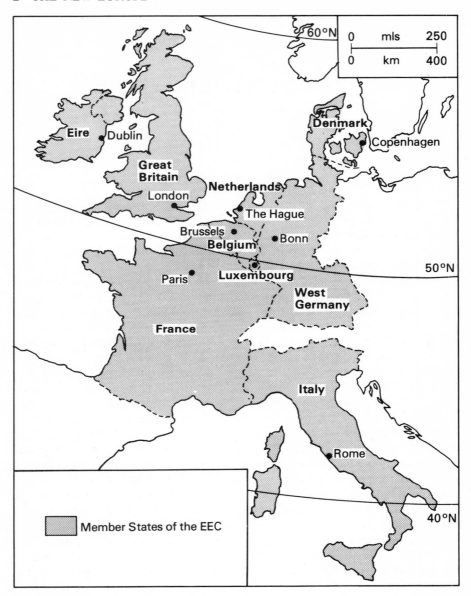

Figure 1.1 Member States of the European
Economic Community.

gave a new efficient mobility to the movement of raw materials and industrial
products. A powerful navy provided maritime supremacy and allowed the
consolidation of imperial possessions over a quarter of the world's surface. The
influx of raw materials from the colonies and the demands of their growing
market served the industries and increased the export trade. The nation states
of Europe, particularly Great Britain, but also France, the Netherlands,

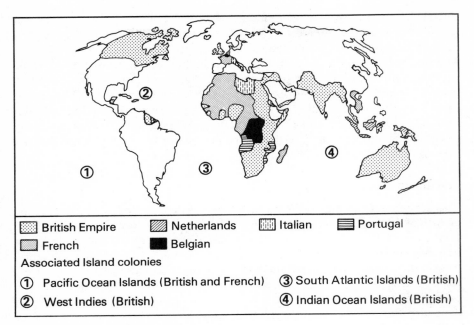

Figure 1.2 Colonial empires of Europe at their greatest extent, post 1918.

Belgium and eventually Germany, became world powers, with large colonial empires (fig. 1.2). The phrase 'workshop of the world' was used to describe Great Britain in the mid-nineteenth century. This was no myth. Great Britain was the first in the field with industrial production, and had little or no competition. In 1870 she produced seventy per cent of the world's ships and despatched huge exports of coal, steel and textiles to all parts of the world. Many of the world's railway systems such as those of Chile, Argentina and India were built with British capital, manufactured products and expertise. At the end of the nineteenth century Western Europe as a whole accounted for approximately ninety per cent of world industrial production.

The loss of world power status

By the mid-twentieth century, however, it was apparent that the economic supremacy of Western Europe could not last. Other factors had emerged. The small nation states of Europe were caught up in the exhaustive process of fighting two world wars, as a direct result of which their stock-in-trade of railways, port facilities and industries was badly damaged. The cost of fighting the Second World War left the UK in debt to the USA, and all the nations of Western Europe had to accept Marshal Aid from the USA. The French railway system had to be completely rebuilt. The German Ruhr was devastated. Production of basic industries throughout Europe was dislocated up to 1948, after which the flow of economic aid through the Organisation for European Economic Co-operation (OEEC) began a slow recovery. The wartime disruption of trade had forced the primary producing countries to look elsewhere for their imports of manufactured goods (often the United States), or make them at home, and after the war these markets were no longer assured to the Western European nations. The change in attitudes and political awareness throughout the world forced the rapid dissolution of the colonial empires so that from 1945 to the mid-1960s practically all the former European colonies became independent. This meant that the sources of raw materials and the colonial markets were no longer under the political control of Europe. Great Britain and France were reduced effectively to nations of approximately 50 million people, Great Britain being very heavily dependent upon imports of both food and raw materials.

The emergence of the 'super-powers'

The declining advantage of Western Europe has contrasted strongly with the growth of the 'super powers', the USA and USSR (and in the near future, China). By the twentieth century the land powers based upon huge continental interiors had overtaken the smaller Western European nation states. These continental powers have emerged with certain basic advantages. Their huge size was once a disadvantage, but now they have efficient internal lines of communication, brought by the trans-continental railway and the airlines. They thus gain from their large land space, huge populations and vast reserves of mineral wealth, which makes them less dependent on world trade. The USA is now in a position where San Francisco and New York, over three thousand miles apart, are in fact only hours distant from each other. The USSR is ninety times as large as the United Kingdom and nine times larger than Western Europe. Apart from their great size and resources the two super powers also dwarf the individual Western European countries in terms of their industrial production. Reference to the steel industry shows the weakness in size of the individual European countries. In 1973 even West Germany's steel output of 49 million tonnes does not bear comparison with that of USSR (131 million tonnes), or USA (139 million tonnes). Figure 1.3 shows that the contrast is particularly dramatic in the case of Great Britain, which was certainly a world power politically, economically and militarily during the nineteenth and early twentieth century. Only in terms of export trade, merchant shipping, and per capita wealth and consumption is there any valid comparison with USA and USSR. The continental powers are practically self-sufficient. Their latitudinal extent and extensive agricultural interiors mean that practically all their food supplies can be produced within their own frontiers. This is contrasted with the very limited temperate zone extent of the individual European powers. The comparisons of food production show why the USA, although the richest country in the world, is not, pro rata, the greatest trading nation. She does not need to trade as do the Western European nations.

The importance of economies of scale

There is also a very important economic factor. In modern technological civilisation the product of a large economic unit is more efficient than the sum of its parts. In a continental unit such as the USA there is unhindered movement

	USA	USSR	UK	EEC 6	EEC 9
Area (1000 km^2)	9100	35000	244	1172	1529
Population (millions) 1975	219	255	55	183	260
Cars per 1000 inhabitants 1973	460	7	234	251	246
Steel production (million tonnes) 1973	139	131	27	122	150
Steel consumption per head (kilogrammes)* 1973	723	516	460	542	516
Energy consumption per head (tce) 1973	11440	5005	5496	4797	4950
Grain production (million tonnes) 1970–72 (average)	214	170	15	75	97
Meat production (million tonnes) 1973	24	14	3	14	19
Motor car production (millions) 1973	8·8	0·7	1·9	8·5	10·5
Exports (million $) 1973	57000	14000*	24374	136908	167931
Crude oil refining production (m. tonnes) 1973	588	na	105	459	578
Coal production (m. tonnes) 1973	537	499	130	140	270
Gross domestic product (1000 m. UA) 1973	1038	na	138	670	835
Merchant shipping (m. tonnes gross) 1973	14·9	17·4	30·2	31·3	65·7

tcs = tonnes of coal equivalent
* estimated
na = not available
UA = EEC unit of account

Figure 1.3 Table of comparative economic resources, 1973.

of raw materials, labour, capital, and the finished product, to all parts of the country, allowing specialisation in favourable localities. By contrast the national frontiers of Europe have hitherto hindered the marriage of, for instance, Ruhr coking coal with Lorraine iron ore. A large population provides a basic and substantial home market. Without this assured home market within which to sell goods it is very difficult for industry to sustain large-scale production. It is not worth investing huge amounts of money in plant and equipment unless a profit is guaranteed, and this profit comes primarily from the home market.

Mass production and assembly-line methods work most efficiently under economies of scale, and when they serve a large market. The American car industry is so large that one single company, General Motors, produces more than the entire British car industry. The more that is produced, the less proportionately each unit costs. Thus the Americans can sustain large-scale production efficiently and at relatively lower cost. Also the cost of industrial technology, research and specialised equipment is now so great that smaller countries have difficulty in finding the money needed for research and development. An example here is the space programme and aero-engine production. What happened to Rolls-Royce in 1971 is a case in point. The very advanced RB 211 engine needed so much research and development money before any payment was forthcoming from US aircraft companies, and the costs escalated so far beyond the estimates, that the Company could not find the money and went bankrupt. The cancellation of the Bluestreak Rocket is a similar example. On the other hand, British and French firms have combined to make possible the Concorde, the most advanced civil aircraft in the world. A study of Great Britain during the mid-twentieth century reveals a prolonged fight for her export markets against increasing, efficient, and often superior competition. There has been such a low growth rate because of the near static home market, a steady invasion by American industry, and a lack of investment in new equipment and industrial technology. One conclusion is that fifty-five million people is not a sufficiently large economic base in the rigorous conditions of modern international competition. The optimum size for a modern industrial state might well appear to be approximately two hundred million people.

Unification in Western Europe

A change of the greatest significance has been taking place in Western Europe since 1945. In its economic context it is a reflection of the relative decline in the status of these nation states since the nineteenth century. The rapid progress made towards economic interdependence is one side of the coin. The other side is that of internationalism. The replacement of the fifteen or so nations of Western Europe by a unified state has never really been an accomplished fact since the days of the Roman Empire, or perhaps since Charlemagne in the ninth century. All attempts since then by individual nations to impose unity upon Europe have resulted in wars, culminating in the devastation of 1945. The revolution in political cooperation which has occurred since then stems from the desire for creating unity, maintaining peace and increasing security. The radical difference is that the movement towards unity is now a step-by-step process, accomplished by agreement between the nations concerned, and is therefore a spontaneous political act from within each nation.

Post-war co-operation in Europe: the initial stages

The need for co-operation

A large number of attempts at increased cooperation emerged out of the economic chaos which faced Europe in 1945. Recovery required a joint programme of economic aid and monetary cooperation which was given form and direction by OEEC, the Organisation for European Economic Cooperation. This involved very substantial American aid which was received by eighteen nations in all. In the sphere of defence, the Western European Union, composed of Britain, France and the Benelux countries, was supplanted in April 1949 by that most important body The North Atlantic Treaty Organisation (NATO). Aimed at the collective defence of North America, the North Atlantic Zone and Europe, this has been one of the most significant and successful steps towards continental security. Political cooperation began in May 1949 with the Council of Europe. This is a consultative assembly in Strasbourg which deals with cultural, administrative and social matters of general interest. It has no executive powers, but is a useful 'talking shop'.

Benelux

In 1947 the Benelux Union was formed by Belgium, The Netherlands and Luxembourg. Although these are three of the smallest nations in Western Europe, it was an initial movement of the greatest significance. The union allowed for the free movement of capital, persons, services and goods across frontiers, for the coordination of economic policy, and for a common trade policy towards countries external to the union. These criteria of economic integration were a pointer to the future.

The European Free Trade Area

The European Free Trade Area (EFTA), formed in November 1959, was a looser association of seven nations with the more limited object of 'the abolition of all tariffs on industrial goods between the seven member states'. These were the United Kingdom, Norway, Sweden, Denmark, Portugal, Switzerland and Austria. EFTA was not a customs union, but was a means of expanding trade and ensuring that a broad alignment in tariff reductions was kept in line with that of the EEC which was already in existence. The United Kingdom certainly saw it as a 'bridge', or bargaining counter for the time when she could negotiate full membership of the EEC. Although the free trade area still functions, it is at a reduced level since the United Kingdom, Eire and Denmark are now members of the EEC.

The European Economic Community (the Common Market)

One market for coal and steel

The European Coal and Steel Community (ECSC) was set up on 18th April 1951 by France, West Germany, Italy and the three Benelux Union countries. A supra-national authority was formed to administer the coal and steel industries of the six countries, and to 'abolish import and export duties, subsidies and restrictive practices, and to establish free and unrestricted movement of coal, iron-ore, scrap, pig-iron and steel between the member countries'. As an experiment in cooperation this was a crucial pointer to the future. Six European

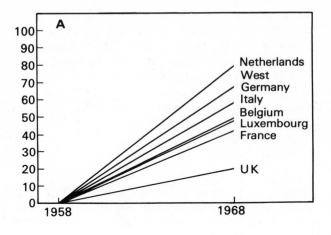

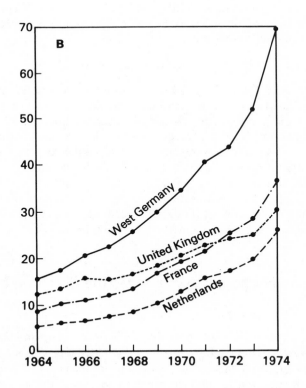

Figure 1.4 Selected growth rates. (A) Per cent rise in real wages 1958–1968. (B) Total export trade (1000 m UA). (C) Index of industrial production (1963 = 100) (D) Growth of Gross Domestic Product (Comparative 1973 figures: USA = 1038; EEC Nine = 835).

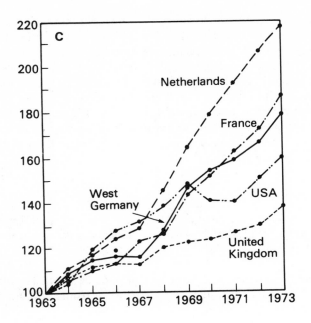

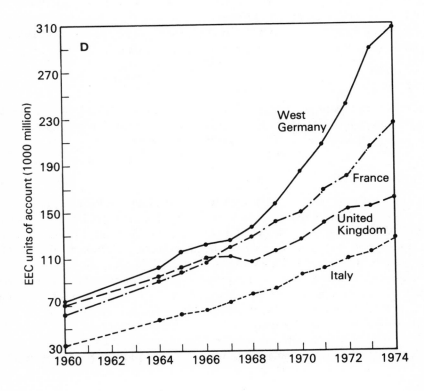

countries had placed a basic sector of their economy into a common pool administered by a supra-national authority. This psychological success has been matched by dramatic practical results. The production of crude steel and rolled products by the 'Six' rose dramatically, from 1952 (42 million tonnes) to 1971 (103 million tonnes). The Heavy Industrial Triangle (chapters 2 and 3) found a new impetus with the cross-frontier integration of its resources. The ECSC also found a successful social and regional role. From 1957 the run-down of the coal industry necessitated plans for the retraining of workers, industrial development loans to overcome unemployment, and the adaptation of the industrial structure of declining areas.

The Common Market

The Treaty of Rome was signed on 25th March 1957. This established the basic tenet of economic integration by means of four progressive harmonisation processes. These were:

1. Internal tariffs: Barriers to the free flow of trade between 'The Six' were to be dismantled and customs duties on goods bought from each other were to disappear in stages.
2. Customs union: All six member states were to apply to external countries a common external tariff. This created a customs union with the six states progressively becoming one trading unit.
3. Internal mobility: There was to be free movement of labour, goods, services and capital between the six member countries.
4. Economic integration: Common policies throughout 'the Six' were to be applied to harmonise transport, industry, energy and agriculture.

Euratom

The European Atomic Energy Authority (Euratom) was set up for the co-ordination of nuclear research and to provide the conditions necessary for the ultimate production of nuclear energy on a large scale.

Economic growth

The most startling measure of success during the 1960s was the rate of economic growth of the 'Six'. Comparisons between the 'Six' and the United Kingdom from 1958 onwards (fig. 1.4) reveal many disparities in terms of growth of real incomes, gross domestic product per head, exports, and indices of industrial production. The Steel Industry (fig. 4.1) is a significant pointer to national growth, and this too shows rapid growth on the continent in contrast with stagnation in the UK. Whilst there are many and complex reasons for this pattern, and whilst the existence of the Common Market may be only partially responsible for the rapid growth, one indisputable fact remains. The EEC Six developed into a large and powerful economic group, capable of comparison with the major world continental powers, USA and USSR (fig. 1.3). Further-

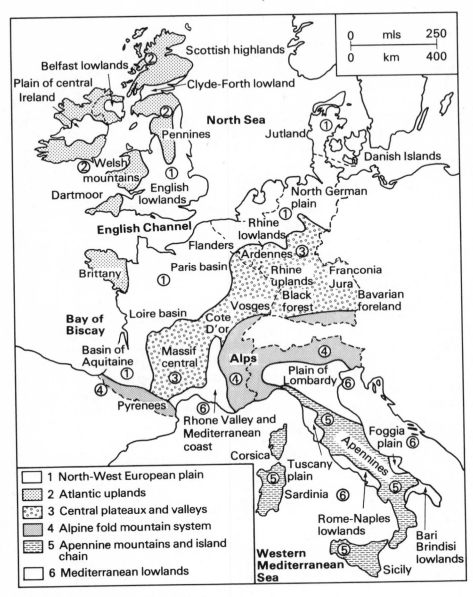

Figure 1.5 Physical regions of the Community.

more, the EEC as a whole is potentially self-sufficient in food. Across Western Europe are large stretches of agriculturally productive lowlands (fig. 1.5). There is a considerable latitudinal extent and a climatic range which gives a wide spectrum of agricultural types, and enables the EEC to be a major food producer. The advantages of scale and latitudinal extent are perhaps the two most significant criteria upon which the success of the Common Market is based.

Policies, progress and enlargement

The customs union and abolition of internal tariffs was completed by 1968, ahead of schedule, and during 1965 the three executives, ECSC, EEC and Euratom, had been merged into a single executive, known as the EEC Commission. Meanwhile the essential policies of economic integration were being created. In 1961 anti-monopoly regulations and steps to create free movement of labour, capital and services were devised. Implementation of the Common Agricultural policy began on 14th January 1962. In 1963 the Yaounde Convention was signed with eighteen African States. This was essentially a preferential trading relationship for the supply of tropical food and raw materials to the EEC in return for aid and a guaranteed market. It marked the emergence of the EEC as a trading unit of world dimensions.

During the 1960s there was a realisation in the United Kingdom that a significant and momentous change had occurred on the continent. The United Kingdom was now a small, highly populated island with a static home market and without the resource base of an empire, and was offshore to a developing continental unit of powerful proportions. On 8th November 1961 the United Kingdom, Eire, Denmark and Norway began negotiations for membership of the EEC. These lasted for nearly a decade, largely because of the intransigence of the French President, Charles de Gaulle, who insisted that Britain was not ready for community membership. Immediately after the resignation of De Gaulle in April 1969, negotiations were resumed and succeeded very quickly. By this stage the original Six had the will to enlarge and strengthen the community, and by 1970 the commission had submitted a plan for full economic and monetary union by 1980. On 1st January 1973 the United Kingdom, Eire and Denmark acceded to the EEC, now enlarged to nine member countries (fig. 1.6). The EEC had entered a new and decisive phase.

	Area (1000 km^2)	Population (millions) 1971	Population (millions) 1975 (estimated)
France	547	51·3	53·1
West Germany	249	61·3	61·6
United Kingdom	244	55·7	57·6
Italy	301	53·9	55·7
Eire	70	2·9	3·1
Denmark	43	4·9	5·1
Netherlands	41	13·1	13·6
Belgium	31	9·7	9·9
Luxembourg	3	0·3	0·3
Total	1529	253·1	260·0

Figure 1.6 Area and population figures.

The Community institutions

The main distinguishing feature of the EEC is its decision-making process (fig. 1.7).

(a) It is essentially a confederation of nation states, each with its own government. The Heads of Government meet periodically at 'Summit meetings', known as 'The European Council'.

(b) The nine governments are represented by one minister each on the nine-man 'Council of Ministers'. This body is the effective link between the national governments and the Commission, and it receives policy proposals from the Commission and takes decisions which are then passed back to the Commission for implementation.

(c) The European Commission is the executive, permanent civil service or workhorse of the community, with its headquarters in the Berlaymont Building in Brussels. It is directed by thirteen members, with France, West Germany, the United Kingdom and Italy having two members each, and The Netherlands, Belgium, Eire, Luxembourg and Denmark one each. The Commission initiates policies, drafts legislation, and administers the day-to-day mechanics of a customs union of 250 million people.

(d) There is also a large body of some 9000 people who are the working secretariat for the Commission and Council of Ministers.

(e) The Court of Justice, which sits in Luxembourg, administers EEC law and arbitrates in disputes involving the community treaties.

(f) The European Parliament at Strasbourg and Luxembourg, is the embryonic political body which it is envisaged will be directly elected during 1978 on a community bases. At the moment its members are appointed by the national governments, and it works on a consultative basis with specialised committees which review policy-making and other community matters.

The EEC consists essentially of nine countries which are increasingly delegating areas of broad economic policy to a common machinery so that decision-making lies between national governments (represented by the Council of Ministers) and the Commission.

The Community budget

The establishment of the EEC as a body acting on a European scale has necessitated the creation of its own independent funds. These have up to now been contributed by the member states on a sliding scale based largely upon each country's relative wealth and size, with West Germany thus paying the largest amount and Luxembourg the least. By 1980 it is proposed that these national contributions will have been phased out and the EEC Commission will have three direct sources of income: ninety per cent of the levies on imports of agricultural commodities; ninety per cent of customs duties; and one per cent of VAT proceeds. The budget is one of the most important elements allowing the EEC to function as an effective body.

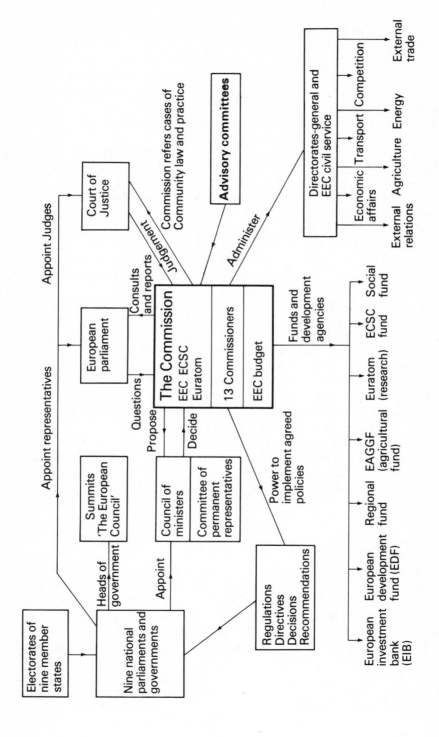

Figure 1.7 The structure and activities of the EEC.

Community funds and agencies

The Community agencies are the practical means by which the policies of economic integration are implemented (fig. 1.7). One of the earliest successes was the ECSC (chapter 2) in harmonising the coal and steel production of the Heavy Industrial Triangle, stabilising the coal industry during its long decline, retraining workers and promoting alternative industrial employment in the former coal areas. The European Social Fund has taken over much of the work associated with the ECSC and has become the principal agency for industrial retraining and social welfare schemes. The Common Agricultural Policy (chapter 6) has been concerned primarily with funds to stabilise farmers' incomes by means of the EAGGF (European Agricultural Guidance and Guarantee Fund). The EDF (European Development Fund) finances economic and social development schemes in countries which have association and trade agreements with the Community. Most important of all is the EIB (European Investment Bank). This works closely with the Commission and provides finance for development and modernisation projects. In the period 1954–1972 it lent 1500 million dollars, much of which went to Italy to support projects like the Val D'Aosta motorway, an essential link in the early integration of Italy with the rest of the EEC. Its work is described in more detail in chapter 10. The latest development was in 1974 with the inception of the Regional Policy (chapter 10). The financial aid available under this agency for any underdeveloped region in the EEC underlines the important principle that economic harmonisation between regions is as important as that between national economies.

The future

The greatest achievement of the EEC has been the progressive lowering of barriers, both economic and psychological, between the member states. The customs union has gone some way towards economic integration, but a great deal remains to be done. There are serious problems associated with the Common Agricultural Policy. The Regional Policy was adopted late in 1974, and energy and transport are posing major problems. Future policies will need to coordinate industry and technology. The environment and social policies are other areas for future negotiation.

Ambitious plans for full economic and political union have been set for completion by 1980, but it is highly unlikely that the EEC will be able to adhere to this time scale. Essential components of monetary union are a European currency, common taxation and fiscal policies and a common budget. An essential pre-requisite of this must be the implementation of direct elections and the delegation of more power to the European Parliament at Strasbourg. This is already planned for 1978 in an attempt to give the electorate direct representation and to move towards a supra-national government. There are already signs of harmonisation in the political field, with the community beginning to pursue external relations (the Energy Conference December 1975) with a single EEC spokesman for all the nine member states. This, for countries such as Great Britain and France with a long tradition of imperial diplomacy, is a revolutionary step. It illustrates the need to build up confidence in integration gradually.

This is the step-by-step process of integration favoured by the Functionalist school of thought. For the alternative Federalist school of thought the progress towards political union is all too slow and faltering.

Nevertheless, much has been accomplished already. The EEC has developed out of the almost ruined European civilisation of 1945. Most of Europe west of the River Elbe has, for the first time in history, joined in a voluntary association for the sake of peace and prosperity. The fragmented pattern of small nation states is in process of being changed into what some visionaries see as the United States of Europe. This unit has not such an extensive land area as the USA or USSR, but it is comparable to them in population and economic power (fig. 1.3).

2

Energy: a variety of sources

The Western European economy is based upon manufacturing industry and therefore has a fundamental requirement for large quantities of energy. Furthermore, energy needs to be available on a long-term, substantial and low-cost basis if industry is to plan and compete effectively. This chapter seeks to illustrate the diversity of energy resources which are now available to the EEC nations, and their changing geographical location.

There are five main primary sources of energy: coal, oil, natural gas, nuclear energy and water power. These are used for the direct production of heat; for industrial purposes, this is frequently converted immediately into electrical energy, which may be regarded as secondary energy. Electricity is perhaps the most significant of all twentieth century forms of energy because of its easily distributable nature and its liberalising effects upon industrial location.

Coal

Coal provided the energy for the industrial revolution which began in Western Europe in the eighteenth and nineteenth centuries. It occurred in thick seams at, or relatively near, the earth's surface and many coalfields such as the Ruhr, or Northumberland and Durham, were by rivers or the sea, facilitating easy movement in the days before a railway network was established. More important in the days of eighteenth and early nineteenth century technology was its versatility. As a source of direct heat it was used as a home fuel, as coke it could smelt iron-ore, and could be used in the manufacture of pottery, glass and in most basic industrial processes. It was the energy source which encouraged the development of steam-driven machinery and the locomotive. Coal powered the railway network of Europe and the navies which maintained British, French, Dutch and German colonies, trade and military supremacy. Its usefulness as an important source of energy has been prolonged into the twentieth century by its availability as a generator of electricity in power stations. In addition to contributing to the early industrialisation of the Continent, coal also dominated the original location of large-scale European manufacturing industry. Coal was low in value in relation to its bulk, being expensive to transport and inefficiently used, so that factories tended to concentrate close to the pit-head. Most nineteenth-century industrial regions developed on or near coalfields. The most industrialised nations of the EEC—West Germany, the United Kingdom and Belgium—

were those with the major coalfields. France and Italy, in particular, lagged behind the other nations because of their relatively poor endowment of coal. Italy
had scarcely any coal at all, and France only one producing field of any real size,
the Nord-Pas de Calais.

The major coalfields

There are two major coal provinces within Western Europe (fig. 2.1). In the
United Kingdom the surface coalfields are found generally north of a line from
Bristol to the Wash, and these gave rise to the concentration of British manufacturing in the Midlands and the North. Each coalfield specialised in a major
branch of manufacturing: for example steel and non-ferrous metallurgy in

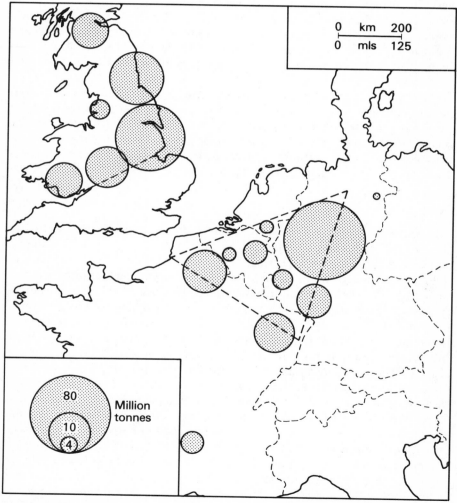

Figure 2.1 EEC coal-producing regions
1973/4 (million tonnes). *Problem:* Identify
each coal field or producing region. What
significant groupings are there?

South Wales, ship-building on the Clyde, and textiles in Lancashire and West Yorkshire. Such manufacturing zones developed their coal-based industrial activities during the nineteenth century and these dominated the United Kingdom economy until the inter-war period when coal was beginning to give way to the pressure of new energy sources.

The second major coal-based industrial area stretches from Lille in France across to Dortmund in West Germany. This contains the Nord-Pas de Calais field of France, stretching into the Sambre–Meuse coalfield of Belgium; the Kempenland and Limburg fields, extending eastwards to Aachen; and the Ruhr in West Germany. At the southern apex of the triangle lies the Saarland coal-basin and the coal and minette iron-ores of Lorraine and Luxembourg. These coalfields contain the vast majority of the manufacturing installations of Western Europe. This is the 'Heavy Industrial Triangle' which in 1952 was responsible for 95 per cent of the coal and 86 per cent of the steel produced in the six EEC countries. It is still the most significant area of heavy industry on the Continent.

Falling demand for coal

Technological changes and the discovery of new energy sources have caused a dramatic reduction in the role of coal since 1945. The exhaustion of the best and most easily accessible coal seams, the labour-intensive character of coal-mining and the expense of transporting it compared to alternative, competitive fuels, has meant that coal has become a very much more expensive source of energy. This process has been accompanied by the demise of the open coal-fire, together with the change in energy consumption from coal to oil and electricity by major users such as the railways, the shipping fleets and the steel industry. The blackening of city buildings and air pollution has caused twentieth-century man to turn to new and cleaner forms of energy. Primary hydrocarbon fuels such as oil and natural gas, the new technology fuel of nuclear energy, hydro-electric

	EEC 6		UK		EEC 9		
	1951	1972	1951	1973 (estimated)	1971	1973 (provisional)	1985 (objectives)
Coal	67	21·5	90	38·0	24·8	22·6	16
Lignite		2·8			2·8		
Oil		59·5		46·0	58·4	61·4	41
Natural gas	33	11·6	10	12·0*	9·5	11·6	24
Hydro-electric and nuclear energy		4·5		4·0	4·4	4·4	19
Total energy consumption (mtce)	353	954	225	307	1205	1437	2252

mtce = million tonnes coal equivalent
* Natural Gas reached a contribution in excess of 1% as recently as 1968. Since then its use in the UK has expanded enormously.

Figure 2.2 Percentages of primary energy consumption. N.B. In 1985 the Commission's medium-term objectives imply a major contribution by nuclear power (17% of the total, with only a 2% contribution by hydro-electricity).

power, and the secondary energy source electricity, have all combined to produce a highly varied energy supply (fig. 2.2). In addition, they are much more easily distributed and transferable by pipeline or cable, and are less bulky and heavy to transport. Coal, therefore, has become a high-cost and inconvenient fuel despite research into increasing its efficiency. As late as 1951, at the beginning of the EEC's existence, coal provided two-thirds of its primary energy and in the United Kingdom the proportion was as high as 90 per cent. Since then, however, although total energy requirements have risen, the share of coal has fallen dramatically, both relatively and absolutely. Coal production by the EEC Six fell from 234 million tonnes in 1961 to 146 million tonnes in 1972 and a similar fall is seen in the United Kingdom figures (fig. 2.3).

	Coal production by country *(million tonnes)*				*Significant collieries*	*Underground workers*	
	1961	1971	1972	1974	1971	1971	1974
West Germany	148·3	117·1	108·7	101·5	67	135 000	109 000
France	52·4	33·0	29·7	22·9	45	60 000	42 000
Netherlands	12·9	3·7	2·9	0·8	5	6 000	1 200
United Kingdom	193·5	147·1	119·5	109·2	292	221 000	169 000
Belgium	21·5	10·9	10·5	8·9	22	24 000	18 000

Luxembourg, Italy, Eire, Denmark, and the Netherlands (1974)—insignificant production

Figure 2.3 EEC coal production 1961–1974. Which countries have the most significant volume of production? Which EEC countries have the most efficient coal industry? In which countries has coal declined most, and why?

The smaller, modern coal industry

It has been necessary to contract and modernise the coal industries of Western Europe considerably (fig. 2.4). The National Coal Board (NCB) of the United Kingdom is an example of relative success in restructuring an old industry into a more competitive form. Several hundreds of the smaller and less productive pits have been closed and production concentrated in modern efficient pits. Productivity has been increased considerably by long-wall coal-face machinery, by power loading, and by the construction of power stations for electricity generation adjacent to the pitheads, thus reducing the transport costs of coal.

The labour force of over a million men in 1914 has thus been dramatically reduced (fig. 2.5). Mechanised coal-cutting and loading has increased from 2 per cent of total production in 1947 to 85 per cent in 1967. The East Midlands coalfield (Derbyshire, Nottingham, Leicester and Yorkshire) has now emerged as the most important region, producing half the United Kingdom total.

The pace of contraction has slowed considerably now that the NCB is producing 120 million tonnes of coal per year, the industry has slimmed to a more efficient size, and it is likely that it may have reached a period of stability, with even expansion possibilities in the wake of the 1973–1974 oil price rises.

Coalfield	1961	1971	1972	1974	Comment
Belgium					
Campine (Kempenland)	9·6	7·3	7·3	6·3	Now the most important Belgian coalfield.
South Belgium	11·9	3·6	3·1	2·6	Massive decline and adjustment.
West Germany					
Ruhr	120·3	96·4	88·9	83·8	Considerable rationalisation. 1974 production stabilised at 84 million tonnes.
Ville (Cologne) (Lignite field)	–	–	110·0	–	Made into briquettes as fuel.
Aachen	8·7	6·8	6·5	6·2	
Saar	16·0	10·6	10·4	8·9	
Lower Saxony	2·0	2·9	2·6	2·2	
France					
Nord/Pas de Calais	26·9	14·5	12·6	9·0	Production cut to one-third since 1961.
Lorraine	14·0	11·5	10·9	9·1	The most efficient French coalfield with considerable reserves of 400 million tonnes.
Centre/Midi	11·2	6·9	6·2	4·8	Small isolated coal basins to be phased out completely.
Netherlands					
Limburg	12·9	3·7	2·9	0·8	Good quality coking coal but with the discovery of natural gas production has declined almost to nothing. In January 1973 only three mines left in operation.
United Kingdom					
Derby, Nottinghamshire and Yorkshire	82·7	68·5	55·8	55·0	The largest and most efficient British coalfield. It contains the newly discovered Selby field with estimated reserves of 500 million tonnes.
Northumberland and Durham	33·7	19·2	15·2	12·9	Considerable rationalisation.
West Midlands	16·1	8·6	6·5	5·4	Large areas exhausted. Production now confined to Cannock, Warwickshire.
Wales	18·2	12·1	9·5	7·4	Considerable exhaustion.
North West	12·8	13·5	10·6	9·9	Main productive area is the North Staffordshire coalfield.
Scottish	17·5	12·5	9·8	8·6	
Kent	1·5	1·0	0·7	0·6	
Opencast mines	8·6	10·6	10·4	9·8	

Figure 2.4 EEC coalfields production (million tonnes).

	Number of miners	Collieries	Production (tonnes)
1947	900 000	908	195
1956	704 700	840	209
1967	409 700	483	184
1971	285 000	292	147
1973	250 000	285	118

Figure 2.5 Changes in the United Kingdom coal industry.

The other major coal province in the EEC has experienced similar problems. Although there has been considerable retrenchment in total production, the pattern varies considerably. Productivity has been constantly low in the small isolated coal basins of the Centre/Midi of France (2200 kg per man shift) and the South Belgian Borinage coalfield (1800 kg per man shift). The Nord/Pas de Calais has always suffered from thin, disturbed seams and, with reserves practically exhausted and mining increasingly expensive, output is being cut back by some two million tonnes per year; it has now been cut to one-third since 1961 (fig. 2.4). By contrast, the most important single coalfield in Western Europe, the Ruhr, is far more productive. Its output per man shift was 3600 kg in 1970 and has now been raised to over 4000 kg. Lorraine is another efficient coalfield with an output of 3700 kg, and has become relatively much more important to France in the last decade. As in the United Kingdom, modernisation and rationalisation in these areas has been undertaken by large-scale authorities. The Charbonnages de France is a nationalised body created in 1946 which successfully increased coal production to a record of 59 million tonnes in 1958 and which has since carried out a controlled reduction. The Societé General of Belgium controls 40 per cent of the coal industry. The Ruhr coalfield was controlled by no less than twenty-six companies, but in 1969 these merged to form Ruhrkole AG which now controls 94 per cent of production in the Ruhr coal basin.

Co-operation in the coal industry

The importance of coal to the economies of Western Europe was recognised by the formation in 1951 of the first agency of cooperation, the ECSC (European Coal and Steel Community). Although it has since been integrated into the EEC treaties, it was the first significant area of economic cooperation and success in the post-war period. By the Paris Treaty of 1951, the original Six decided to remove internal price barriers and transport discrimination, customs duties and quotas on coal, coke, pig-iron, scrap and steel, thereby establishing a single market for these products. For the first time in history the great resource area of the 'Heavy Industrial Triangle' could be considered as one efficient geographical unit. Instead of four groups of national coalfields, separated by national frontiers, there was now a single resource of some 230 million tonnes of coal per annum on the market at a common price. More significantly, this cooperation had a major psychological value in pooling the resources of an area which had been a major bone of contention between France and Germany for over 150 years.

ECSC policy experienced a marked change in emphasis due to the changing role of coal. In 1951 coal played the largest part in energy supplies, providing 67 per cent of total energy of the original Six. This was a period of rapid post-war industrial growth and with an acute shortage of fuel, priority was given to the maximum output of coal. As an example, French production rose to a high point of 59 million tonnes in 1958.

During the 1960s this pattern changed dramatically. The ECSC controlled and guided the decline in coal production caused by competition from oil and natural gas, and cheaper imported non-Community coal. There was a phased reduction of output, and closure and amalgamation of collieries to create fewer but more efficient units. Annual demand for coal in the original Six dropped from 245 million tonnes in 1950 to 201 million tonnes in 1968 (fig. 2.2), and coal now provides less than a quarter of total energy consumption. In the United Kingdom, although the picture of decline is similar, the degree of dependence upon coal is much greater than on the continent, with coal still providing 40 per cent of total energy requirements. The improvement in the efficiency of the coal industry has been remarkable, with modernisation and mechanisation of collieries, Community grants for retaining redundant miners, housing grants, safety techniques examined and improved, and research into new uses for coal and its by-products. Particularly in the Franco–Belgian coalfield, there has been a wave of development of new industrial estates in the decaying mining areas. Altogether, about half a million workers have been retrained. The basic achievement of the ECSC has been to adapt its policies to periods of expansion and contraction and to have aided the restructuring of an ailing industry.

It is relevant at this stage to consider a third major period in the policy-making of the ECSC. From 1974 onwards, the costs of petroleum have increased dramatically because of the actions of the OPEC (Oil Producing and Exporting Countries) cartel. The French authorities have calculated that in early 1974 the production price of coal was 180 francs per tonne, as opposed to that of imported oil which was 250 francs per tonne. Two new developments would seem likely: the urgent tapping of the newly discovered hydrocarbon resources in the North Sea and adjacent continental shelf, and the re-examination of energy policies in the light of the new more highly competitive position of coal.

Oil

The consumption of oil in Western Europe has increased massively since the 1950s, at an average rate of 10 per cent per year. This is due partly to the relatively low cost of production of the refined product, vis-a-vis coal, and partly to the enormous advantage of oil in servicing large, expanding and non-competitive markets such as motor and aviation fuels. In addition, oil was competitive in the production of electricity in thermal power stations, and in home heating as well as in giving rise to by-products such as artificial fibres and plastics.

	Production	Imports
West Germany	6191	103319
United Kingdom	411	111646
France	1175	129814
Italy	1093	120236
Netherlands	1574	63927
Belgium	0	30398
Luxembourg	0	
Denmark	86	9363
Eire	0	2625
Total	10530	571238

Figure 2.6 EEC consumption of crude oil (1000 tonnes), 1974.

Consumption of oil by the enlarged EEC was over 580 million tonnes in 1974 (fig. 2.6). This represented approximately one-third of the international movement of oil since nearly all had to be imported, mainly from the Middle East. The oil proportion in the total fuel bill rose from 25 per cent in 1958 to 60 per cent in 1972 (fig. 2.2). Yet the EEC could produce only 5 per cent of this oil from its own reserves. This dependence on imported oil is therefore one of the EEC's most vulnerable points, both from a strategic point of view and in terms of pressure on the balance of payments.

In spite of this obvious weakness, the EEC relies upon oil for approximately 60 per cent of its energy requirements. The low cost oilfields exploited in many parts of the world are supplemented by ocean-going supertankers of one hundred thousand tonnes and over dead weight. These carry crude oil to the principal estuaries of Western Europe, at which point the oil is refined and then carried by pipe-line, road or railway. This is a well-integrated production–supply pattern, largely under the control of the major Western oil companies which, during the 1960s, allowed a huge expansion of low-cost industrial production. The pattern of oil refining in the EEC is almost entirely of coastal, riverside or estuarine refineries with ocean terminals for crude oil input (fig. 2.7). As consumption has increased so the refining capacity has enlarged dramatically. In the original Six, the refining capacity increased from 90 million tonnes in 1958 to 360 million tonnes in 1967, and in the enlarged EEC it reached 540 million tonnes by 1973.

A very important feature of relative costs of energy is seen in government controls. In the UK there has been a 40 per cent tax on fuel oil to bring its cost up to that of coal. Without this tax oil would have been so cheap that coal would be completely uncompetitive, and the tax was devised largely to arrest a too severe decline of coal with the associated problems of unemployment and the run-down of whole regions that would have followed. Even with the tax, oil was roughly competitive with coal.

Another aspect of this complex supply situation is the attempt to diversify

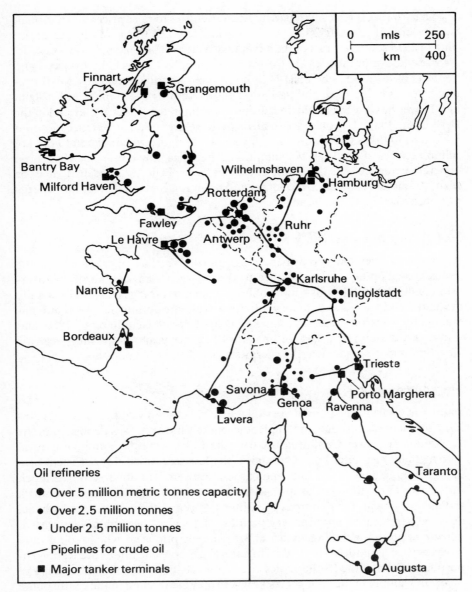

Figure 2.7 EEC oil-refining capacity. (From
D. J. Sinclair)

sources of supply so reducing the strategic risk of over-dependence upon any
one area. In 1958, the Middle East supplied 77 per cent of the original six EEC
countries' oil, whereas by 1968 this had fallen to 52 per cent. Today, North
Africa (Libya, Algeria and Mauretania) supplies one-third of the EEC's oil
requirements and increasing amounts are coming from the Far East. The UK is
taking more oil from Nigeria.

Furthermore, the recent moves by Arab countries to raise prices and nationalise Western oil companies have ended the low-cost advantage of oil. The beginning of 1974 saw a reversal of the advantage which oil has had for over a decade. As a result, exploration within the whole community has been intensified. Land deposits of oil have been disappointingly small and there are only small producing fields in the Lacq and Parentis areas of Aquitaine–Pyrenees, at Emsland and Lower Saxony in the North European basin, in the Rhine Valley and in the Paris basin. In the UK there are small fields in the Trent Valley, but these account for only 180 thousand tonnes of oil a year, a tiny figure when related to the 111 million tonnes of total UK consumption. There has, however, since 1965, been concrete evidence that the whole energy pattern of the enlarged EEC may be revolutionised by the discovery of oil and natural gas in an entirely new energy province, the North Sea basin.

North Sea gas and oil

A completely new energy province, the North Sea, has emerged during the 1960s, and its potential importance to the enlarged EEC can hardly be overestimated. This indigenous supply of both oil and natural gas has yet to be fully evaluated and estimates as to its value range from the optimistic view that it has enough hydrocarbon reserves to make Europe self-sufficient in oil by 1980, and that this situation might last for upwards of twenty years, to the more realistic view that it may supplement the energy supplies by at least one-third.

The source rocks

In the early part of the Permian period (circa 250 million years ago) the Hercynian Continent was eroded and the Rotliegendes sandstone was deposited in the North Sea area over Coal Measure deposits which were the source of natural gas (methane). In later Permian times a shallow sea, called the Zechstein Sea, in which large deposits of salts and carbonates were laid down, covered much of the area of north west Europe and the North Sea. Later the North Sea was a sedimentary basin for hundreds of millions of years, throughout the Triassic, Jurassic, Cretaceous and Tertiary periods, and so has become a vast area of marine deposits, including hydrocarbons, interruptions of which could only have been on a minor scale. The main natural gas concentrations are trapped in porous sections of the Rotliegendes and below the impermeable salt layers. The oil occurs mainly in the younger rocks where they are thickest in the centre of the North Sea.

The discovery of North Sea wealth

Exploration on the continent of Europe and in the United Kingdom, from the 1930s onwards, provided evidence of small oil and gas fields, but there was little encouragement to undertake the expense of searching for and developing resources under the North Sea on this evidence alone. In addition, marine technology in this field has had to develop very rapidly during the last few years to be capable of constructing and maintaining the large semi-submersible platforms necessary for drilling in up to 200 metres of stormy seas.

At Slochteren, a village in the Groningen province of Northern Holland, Shell and Esso struck natural gas in enormous quantities on 14th August 1959. Further drillings confirmed the vast size of the find—the estimated reserves of gas in this field are 2400 million tonnes of coal-equivalent. It may seem strange that a major gas field like this one at Slochteren had remained undiscovered for so long. One reason was the great depth of the gas, over 3 km below the surface.

Studies of the rock structures beneath the North Sea began with an airborne magnetometer survey of the entire area from southern Norway to the Straits of Dover, which indicated broad areas within which hydrocarbons were likely to be found. These are normally dome-like zones in which the oil and gas are trapped beneath impermeable rock layers. The first seismic survey of the United Kingdom part of the North Sea began in 1962 as a joint enterprise of Shell, Esso and British Petroleum. In July 1964, the Continental Shelf Act defined the territorial areas of the North Sea for the seven nations bordering it. The boundaries between the areas of the states concerned were defined by reference to a 'median line' (fig. 2.8). Concessions were granted to 23 consortia to drill for natural gas in specified 'blocks' in the United Kingdom area, each about 250 km^2 in area.

Natural gas

The first major strike of natural gas was made by British Petroleum late in 1965 in the Rotliegendes sandstone, some 70 km off the Humber estuary. An 80 km pipeline under the sea brought the first experimental quantities of gas from the under-sea wells to Easington on Humberside early in March 1967. The Gas Council has constructed a 60 cm feeder main, 120 km long, from Easington across the Humber to feed into the existing Canvey–Leeds methane pipeline. By May 1967, out of some 50 odd wells, 16 had shown really significant amounts of gas—a phenomenal score by all past drilling experience. So far, six large gas fields have been located, namely West Sole, Indefatigable, Ann, Viking, Leman Bank and Hewett (fig. 2.8). The possibility of gas fields extending to the mainland has also emerged with the discovery by Home Oil of a substantial find in Yorkshire, but, in general, the gas-bearing horizons stop offshore. A second pipeline brings gas to shore at Bacton in Norfolk, from where it is fed into the Canvey–Leeds pipeline near Rugby.

Natural gas has become a substantial element in the energy pattern of the EEC in the last decade and in 1973 143 million tonnes of coal-equivalent produced about 12 per cent of total energy consumption. In view of the massive reserves in the Dutch Groningen field and the United Kingdom and Dutch sectors of the North Sea, and with the present discoveries estimated to last for some 30 years, natural gas is a long-term economic factor.

The oil discoveries

The oil companies discovered significant evidence of crude oil deposits as well as natural gas in the North Sea. Whilst natural gas is present in the Rotliegendes

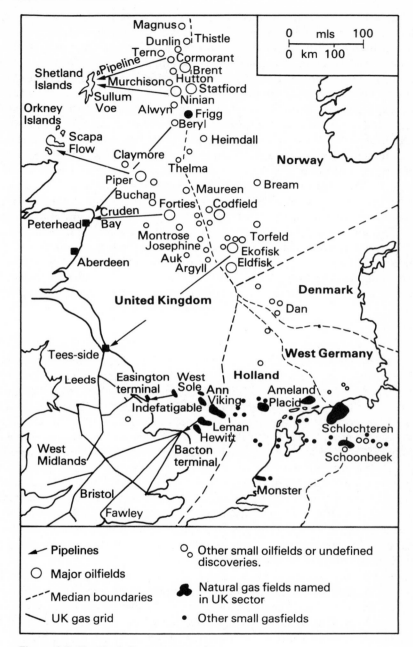

Figure 2.8 The North Sea energy province.

and Bunter sandstones found to the south of the Humber estuary, oil-bearing layers are to be found in the younger Cretaceous, Jurassic and Tertiary rocks in the Scottish and East Shetland Basin. The northern part of the North Sea is extremely hazardous, especially in winter. Nevertheless, the prospect of large indigenous supplies of oil to Western Europe was such a great attraction that during the latter part of the 1960s exploration drilling rigs began to move north from the gas deposits. More recently larger rigs have been built for the deeper water areas. The United Kingdom has shown the greatest interest, partly because of her large offshore sea area and partly because of her enormous consumption of oil, but exploration has continued over the whole area. So far, results are very encouraging, with 30 consortia of the major oil companies working in the area and, quite apart from oil, creating a new marine industrial technology in the shape of the offshore drilling platform. The National Coal Board is involved with the major oil companies in oil exploration as a natural extension of its offshore drilling for coal. The British National Oil Corporation (BNOC) has been created as a Government-owned body to participate in this rapidly developing industry.

Norway and the United Kingdom appear to have gained the major share of this new natural resource as most deposits of oil lie along the median line dividing British from Norwegian waters. Norway, having a much smaller population, will benefit in per capita terms more than the United Kingdom, although in any case the whole of Western Europe should benefit from having a politically stable source of oil.

Assessing the importance of the oil

Economic revival has already come to ports like Stavanger and Aberdeen. It is difficult to substantiate and quantify the discoveries of oil so far made. However, the following facts are based upon a broad assessment of many reports:

1. Oil exists in vast quantities between the Tyne estuary and the Shetlands, and there is enough to last up to fifty years. There are still many areas where no licences have been issued.
2. The North Sea is likely to yield 20–30 viable oilfields.
3. BP estimate that from 3 to 5 million barrels of oil per day is the likely production pattern from the North Sea by 1980. The present UK consumption of oil is 2 million barrels per day.
4. Production from present discoveries in the UK section should reach 40 million tonnes by mid 1977 and 125–140 million tonnes per year by 1980.
5. As the present UK consumption of oil is 110 million tonnes per year, she will be self-sufficient in oil by 1980, and will probably be a net exporter of oil during the 1980s.

The principal oilfields in 1975 (see fig. 2.8) are:

(a) **The Norwegian Group.** Ekofisk is an oilfield in the Norwegian sector discovered by Phillips Oil consortium. Its position is 290 km west of Stavanger and its probable capacity gives reserves of oil half as large as Alaska's Prudhoe Bay. Production is likely to be half a million barrels per day for at least 35 years. The problems of landing the oil are, however, very difficult. The Norwegian trench, 250 metres deep, prevents a pipe from being built to Norway and has been the deciding factor in the construction of a pipeline to Teesmouth in the UK. Also, the UK oil and gas market is much larger so that the prospects for piping the oil to Teesmouth are much more viable economically.

Around Ekofisk are a number of other fields, the Torfeld and West Ekofisk, whilst much farther to the north are four fields of importance, Codfield, Heimdall, Statfiord (which straddles the median boundary and is therefore of value to both UK and Norway) and the Anglo-Norwegian Frigg gas and oil field..

(b) **The Forties Group off East Scotland.** The Forties field was discovered by British Petroleum 160 km east of Aberdeen, and is capable of producing 400000 barrels of oil per day (one sixth of current UK consumption). The pipeline bringing the oil ashore to Peterhead became operative during 1976. This group of oilfields stretches, however, from the smaller Auk and Argyll fields northwards to the Piper field, another large discovery from which a pipeline is planned to Scapa Flow in the Orkney Islands.

(c) **The Shetland Group.** This is the richest series of strikes so far. At least six large fields have been discovered, the best known being the giant Brent field, which is expected to yield 500000 barrels per day. These oilfields are to share a pipeline which brings the oil ashore at Sullum Voe in the Shetland Islands. The Brent field came on stream in late 1976.

Other strikes, of a minor nature, have been made in the Dutch and Danish sectors, but interest is already moving towards the Minches of West Scotland, north towards Rockall and Iceland, and into the Irish Sea. Drilling has already begun in the area between Wales, Cornwall and Eire, known as the Celtic Sea. Finally, the United Kingdom and France have begun discussions regarding the median line through the English Channel. This new energy province is of critical importance in promising to counteract the most significant deficiency in the EEC's energy supplies.

Nuclear energy

Nuclear energy is seen by many as the long-term energy source of the future, although there are enormous problems of pollution and waste-disposal still to be overcome. Its economics are not simple because they are related to the availability and efficiency of competing fossil fuels, and because nuclear energy has not yet attained its optimum operating efficiency. Nevertheless, it already appears to have the greatest potential for technological improvements and therefore cost reduction. Its great advantages are that its fuel, uranium, is needed in relatively small quantities and is therefore easily transportable; its main use is the generation of electricity, that most flexible form of secondary energy; and the development of the fast-breeder reactor gives the prospect of vastly increased energy from each tonne of uranium and its by-product, plutonium, which is produced in greater quantities than it is used. Although construction costs of nuclear power stations are higher than those of a conventional thermal power station, generating costs are now lower. Lastly, the increasing cost of oil during 1974 has led the major industrial nations to think seriously about a reduction in fossil fuel consumption and an increased programme of nuclear research. The drawbacks of nuclear energy include safety factors, disposal of nuclear waste and the uncertain research factor. Plutonium, in particular, remains radio-active for periods up to 200000 years.

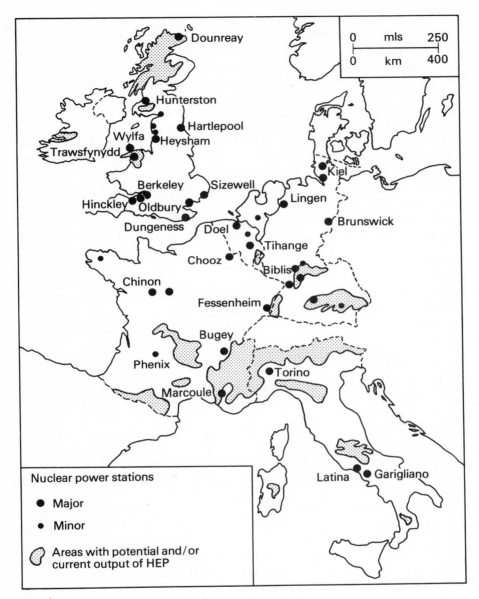

Figure 2.9 Nuclear and hydro-electric
power capacity in the EEC.

The UK led the world with its installation of nuclear power stations (fig. 2.9).
As a highly industrialised country with an independent military deterrent, declining coal production and expensive oil imports, there has been a long-term
nuclear programme since the 1950s. Nine Magnox Mark I reactors have been
built. Berkeley, finished in 1962, had running costs of 1·25 pence per kWh. The
last one, Wylfa, generates electricity at 0·70 pence per kWh. The Mark II, or

advanced gas-cooled reactor, is now being built at Dungeness 'B', Hinkley 'B', Hunterston 'B' and Hartlepool, and generating costs are expected to be 0·52 pence per kWh. One of the latest coal-fired power stations, Drax, in Yorkshire (1971), generates at approximately 0·53 pence per kWh, and Pembroke oil-fired power station, 0·59 pence per kWh. The second generation AGRs, now being built, are much larger than the original power stations, but these have been subject to long delays because of development problems, and the UK is now considering the purchase of American or Canadian reactors. From an average 400 megawatts in the 1950s to 1250 megawatts in the 1960s, the projection for Heysham power station is 2500 megawatts. In 1973 the UK had fourteen nuclear power stations (two experimental, eight Magnox and four AGR), with a total capacity of 13000 megawatts. And yet, despite the initial start, the programme contributes only 10 per cent to the national grid.

The original Six have embarked on a similar but more modest programme and their efforts have been aided by cooperation in the form of Euratom. This body was set up in 1958 as part of the Common Market and was aimed at a coordination of European energy production. In 1970, installed nuclear capacity was 400 megawatts, much smaller than that of the UK. However, a large increase is projected by 1980 with a capacity of 40000 megawatts supplying about 25 per cent of total electricity output. France, in particular, has begun a very ambitious programme of nuclear energy since the dramatic rise in oil prices in 1974.

Hydro-electric energy

Hydro-electric energy is one of the less important sources of primary energy in the community. In the UK production is confined to the Highlands of Scotland and Wales and, although in 1968 the Scottish HEP Board produced 3900 million kWh, this was only about one per cent of total electricity production. The high relief areas of the Alps, Apennines, Central Massif and Central South Germany, and major rivers such as the Rhine and Rhône (fig. 2.10) are the principal areas of HEP generation on the Continent (fig. 2.9). The primary energy contribution of HEP to the original Six in 1965 was about 6 per cent. Any increase here is unlikely because most of the best sites have already been harnessed, and the relative contribution to energy supplies has declined to 4 per cent of the total in 1973 (fig. 2.2).

The Shannon basin project in Eire harnesses the energy of the tides. A similar scheme is in operation in the Rance estuary in Brittany, and there are possible schemes suggested for the UK on the river Severn, at Morecambe Bay, and at the Wash. The number of sites are limited, and this source of energy cannot be expected to make a significant overall contribution in the immediate future.

Electricity

The transformation of the primary fuels described in this chapter into the secondary source electrical energy is one of the most important single aspects of the energy revolution. The generation of electricity depends upon the use of coal, oil and natural gas in thermal power stations, together with nuclear power

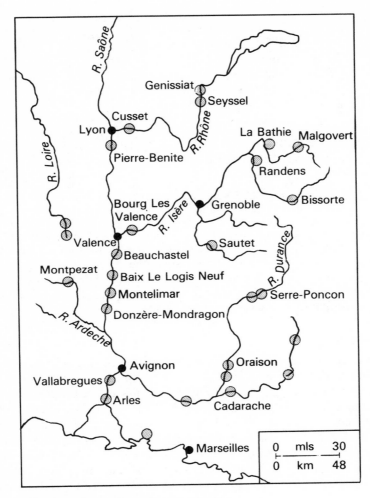

Figure 2.10 Hydro-electric power in the Rhône valley.

stations and hydro-electric power stations (see fig. 2.11). The data given in fig. 2.11 hides considerable variations between the nine member states. The United Kingdom uses a higher proportion of coal, and nuclear energy provides 10 per cent of her electricity. In France 30 per cent and in Italy 35 per cent of total electricity production is from HEP. The Netherlands generates a very high proportion of electricity from natural gas.

Production of electricity has more than doubled in fourteen years. In West Germany it rose from 111 to 293 million kilowatt hours, and in the UK from 129 to 254 million kilowatt hours between 1960 and 1974. This has been accompanied by a much greater efficiency in production and transfer over the past two decades. The same amount of primary fuel as used in 1958 will now generate 45 per cent more electricity and the super-grid at 400 kilovolts will now transfer it over large areas with a minimal loss of energy.

Conventional thermal power stations		
Coal	28·0	
Petroleum	28·9	
Lignite	8·0	81·4
Natural gas	13·2	
Town gas	3·3	
HEP	12·4	
Nuclear power	6·2	

Figure 2.11 Electricity production (%) for the nine EEC countries, 1974.

Electricity has enormous advantages. It is a clean form of energy, and, in the long term, may well be generated by nuclear power, probably completely replacing the fossil fuels. Most important of all, the distribution of electricity via the grid over large areas of Western Europe has helped to break down the old pattern of heavy industrial regions restricted to the coalfields in favour of a widespread and flexible distribution of industry.

Conclusion

The reduction in the importance of coal, matched by a rapid rise in oil consumption and the growing use of natural gas and nuclear energy, together with the local importance of hydro-electric power, has created a great variety of energy sources in the EEC of the 1970s (fig. 2.2). The new situation where imported supplies of oil are now both expensive and uncertain makes the energy policies of the 1960s out-of-date. The North Sea supplies of oil and natural gas are vital, and there is a need to pursue programmes of nuclear fusion research and the possibilities of tidal and solar energy, so that in the long-term fossil fuels can be dispensed with. Most important of all, the EEC needs to agree on a common policy to coordinate and rationalise supplies and distribution of energy resources. The difficulties of formulating a common energy policy arise largely from the differences in attitude between countries like the UK, with her large and diversified indigenous supplies of energy, and Italy and France, who are heavily deficient in energy resources.

The Commission published (November 1974) its medium-term guidelines up to 1985 (fig. 2.2), which specified a deliberate policy aimed at economising energy supplies, a fast rate of construction of nuclear power stations, an effort to increase supplies of indigenous natural gas and oil, efforts to maintain hard coal production at its present level, and a reduction in the Community's dependence for energy supplies on the rest of the world.

3

Industry:
locational change and
complexity of structure

In the enlarged EEC the process of industrial change is rapid and often dramatic. Great Britain was the world's first modern industrial power, followed closely by Germany, and in varying degrees by the other West European powers. A significant characteristic during the nineteenth century was an overwhelming reliance upon heavy and staple industries. In the 1880s the United Kingdom produced about 80 per cent of the world's ships; as late as 1907 coal, iron and steel, and textiles accounted for 46 per cent of her gross domestic product and 70 per cent of her exports. The twentieth century has witnessed the relative decline of these basic industries, as they are merely the first stages on the road to a mature industrial society. The growing complexity of industrial structure has meant that they have been supplemented by the assembly-line techniques of the car industry, the technical accuracy of the machine-tool industry, the consumer-based light industries, and science and technology-based, sophisticated and specialised industries. Associated integrally with this is the increasing dispersal of location, caused largely by the freeing of industry from coalfield locations and its tendency to become 'foot-loose'. This chapter will deal with these changes and analyse the causatory factors which fall into three major areas:

(a) Free market factors of location;
(b) Industrial production, organisation and financial factors;
(c) Government intervention and supra-national factors.

Free market factors of location

Industrial location has traditionally been affected most by the availability of power, raw materials and skilled labour, by market potential, and by transport facilities. It is the changing relative importance of these factors which sets up decline or growth in, and disparities between, regions. The occurrence and extent of the older coalfield industrial areas (figs. 2.1, 2.4, 3.1 and 3.2) illustrates the essential importance of coal as the original location factor, due primarily to its

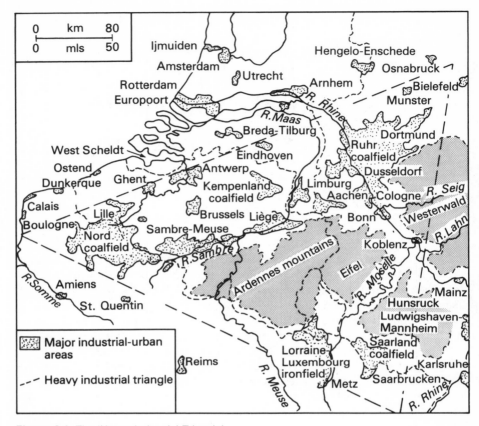

Figure 3.1 The 'Heavy Industrial Triangle' of north-west Europe.

The Sambre-Meuse valley, with a ribbon of settlement, coal-tips in the background and factory chimneys adding to the features of an old industrial landscape.

bulk and weight, which prohibited extensive movement, but also because it suffered little competition for over a century. The most significant areas of 'heavy' industry are still coalfield-located, although they owe their survival and present position partly at least to new factors which have tended to preserve geographical inertia.

In these coalfield areas there is a predominance of heavy industry or old staples like textiles, and a tendency to an easily distinguishable single industry in each area, based upon the original local raw materials. Such an emphasis is summed up in the term 'monotechnic'. The Ruhr, the Potteries, Liège and Tyneside all have this characteristic dominant industry, although less so than in the past. The age of development of such areas means they also have a large proportion of old and obsolescent housing and factories, and land is often in short supply with cramped old-fashioned factories competing for room to expand.

The northern part of the United Kingdom

On a general map of the EEC (fig. 3.2) the areas dominated by long-established heavy industry are dispersed around the margins of the highland zone of the United Kingdom. Individually, however, they are easily definable regions. Dense clusters of industry are found in central Scotland along Clydeside, in the north-east around Newcastle-upon-Tyne, and at Teesside. These are the traditional areas of heavy industry which specialise in iron and steel, shipbuilding, marine engineering, and heavy structural engineering, with chemicals particularly on Teesside. East Lancashire, centred on Manchester, and West Yorkshire are the two areas traditionally associated with the textile industry, but the shipbuilding and chemicals associated with Merseyside, and the Sheffield steel industry are also integral parts of these regions. The West Midlands conurbation was originally dependent upon the steel and metallurgy of the 'Black Country', but is now one of the most varied, complex, and sophisticated engineering regions in Europe. Mention must also be made of one of the most successfully monotechnic industrial areas anywhere in the world, the North Staffordshire coalfield, which continues to produce high-quality china, pottery and earthenware goods. It deals with a high-value product in great consumer demand, and herein lies its success. At the other end of the scale lies a region which emerged because of its coal supplies, and which developed steel and engineering industries, but which is so isolated geographically that it has now become one of the worst unemployment problem areas of the United Kingdom. This is the Cumberland coalfield, centred upon Whitehaven and Workington.

In Wales, there are coalfields at both northern and southern extremities. The small North Wales coalfield between Wrexham and the Dee developed a small but important steel and chemical industry. The area is relatively isolated and the medium-sized Shotton steel works on Deeside is under sentence of closure as part of the rationalisation programme of the British Steel Corporation. South Wales is the classic example of intra-regional migration towards coastal locations such as Port Talbot and Llanelly. The weight factor of coal produced in confined valleys such as the Rhondda and Taff has become less important than

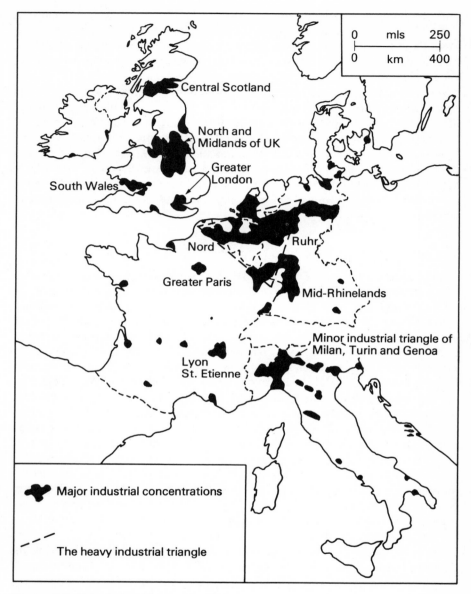

Figure 3.2 Major industrial areas in the
EEC Nine.

the low cost of imported raw materials for the steel, tinplate and metal-process-
ing industries.

The 'Heavy Industrial Triangle'

This zone is a vaguely defined area denoting the principal area of industrial
activity in the EEC, but in its original concept it marks the area within which

most of the coal, staple industries, steel-making and heavy engineering of continental Europe are found (fig. 3.1). Bounded at its apices by the Nord coalfield of France, the Ruhr coalfield of West Germany, and the Lorraine iron-ore field, it contains even now (1976) 95 per cent of coal production of the original Six, and nearly 60 per cent of their steel-making capacity. The French Nord-Pas de Calais zone stretches in an arc from Dunkerque to Lille and through into Belgium as the Sambre–Meuse coalfield. Mons, Charleroi and Liège are the central industrial foci in the Sambre–Meuse valley and are important for textiles, heavy metallurgy, chemicals and glass. Small extensions of industry are found north-east in the Kempenland, a more recently-developed concealed coalfield, where Genk and Hasselt are chemical and metallurgical centres. Across the Dutch border is the small Limburg coalfield, around Maastricht, and in West Germany lies the small Aachen coalfield. The Ruhr is the greatest concentration of all, and extends from its Duisburg–Dortmund axis south to Cologne, and north towards Munster. The southern apex of Lorraine based upon Minette iron-ores and a modern coalfield, includes the steel and engineering centres of Nancy, Thionville and Metz, and extends into Luxembourg. Slightly to the north-east is the Saarland, an old coal and metallurgy region with Saarbrucken and Volklingen as the principal towns.

The Nord/Pas de Calais coalfield

This provides a useful case-study which illustrates the decline and change in these old manufacturing zones in the twentieth century. In 1962 it had over half

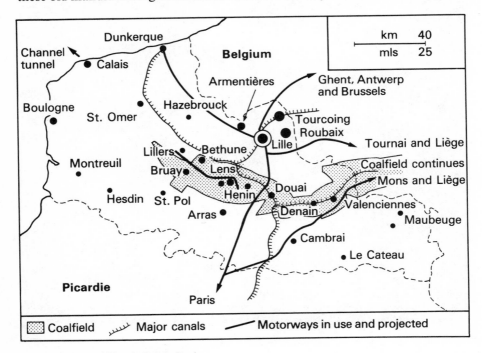

Figure 3.3 Nord/Pas de Calais Region.

its total employment (335000 out of 607000) in three staple industries: coal, steel and metallurgy, and textiles. The coalfield, stretching from Bruay to Valenciennes (fig. 3.3) has been badly affected, with coal production falling from twenty-seven million tonnes in 1961 to fifteen million tonnes in 1971 and to nine million tonnes in 1974. Under the latest rationalisation plan, it is due to cease production altogether in 1983, since even with recent changes in the costs of other primary fuels, notably oil, it is a very high-cost coalfield. The seams are thin and disturbed, productivity is low, and reserves are practically exhausted. Excessive investment costs required in a poor and declining resource are therefore ruled out. The legacy of the area, in addition, is a cluster of small mining towns known as 'cités minières' with all the environmental disadvantages of obsolescence and a need for urban renewal. The Nord is referred to as the 'Pays Noir'.

The textile industry lies mainly to the north of the coalfield itself at Lille, Roubaix, Tourcoing and Armentières. It is based on wool and cotton and has

Lille. The crowded factories and haphazard distribution of buildings, the railways and the canal are typical of an old industrial landscape.

experienced severe contraction, with employment reduced from 224000 in 1931 to 168000 by 1954, and 102000 by 1967. Foreign competition, a slowness to introduce up-to-date machinery and loss of markets to synthetic fibres are the main causes in this decline, resulting in the closure of many small firms and re-grouping of others.

The Douai–Valenciennes area has traditionally been the centre of the steel and heavy metallurgical industries, with specialised steel and machinery to the south in Arras, Cambrai and Maubeuge. Employment is relatively more stable, and production of steel in the whole area has actually increased, entirely owing to the new integrated Usinor steelworks at Dunkerque which produces over 4 million tonnes, or over 80 per cent of the region's steel output. Here is the essence of the Nord's problem. The older parts of the coalfield have an over-dependence upon heavy metallurgy. Factories are often small and in inconvenient situations with obsolete machinery. There is a lack of light industry and of the specialised high-value products which would help to diversify the industrial structure.

The region needs adjustment and diversification away from basic industries, together with the renewal of its equipment. However, it has great potential advantages, the foremost of which is that there are 60 million people within 300 kilometres, forming a huge consumer market. A large adaptable labour force has the potential to attract capital investment on a large scale and many new industrial estates have been sited in the coalfield towns. New industries include plastics, petrochemicals, cars and components, electronics, and consumer durables, giving a total employment potential of 70000. The old canal system has been upgraded with deepwater channels taking 3000 tonne barges from Dunkerque to Lille and Paris. Finally, there is the new motorway infrastructure and the future link with a possible channel tunnel. The real value of the motorway network is that it places the Nord athwart the Paris–Lille–Brussels axis.

Industrial adjustment

There is a continuing major significance for the coal-based industrial areas in spite of the radical changes now taking place. The process of geographical inertia is based largely upon their skilled labour supplies, traditional industrial linkages and their large urban consumer market. With the commitment which national governments now have to aiding these old industrial regions, and with the EEC's regional aid policy, these areas will continue to attract capital investment on a large scale. The problem of the residual staple and heavy industries, and the resulting imbalances, must be corrected by the lengthy process of diversification into new industries.

Of great significance is the position of each industrial area relative to its national economic core. It is arguable that the Nord/Pas de Calais, Belgian Borinage, Ruhr and West Midlands, are in a favourable position, lying as they do close to the core areas and in the mainstreams of activity. The north-east of England, and the Scottish coalfields, both of which lie close to the oil and natural gas resources of the North Sea, may well have a similar advantage. The North Sea littoral is certainly likely in the future to be a major area of concentration for industrial development and it may well have a revitalising effect upon these older coal-based industrial areas. By contrast, industrial regions lying on the periphery of activity within Western Europe face adjustment in a more difficult context. South Wales and the small industrial areas around the French Massif Central such as Décazeville, Alés and Commentry have no such advantages of centrality and the process of industrial adjustment will take longer, and may not be as successful.

Imports of raw materials

These are becoming increasingly important. Iron-ore, associated with coal in the blackband deposits of the industrial revolution, is now left in such small uneconomic quantities that the steel industry imports the bulk of its iron-ore from Sweden, Spain and North Africa, whilst only French Lorraine and Northampton produce any significant home quantities. Oil has had the most important single effect, but all forms of raw materials which are heavy, bulky and costly to transport overland are increasingly causing industrial concentrations to develop on coastal, estuarine and major waterway sites. Heavy processing industry, including steel, non-ferrous metals, oil-refining, chemicals and petrochemicals, cement and electrical power generation, needs to be sited at low-cost importation points, with good facilities for transhipment inland and large flat sites for construction of installations. The coastal ports are increasingly

Antwerp. An industrial zone based upon break-of-bulk raw materials, with dockside oil-storage and a petroleum refinery in the foreground.

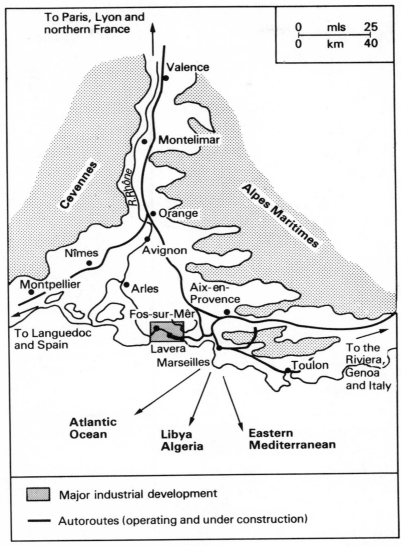

Figure 3.4 Fos-sur Mer/Lavera industrial zone.

the cheapest points at which receipt, processing, manufacture and distribution can take place (fig. 3.2). The sea-coast from the Seine mouth to Denmark is the single most important stretch, with the Seine estuary (Le Havre), Boulogne, Dunkerque, the Rhine estuary (Rotterdam and Antwerp), Bremen and Hamburg, Kiel and Copenhagen being the main ports. On the Mediterranean coast are Genoa and the Marseilles–Rhône area (figs. 3.4 and 3.5), whilst in the United Kingdom the nodal points for new heavy industry are Thameside, Teesside, Severnside, Humberside, Merseyside and Southampton Water. The im-

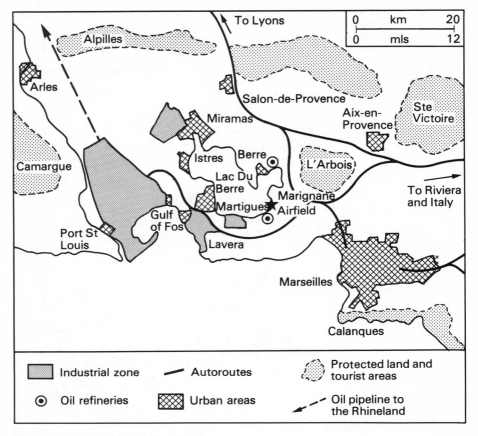

Figure 3.5 The position of Marseilles.

portance of river ports in France and Germany must also be recognised and in particular Rouen, Duisburg and Mannheim are centres of major industrial concentrations related to their waterside sites.

'Footloose' industry

The liberation of certain types of manufacturing industry from the confined zones of the coalfields and the waterside raw material input points, has been achieved by a number of factors acting in conjunction. These are: the widespread cheap transmission of electricity; the development of fast transport links especially roads, so that movement of raw materials is cheaper and more efficient; the growth of light industry, precision engineering and science-based industries in which a greater emphasis is placed on skilled labour than on raw materials; the new significance of the market and labour supply cost factors. The transfer of electrical power via a national grid neutralised the effect of bulky fuels, and industry has become 'footloose' with many factors being important in the siting of factories. Labour costs in a wealthy society such as that of Western

Europe are often the single largest element in manufacturing overheads, whilst the consumer goods destined for the market need to be adjacent to that market, or within easy transport distance. The growth of the trading estate is associated with this trend, involving planned industrial sites with facilities such as electrical power, water supply and factory space, close to suburban housing areas and major routeways.

Manufacturing in cities

The most significant positive development relating to market and labour supply factors has been the growth of major manufacturing areas associated with any large centre of population: the city, the conurbation, the capital city region. Greater Paris, Greater London, Brussels, Frankfurt, Copenhagen and Milan all have one major resource—population. Labour requirements are abundant female labour, well-qualified graduates for the research and managerial staff, and a pool of skilled labour and technicians for the operation of complex machinery.

The mass-market production techniques require areas with a high purchasing power and with an income level above average. Finally, the complexity of modern industry, needing frequent contact and movement by executives, requires good communications and locations near motorways and airports. All these factors have tended to favour the growth of manufacturing in and around the cities of Europe.

The Daimler–Benz Car Assembly plant at Sindelfingen, near Stuttgart. Notice the 'greenfield site' and the planned and extensive factory layout.

The 'minor industrial triangle' of Milan–Turin–Genoa in Northern Italy owes its origins to the accumulation of capital from trade in the medieval city states of the Plain of Lombardy. The line of industrial towns from Turin to Venice, based upon the historic advantages (see chapter 16) of Northern Italy, has meant that it, rather than the national capital city of Rome, has become the industrial core of the country.

Other major city regions are those in the middle Rhineland, such as Frankfurt, and the southern German cities of Munich, Stuttgart and Nuremberg, noted for their wide range of high-value components and precision engineering. The cities of Saxony, particularly Hanover and Brunswick, are important for vehicles and components. Greater Lyons, third city of France, stands in the centre of the Rhône–Saône corridor. Originally a silk manufacturing centre, it has become important for engineering, metallurgy and chemicals, with an impressively varied industrial structure.

Greater Paris and Greater London, both with about eight million people, are capital cities of world rank, and have an extremely varied manufacturing base. Their political, financial and commercial wealth has been responsible for the creation of a 'metropolitan structure of industry'. This includes a complete range of industrial types over the whole city, ranging from the heavy industry of the river and port areas to the specialised industries of the central area.

The industrial structure of Greater London

A study of five type zones illustrates the factors involved in the concentration of manufacturing in a major capital city (fig. 3.6).

1. **Thameside** This is a most distinctive zone with a role as the transhipment point and dockside area for the primary processing industries. It stretches downriver from the original port in the Pool of London above Tower Bridge out past Woolwich and Greenwich to Dagenham and to Lower Thameside at Purfleet, Thurrock and Northfleet. The evolution of this zone typifies that of all the European estuary-based port areas: the decline of the inner areas and the movement outwards to the deeper and more accessible water near the open sea. London docks have now moved to Tilbury and possibly in the future may extend out to Maplin sands. The food-processing (flour and sugar, etc.) of the inner docks of Royal Victoria and Silvertown is succeeded by heavier and more noxious industries downstream: vehicles at Dagenham, and cement, explosives, paper-making, oil refining, and petrochemicals out through Northfleet and as far as the Isle of Grain.

2. **Inner London (north-east crescent)** This was another nucleus of London's industry in the nineteenth century, with a crescent of small workshops from Whitechapel through Bethnal Green and Hackney to Finsbury, Clerkenwell and Camden Town. Sixty years ago the bulk of London's industry lay within this area, but considerable migration has taken place out of the cramped quarters and decayed inner suburbs to outer London and the New Towns. The East End is, however, still a major element in London's industrial geography. The main industries are clothing and furniture, food, drink and

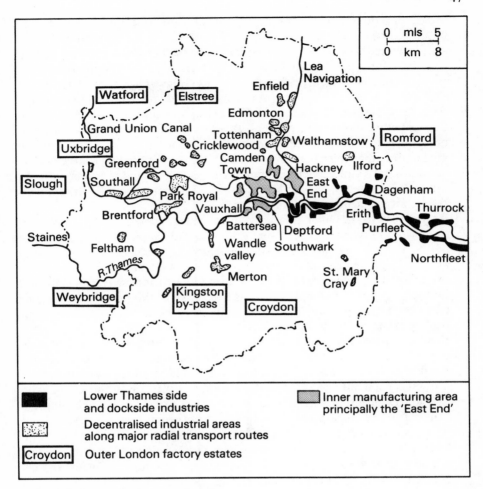

Figure 3.6 Greater London manufacturing areas.

tobacco, printing and specialised instrumental engineering. The most interesting feature is the distinctive pattern of 'quarters', as in Whitechapel, which has some 900 small workshops in adapted and congested premises devoted to clothing manufacture.

3. **Radial transport lines of industrial concentration** Decentralisation along main roads and railway lines followed the growth of transportation facilities, and in particular the coming of the lorry during the interwar period, 1919–39. Significant industrialisation occurred between 1900 and 1914 in the Lea Valley, from Tottenham and Edmonton towards Enfield with the introduction of workmen's train-fares and the growth there of working-class housing. Much of the former East End industry migrated there, in a linkage process along the nearest line of communication. The move from cramped inner sites was also a powerful factor in the growth of these manufacturing sites along

radial lines of communication. Much of the industry in the Lea Valley is a natural continuation of that of the East End: furniture, clothing and shoes, supplemented by electrical engineering. Most of the other areas with factory concentrations, particularly those in West London, depend upon road transport: Colindale and Cricklewood on the Edgware Road; Park Royal, Perivale, Wembley and Greenford along the A40 and Western Avenue; and Brentford, Feltham, Yiewsley and West Drayton along the A4/M4 wedge to the west of the city. The Great West Road (A4) illustrates the great variety of new, planned factories. Here, engineering products, particularly electrical, are dominant, but also there are also consumer goods needing a large market, labour supply and efficient communications (e.g. branded foods, pharmaceuticals, cosmetics, plastic kitchenware, radio and scientific instruments, refrigerators, vacuum cleaners).

4. **Factory estates in Outer London** A more recent growth, these show many similarities to type (3), being usually along radial routes, but they have often been planned to take account of the movement of population out of London, and the associated labour supply. Croydon, Staines, Uxbridge and Elstree are examples, with mainly light and consumer goods factories. The movement of industry out into London's new towns is also part of this process. Perhaps the best example of an outer industrial estate is, however, Slough, a composite trading estate established in the 1930s.

5. **Central London** The central areas of most of the metropolitan cities also contain additional activities which are a reflection of their position in national life. The manufacture of fashionable clothes, jewellery and other luxury goods, is often carried out very close to the marketing centre, as in the West End of London adjacent to Oxford Street and Bond Street. The publishing and printing of periodicals and newspapers is another such specialised industry which is carried out in the City of London. Finally, the essential services of finance, business services and insurance (so essential to industry as a whole) are controlled by the City of London. On the Continent, Dusseldorf and Frankfurt also provide this facility on a large scale.

The organisation, control and financing of industrial production

The mass production techniques of twentieth century industry have inevitably led to basic structural changes in industry, which in turn have led to locational changes as the small workshops of the nineteenth century have become the large factories and the vast corporations of today. Many of the problems of industrial areas such as Lancashire or the Franco-Belgian coalfield arise from the decline of staple industries like cotton and their replacement by sophisticated industries such as radio and electronics, often not tied to the same location. The key to structural changes lies in the economies of scale which can be achieved by mass-production, integration of the means of production, and large-scale capital investment, research and technology in industry. The large units may be typified by giant corporations such as British Petroleum, Imperial Chemical Industries or Volkswagenwerk (fig. 3.7).

Rank	Company	Headquarters	Main activity	Sales (£1000)
1	British Petroleum	UK	Oil industry	9 305 600
2	Royal Dutch Petroleum	Netherlands	Oil industry	8 266 600
3	'Shell' Transport & Trading	UK	Oil industry	6 845 378
4	Unilever NV	Netherlands	Food, detergents, toiletries, etc.	5 872 400
5	Philips' Lamps	Netherlands	Electronics and electricals	4 308 000
6	Cie. Francaise des Petroles	France	Petroleum products	4 109 100
7	IRI	Italy	State Industry Holding Co.	3 956 800
8	BASF (Badische Anilin)	Germany	Chemicals	3 884 400
9	August Thyssen-Hutte	Germany	Iron, steel, chemicals	3 740 800
10	Hoechst	Germany	Chemicals	3 575 400
11	British American Tobacco	UK	Tobacco and cosmetics	3 488 000
12	Bayer	Germany	Chemicals	3 341 400
13	Veba	Germany	Chemicals, electricity, glass, transport	3 197 220
14	Siemens	Germany	Electronics, electricals, engineering	3 048 800
15	Volkswagenwerk	Germany	Motor vehicles	3 008 100
16	Imperial Chemical Industries	UK	Chemicals, fibres, paint, etc.	2 954 800
17	Electricity Council	UK	Electricity generation	2 656 000
18	Unilever Limited	UK	Food products, detergents, etc.	2 440 800
19	Daimler-Benz	Germany	Motor vehicles	2 395 600
20	Shell-Mex & BP	UK	Petroleum distributors	2 339 000
21	Mannesmann	West Germany	Steel and mechanical engineering	2 332 000
22	British Steel Corporation	UK	Steel	2 255 800
23	Pechiney-Ugine	France	Chemicals, aluminium	2 132 500
24	AEG-Telefunken	West Germany	Electrical engineering	2 121 800
25	Petrofina	Belgium	Petroleum products	2 087 500

Figure 3.7 EEC top twenty-five industrial groups, 1974. (Source—*Times 1000 Review*)

Mass production and the specialisation of labour

The many processes required by the assembly of components, the increasing substitution of labour by machinery, and the concentration of processes in large factories have led to high capital costs and a need for continuing large-scale investment. Integration of related processes occurs as a means of cutting costs of production and increasing efficiency. Horizontal integration is the control by one group of most or all of the productive capacity in one stage of manufacturing. Added to this is vertical integration where in many cases economies can be made by bringing together successive processes on the same site. Substantial savings in fuel, transport and other overheads give increased efficiency, lower costs of production and economies of scale. Ford Motors (United Kingdom) have a vertically integrated plant at their Dagenham factory capable of producing cars through all stages of manufacture and assembly. The man-made fibres group Courtaulds illustrates both aspects of integration very well. They have a 'Northern Textiles Division' to coordinate their control of over one-third of the Lancashire cotton spindles. In addition, they also control production stages from the raw materials (wood pulp and chemicals) to the initial production stages (spinning, weaving, knitting and bonded synthetic fabrics) and finishing (dyeing, printing, hosiery, garments and marketing) as well as textile engineering.

The assembly line, which dominates the car industry, the aircraft industry and much of the electronics industry, requires thousands of components which are produced in separate specialist factories and then transferred to the assembly factory. Industrial linkage of subsidiary component factories by transport is therefore essential. This type of industrial association is best known as 'regional swarming', one of the best examples being the West Midlands conurbation with its associated towns having a high proportion of their industry geared to producing components for the vehicle industries of Birmingham and Coventry. Older industries such as cotton textiles, iron and steel, and shipbuilding, have for decades had a tendency to cluster in their traditional resource areas. The remaining UK shipyards have amalgamated, for example, the Swan-Hunter Company on the Tyne and Wear, and Scott-Lithgow on the Clyde.

The giant industrial corporations

These illustrate the technological superiority of size: Imperial Chemical Industries of the United Kingdom has become a significant multi-national corportation which has almost a conglomerate structure. It controls many types of both basic and sophisticated chemical products (fig. 3.8). With over 60 manufacturing plants in the UK and 38 either wholly owned or subsidiary companies in the rest of the EEC, it can claim to be European in outlook (fig. 3.9). Its world stature is illustrated by the further 270 subsidiary and associated companies in the rest of the world.

Imperial Chemical Industries in the United Kingdom operates in both chemicals and synthetic fibres in a virtual monopoly situation. But the monopoly is within the United Kingdom and provided there is government regulation and protection of the consumer, no great problems arise. The severe competition which ICI faces is from its counterparts in the United States of

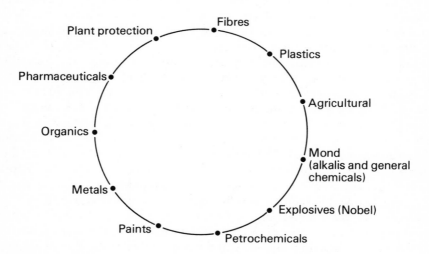

Figure 3.8 ICI Divisions. (From Imperial Chemical Industries)

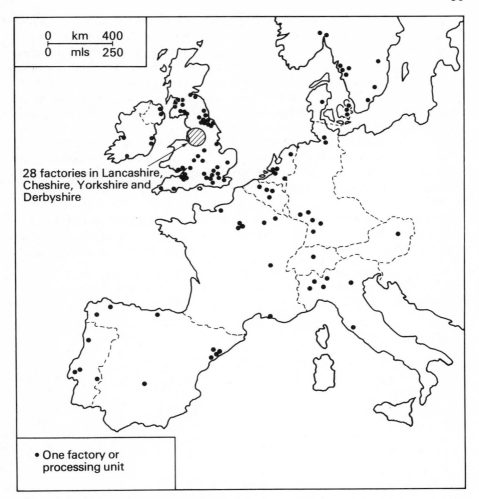

Figure 3.9 ICI established in western Europe. (From Imperial Chemical Industries)

America, Dupont and Union Carbide, and in Europe, Montedison and Hoechst. An indication of the power of large companies in terms of total capacity is in the United Kingdom where the fifty largest companies produce nearly half the national turnover. Even more extreme is the case of Holland, where 35 per cent of production is from three companies: Philips Electrical (Eindhoven), Royal Dutch Shell and Unilever NV.

The survival of small-scale industry

Industry in the EEC is not all controlled by large companies. In fact, much of the industrial structure is small and fragmented, at least by American standards. In general, France and Italy entered the 1960s with a predominance of small production units, family firms, a lack of rationalisation and the survival of small workshops. This was a reflection of the fact that the industrial revolution in France was late, slow and incomplete. On the whole, the United Kingdom and West Germany have the largest units, reflecting their more mature and sophisticated industrial structure. Quite dramatic changes have, however, occurred with the dismantling of tariffs and the increased production and movement throughout the EEC, creating direct competition and the need for enlargement and rationalisation. Direct government intervention created a spate of mergers in all community countries. In France, particularly, since 1967 there has been considerable activity. Two steel giants are between them now responsible for the bulk of production: one, Wendel-Sidelor/Moselle Siderurgie produces 7·25 million tonnes of crude steel, 35 per cent of French production. Usinor-Lorraine-Escaut, with 16 steelworks, controls 33 per cent of production with 6·25 million tonnes capacity. In textiles, Lainiere de Roubaix and Filatures et Freres of Tourcoing are now merged into one of the largest companies in Europe. The tables of the largest European companies (fig. 3.7) and comparable European and American companies (fig. 3.10) serve to highlight several interesting facts:

(a) American companies usually head the 'league table' by large margins.
(b) The United Kingdom, West Germany and Holland have the largest companies in the EEC.

	CHEMICALS			CARS	
Rank	Name	Sales	Rank	Name	Sales
1	BASF (Badische Anilin) (West Germany)	3900	1	General Motors (USA)	14400
			2	Fords (USA)	10800
2	Hoechst (West Germany)	3600	3	Chrysler (USA)	5000
3	Bayer (West Germany)	3300	4	Volkswagenwerk (West Germany)	3000
4	Du Pont (USA)	3200	5	Toyota (Japan)	2300
5	ICI (UK)	3000	6	Fiat (Italy)	1900
6	Union Carbide (USA)	2400	7	British Leyland (UK)	1600
7	Dow Chemicals (USA)	2300	8	Renault (France)	1175
8	ENI (Italy)	2000			
9	Rhône-Poulenc (France)	2000			
10	Monsanto (USA)	1600			

	ELECTRICAL AND COMPUTERS			AIRCRAFT/AEROSPACE	
Rank	Name	Sales	Rank	Name	Sales
1	General Electric (USA)	6100	1	Boeing (USA)	1700
2	IBM (USA)	5800	2	Lockheed (USA)	1500
3	International Telephone (USA)	5100	3	McDonnel Douglas (USA)	1400
4	Philips (Netherlands)	4300	4	Hawker Siddeley (UK)	636
5	Western Electric (USA)	3400	5	Sociéte Nationale (France) Aerospatiale	467
6	Siemens (West Germany)	3000			
7	Westinghouse (USA)	2600	6	Dassault/Breguet (France)	350
8	AEG-Telefunken (West Germany)	2100	7	British Aircraft Corporation (UK)	271
9	RCA (USA)	2100			
10	Hitachi (Japan)	1700			
11	General Electric (UK)	1100			

Figure 3.10 Table of industrial comparisons (approximate sales in million pounds), 1974. (Source—*Times 1000 Review*)

(c) Oil, chemicals, cars, electrical goods and food tend to be the products of the largest companies.

(d) The Italian IRI, the United Kingdom Electricity Board and the British Steel Corporation are the largest state enterprises.

(e) Irish industry is small-scale and fragmented. The largest Irish company ranks equivalent to the 250th United Kingdom company. Belgian industry also is on the whole fairly small-scale. The largest Belgian company ranks twenty-fifth and the largest Danish company forty-third.

(f) Some giant companies dominate the industrial structure of Italy: Fiat (cars), Montedison (chemicals), Pirelli (tyres), Snia-Viscosa (synthetic textiles), Finsider (steel), and ENI (oil and natural gas).

Industry and technology

Industry has moved into a very sophisticated stage of development during the mid-twentieth century. The replacement of many traditional raw materials with synthetics, particularly in plastics and textiles, is one example of this. More important is the influence of technology with certain sectors of the economy assuming key roles: space satellite technology; aero-engines and aircraft; radio and electronics; nuclear technology; automation systems and computers. These require vast expenditure on research, which has led to the existence of a 'technological gap' between Europe and the United States and to the invasion of American industry into Europe in these key sectors in an attempt to control the fastest growing industries. Comparisons can be made between the smaller national European companies and the larger American ones (fig. 3.10). In the advanced sectors of the economy, three factors are crucial; the relatively small home market of each EEC country and the financial difficulty of sustaining projects to the stage of commercial viability; the unwillingness of governments to pay indefinitely for projects costing millions of pounds; the smaller European market in military weapons; the difficulty of countering the sales capacity of the Americans.

European aircraft manufacturers have suffered in particular because of the great market benefit reaped by the Americans from their large home military commitments and widespread use of civil aviation products. The United States Airforce has 52 000 aircraft, compared with 25 000 for all the countries of Western Europe. The United States produces 60 per cent of the world's aircraft. The aerospace industry shows a similar picture with continued cancellations of costly European projects such as the Blue Streak rocket. Nevertheless, there has been a spirited attempt to continue to compete, with the United Kingdom having seventeen types of missile in production 1972–73. The UK and France have also put satellites into orbit. These, however, are the only two members of the community to have any experience of advanced aerospace technology.

In nuclear technology the position is better. In Europe generally there has been a realisation of the immense benefit that this energy source can give, and cooperation in the form of Euratom has been, though only partially successful, a valuable pointer to the future and to the possibilities of energy from nuclear fusion. The United Kingdom, in particular, has led the world in the research field. Partly due to her world-power status in the 1940s, and partly because of the need to replace energy sources which are becoming increasingly expensive, research and development has continued both in the military field and in the civil application of nuclear energy. France has latterly embarked upon a nuclear deterrent, and both countries have a large pool of nuclear technology. The thirteen nuclear power stations in the United Kingdom (chapter 2) are an example of a considerable pre-eminence in the production of what may well ultimately be the cheapest form of electricity. France and West Germany have also embarked on a large programme of nuclear power stations (fig. 2.9).

The electronics and electrical engineering industry is one of the fastest-growing sectors of the economy, by an estimated 10 per cent a year. American companies dominate the field, and command about 80 per cent of the world sales in electronics, computers and tele-communications. The large European companies are Philips of Eindhoven, Siemens of West Germany, and General Electric of the United Kingdom, but even they are small compared to some of the United States giants. In computers, only the United Kingdom has an indidual industry outside United States control. International Computers Ltd, the United Kingdom company, has 3 per cent of world sales, whereas IBM, the American company, has 75 per cent. It is in this sector, with its telecommunications and automation systems, essential to the sophisticated economy, that Europe lags considerably behind the USA.

Related directly to this is the invasion of American industry by the injection of capital and extension of ownership and management into the European scene. Certainly outside investment is generally advantageous, with the stimulation it brings in new factory growth and employment, higher wages and rationalisation. The real problem is when this leads to excessive outside control of key industries, because these are vital to the technology and growth of the country concerned. The selectivity of United States control of British industry is shown in Figure 3.11. In the United Kingdom American companies own 10 per cent overall of British production, but six key industries – electronics, cars, drugs and medicines, petroleum, computers and office machinery, and tractors – have absorbed 75 per cent of total United States investment. Throughout the EEC the

Industry	Percentage United States control
Cars	55
Computers	45
Petroleum	40
Agricultural machinery	41
Medicines and drugs	23
Instruments	17

Figure 3.11 Degree of United States control of Key British industries, 1973.

position is similar. Cross-frontier EEC mergers to give European industrial units of comparable size to the American ones, serving a large home market of 250 million people, are a possible remedy.

Government intervention and supra-national factors

Government intervention has occurred principally because of the need for adjustment in the complex economies of the EEC countries, and has three basic aims: to control areas of production which are basic to the economy; to support high technology and research industries; and to support declining industrial areas. It is in the United Kingdom that state intervention has reached its greatest extent, but France and Italy also furnish good examples.

Nationalised (state-controlled) industries

In the United Kingdom nationalised industries are very big business and include some of the largest employers in the country. Although initially associated with a socialist political viewpoint, the state controlled corporation is now generally accepted for economic reasons. It has been recognised that in certain areas basic to the economy, there is great value in the concentration of power in the state rather than in private hands. In theory at least an overall planning view can be secured, the resources of the state are available for investment, and integration and large-scale operations are assured. All essential services and many production industries are included as follows:

Communications: British Rail, British Airways; National Bus Company and British Road Services; posts and telecommunications.
Energy: Electricity and Gas Boards; National Coal Board; United Kingdom Atomic Energy Authority.
Basic Industries: Steel; in late 1976 the shipbuilding and aircraft industries were taken into state control.

In France the state owns and operates large sections of the economy: the Charbonnages De France (coal-mining, power stations and chemicals); Electricité De France; Gaz De France; SNCF (French Railways); SNECMA (aero-engines). A variation on direct control is the Renault Car Company where government control is vested in a director-general and day-to-day running is left very much in the hands of the company management. In Italy IRI (Instituto Per La Reconstruzione Industriale) originated as a financial rescue operation in 1933 and has since grown into a state corporation which controls the telephone system, Alitalia Airways, the Autostrada Del Sole and Finmare (the merchant marine). It has shares in Finsider (steel) and other engineering, textile and chemical companies. A more recent development has been ENI (Ente Nazionale Idrocarburi), set up in 1953 with the object of capitalising on the newly-discovered oil and gas reserves in the Po valley and given a monopoly of prospecting in Italy. With its headquarters near Milan, it now controls oil refineries of over 8 million tonnes capacity, petrochemical plants, tanker fleets and oil pipe-lines from Pegli and Trieste to Ingolstadt in southern Germany.

Active intervention and guidance in regrouping and financial aid

This is even more widespread than direct government control. Where technology has dictated larger units, and the national interest has been at stake, persuasion and guidance has brought results. In the United Kingdom aircraft industry, famous names such as Fairey, Avro, Bristol, Supermarine, Vickers and De Havilland were merged into two giants, British Aircraft Corporation and Hawker-Siddeley, and subsequently nationalised (1976). Rolls-Royce, the largest aero-engine manufacturer outside the United States of America, could not be allowed to disappear and so the company's bankruptcy in 1971 was annulled by the expedient of a financial takeover by the government. The United Kingdom government is a controlling shareholder in British Petroleum, and recently has acquired effective control of British Leyland. In industries where there has been persistent intense foreign competition, and an industry has remained at an inefficient level of production with too much labour, or organised in small units more akin to the nineteenth century, then regrouping and controlled reduction of output is necessary. Two severe cases have been the United Kingdom cotton and shipbuilding industries. The Charbonnages De France has established a gradual reduction target in the French coal industry. In the United Kingdom statutory powers backed by financial resources, were given to the Industrial Reorganisation Corporation and subsequently the National Economic Development Corporation, to enable such beneficial changes to be made.

Support for declining industrial regions and relocation policies

Specific areas of severe decline have been the major preoccupation of the EEC governments during the past two decades. The efforts of the Italian government to promote industrialisation and to raise living standards in the south have been made through IRI development projects such as integrated steelworks, paperworks, cement works and various land-improvement and marketing schemes. The most important move, however, has been the setting up of the Cassa Del Mezzogiorno in 1950 (chapters 10 and 17). In France the Sociétes de Development Regional (SDR) are aimed at stimulating investment and attempting to persuade industry to move to those areas with contracting staple industries and those which are shedding excess agricultural workers. The Nord-Pas de Calais fits the first category and the south and west of France the second. In the United Kingdom the designation of development areas of three grades of severity has been accompanied by fiscal measures to improve their attractivity and stimulate industrial growth. Trading estates with light industry and new roads and towns are all part of the complex operation required to arrest industrial decline. The concept of the regional problem is, however, much wider and is dealt with more fully in subsequent chapters.

The EEC and its industrial policy

Finally, and most important for the future, is the effect of the enlarged EEC upon the home market of each of the nine members. The creation of a large integrated market of 250 million people has already been a factor in industrial growth, as seen in the large increases in production in West Germany, and the other members of the original Six (fig. 1.4). The future international proficiency of EEC industry depends on two evolving factors: cross-frontier mergers and the industrial policy of the EEC itself.

The problem with cross-frontier mergers is that financial and legal liability problems arise which are difficult to overcome. The future obviously lies with companies which can trade in all parts of the EEC as a single unit, to take advantage of the economies of scale. So far, however, there has been very little movement in this direction. Even attempts such as the loose association of Dunlop and Pirelli have foundered because of massive Pirelli losses having to be paid for by Dunlop. Many companies such as British Leyland have solved the problem temporarily by having links with continental companies and agreements to build cars under licence. Their agreement to build 'Minis' under licence at the Italian Innocenti factory resulted eventually in them buying up the Innocenti company, but during 1975 Leyland's Innocenti factory had to be closed because of financial problems.

It is logical that a common industrial policy should be worked out. This implies the completion of a common market for industrial goods, and is an important and essential step towards the attainment of full monetary and economic union. The steps which need to be taken include:

(i) free movement for all industrial goods and removal of any remaining tax-discrimination throughout the market;
(ii) new tax rules which encourage cross-frontier mergers and takeovers;
(iii) the establishment of a European company statute and a common patent convention;
(iv) freedom of movement of capital;
(v) freedom of establishment and the right of persons to engage in business throughout the community;
(vi) common policies for scientific and technical development in regard to technical standards (metrication and other measurements in the United Kingdom); safety standards; regulations of food quality; integration of the telecommunications network and equipment.

4

The Iron and Steel Industry: integration and rationalisation

This chapter and the next will give some detailed consideration to particular industries and their changing locations and structure. The steel industry, automobiles, textiles and chemicals have been selected because of their very significant contribution to the Western European economies, and because they exemplify many of the processes of change which have been discussed in chapter 3.

The steel industry is an important index of the relative wealth and stage of development of any particular country. It is traditionally a major employer of labour, and requires high capital investment and therefore has a tendency to locational inertia. Steel is a basic material which is used in almost every part of industry, transport of all types, construction and engineering, both heavy and sophisticated. It is therefore greatly involved in the complex patterns of modern industry.

The EEC is one of the world's major steel producers (fig. 4.1) and this chapter analyses its development in terms of four themes: the growth of national in-

	1964	1971	1973	1974	*Percentage growth* 1952–1967
West Germany	37·3	40·3	49·5	53·2	97
France	19·8	22·8	25·3	27·0	81
Italy	9·8	17·5	20·9	23·8	337
Belgium	8·7	12·4	15·5	16·2	89
Luxembourg	4·6	5·2	5·9	6·4	49
Netherlands	2·6	5·0	5·6	5·8	389
EEC (Six)	82·8	103·2	122·8	132·4	114
UK	24·7	24·2	26·6	22·4	39
Denmark	neg.	0·5	0·5	0·5	–
Eire	neg.	0·1	0·1	0·1	–
EUR-9	–	–	150·1	155·6	–

Figure 4.1 EEC steel production (million tonnes).

dustries up to 1945; government intervention and control; the supra-national factor; and contemporary locational and structural changes.

The main stages of growth of the United Kingdom steel industry

The early nineteenth century

During the industrial revolution coal was the critical determinant of location. The coalfields contained blackband iron-ore and often had limestone available nearby, and coal, being heavy and of low value in proportion to bulk, was costly to transport very far. In addition, early iron and steel technology was relatively inefficient, requiring large quantities of coal in proportion to iron-ore, and the means of transport available could not cope with such a situation. For these reasons the coalfields were unrivalled sites for steel-making—amongst them South Wales, Durham and the 'Black Country' of the West Midlands.

The 1870s to 1930s

Improvements in iron-smelting techniques, allowing a more efficient use of smaller quantities of coal and hence lower fuel costs, made it less essential for steel-making to be tied to the coalfields after the mid-nineteenth century. Two new steel conversion processes also contributed to this trend. The Bessemer converter in the 1850s, modified by Thompson-Gilchrist so that high-phosphorus iron-ores could be utilised, allowed increasing use of the abundant, though lean, ores of the Jurassic scarplands of Cleveland, Lincolnshire and Northampton. In 1873 the open hearth furnace enlarged the scale of steelmaking and was to dominate the scene until the 1930s. It has remained of major importance and is particularly useful in re-melting scrap-iron. The iron-ore fields became location sites for new steelworks, established on 'greenfield sites' (entirely new locations with no previous industrial characteristics). Corby, opened in 1935, was a good example of this, and the areas around Northampton and Scunthorpe became major iron and steel manufacturing zones in the first half of the twentieth century.

This increasing complexity of location was compounded by changes in the supply of raw materials which began during the early twentieth century. Imports of foreign ores from Sweden, Canada, Spain and North Africa increased rapidly, partly because of larger ore-carriers, and partly because of their higher ore-content, two or three times as high as the lean Jurassic ores of Northampton. There was a growing tendency for steelworks to be located at ports and estuary sites around the coast. The natural growth points became the South Wales coast between Cardiff and Swansea, Teesmouth, the Dee estuary and the Manchester Ship Canal. These coastal zones adjacent to already existing coalfields and iron and steel producing regions were in an excellent position for the low-cost assembly of all necessary materials. Teesmouth was a good example, having an abundant supply of ore in the nearby Cleveland hills, coking coal from southwest Durham 40 km away, limestone from Weardale, flat estuarine land for the construction of large factory areas, and, most important, the estuary, which allowed the import of rich Spanish and Swedish ore.

The decline of formerly important areas was beginning, but was complicated by the effects of the great depression of the 1930s. Inertia kept the original locations on the coalfields in existence but, economically, their long-term operating efficiency was low. They were often in small congested works, with exhausted iron-ore and uneconomic coal and requiring imports with high transport costs. The Ebbw Vale Steelworks was one such case, closed during the 1930s slump and later reopened in 1938, largely as a social measure to help combat the serious long-term unemployment problem in the mining areas of South Wales. This structural problem of reconciling the development of new growth areas, whilst maintaining employment in run-down regions as a social service, has continued to affect the steel industry to the present day.

Post-1945

By 1945 the UK steel industry had completed the second stage of its evolution. It was a large-scale industry with a network of factories in seven traditional regions (fig. 4.2). There was, however, an unintegrated structure and much

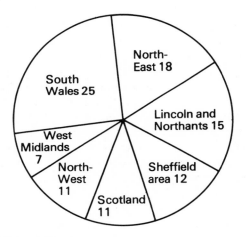

Figure 4.2 UK steel production, 1965—
percentages by traditional regions.

duplication of products. Control was in the hands of many private companies, often in small factories, undercapitalised, and with obsolescent equipment. The processes of change begun in the 1930s were continued and intensified: the movement to the coast; technological change and the increasing advantages of size gained by amalgamation and concentration in large factories; and the residual areas of steelworking maintained by inertia and increasing state intervention. Port Talbot (1947) and Llanwern, in particular, are examples of favourable sites for large integrated steelworks built on extensive areas of flat land and using low-cost imports at deep-water access points. Inland sites have appeared increasingly uneconomic in recent years, a conflict of interests emerging over many old steel-working areas where government intervention has stopped the closure of unprofitable works for social reasons. Ebbw Vale, Consett and Workington are all examples which have been retained, but they have a low cost-effectiveness and are part of the government's social support policy for declining areas, rather than having any real economic future. On the other hand, some areas have adapted their former advantages to new ones. The 'Black Country' has kept a remnant of its former steel-making capacity because it is adjacent to its market, the engineering and car factories of the West Midlands, and because it has local supplies of scrap-iron.

New processes

Technological progress has continued rapidly with two new factors: the basic oxygen, or LD, process and the electric arc furnace. The separate processes of iron-making, steel-making and finishing are increasingly being dealt with together in large integrated works. Internal costs are lower and economies of scale and greater efficiency are achieved. The open hearth furnace is rapidly being replaced by the basic oxygen converter which combines three great virtues: the rapidity of the Bessemer converter; the scrap-consuming ability of the open hearth furnace; and a facility for large-scale production. Two such converters can produce four million tonnes of steel per year. The entire UK production of approximately 26 million tonnes could thus be obtained from 14 converters in 7 steelworks. The likely pattern for the next decade is therefore rationalisation and concentration in fewer larger units. In 1969 open hearth furnaces still accounted for 51 per cent of capacity, and basic oxygen converters only 34 per cent. By 1980 it is expected that 80 per cent of steel will be produced from these converters, with the remaining capacity in electric arc furnaces. This last one is a specialist process often used for very high quality and alloy steels.

Nationalisation

The final element is Government intervention. There were thirteen major steel companies, some very large, such as the Steel Company of Wales, but there was too much product duplication, wasteful internal competition and a lack of the scale required for international competition. Since 1967 90 per cent of the steel industry has been nationalised as the British Steel Corporation, with a few private sector companies concentrating on alloy and specialist steel products. The main changes are as follows:

1. Re-organisation on a product basis, with area specialisation creating greater efficiency. The principal types of steel are general and heavy steels, tubes, sheet steel, strips and bars, and special alloy steels. Wales has traditionally specialised in sheet steel. Corby is the headquarters of the Tubes Division; South Teesside is headquarters of General Steels, and Sheffield of Alloy and Special Steels.
2. The new investment programme estimates that the British Steel Corporation will need capacity of up to 38 million tonnes in 1980–81.

A steelworks landscape in the Don Valley,
near Sheffield. These older factories are part
of British Steel's 'Special Products Division'.

3. A large new fleet of ore-carriers is to be developed to gain from the economies
   of large-scale sea transport, and Port Talbot (150000 tonnes capacity),
   Immingham (100000 tonnes), Redcar (200000 tonnes) and Hunterston
   (350000 tonnes) are to be developed as ports for this purpose.
4. Rationalisation and modernisation means in effect the expansion of five
   main heritage (traditional) steel-making areas. In Scotland, Ravenscraig is to
   be increased to 3·2 million tonnes capacity. An electric arc plant is to be built
   at Hallside and there will be a direct ore-reduction plant at Hunterston ore

The Anchor Development at British Steel's
Appleby Frodingham Works, Scunthorpe.

terminal. With modernisation of the tube works at Clydesdale, total capacity will be 4·5 million tonnes. In Wales, Port Talbot will raise capacity to 6 million tonnes and Llanwern to nearly 4 million tonnes (10 million tonnes in all). In England there are three areas. In the North-East Lackenby is to be expanded and adjacent to it a completely new complex at Redcar on the south bank of the Tees is to be developed. The combined capacity will exceed 12 million tonnes. On Humberside a substantial increase in the Anchor Works at Scunthorpe will raise production to 5 million tonnes. At Sheffield/Rotherham, the capacity for stainless, alloy and special steels will be expanded. This is a more specialised market, but production will be in the region of 2 million tonnes. Thus, the future favours a few large integrated coastal steelworks of 6 million tonnes capacity. There will also be room for a new breed, the mini-mill, using electric arc processes for smaller scale specialist alloy steels where the advantages of scale are not so crucial.

5. A reduction in the workforce is a necessary corollary of modernisation and by 1981 it is estimated that 180000 will be the required workforce. This involves a substantial reduction from 257000 (1967) to 230000 (1973), 208000 (1975) and 180000 (1981). This should produce a stable and efficient steel industry.

6. The modernising and resiting of steelmaking plant undoubtedly affects some areas adversely, a continuation of the problem first seen in the 1930s. Shotton-on-Dee, East Moors (Cardiff), Consett, Ebbw Vale and Hartlepool are old obsolescent plants which face closure. The Shotton works is one example where a whole region is almost completely dependent on one factory; 80 per cent of north-east Flintshire is dependent upon it for employment, and for Ebbw Vale the prospects may seem like the great depression all over again. In terms of traditional regions (fig. 4.2) it would appear that the West Midlands and North-West will be phased out from steel production entirely.

7. The British Steel Corporation needs modern large-scale plants equipped for new technology and high volume production. The expansion of these necessitates a run-down of old, badly-located plants; commercial viability has to be tempered by adjustments to meet the human problems involved. Possibly 38 million tonnes capacity for 1981 is an over optimistic forecast, when for much of 1975 the steel industry was operating 20 per cent below capacity.

Steel on the continent: the dominance of the 'Heavy Industrial Triangle'

Germany: the Ruhr

Prior to the establishment of the Community, the steel industry on the continent was related almost entirely to the central coal belt and its associated supplies of iron-ore. The original definition of the 'Heavy Industrial Triangle' (fig. 4.3) is based upon the Ruhr, the Nord/Pas de Calais and Sambre–Meuse coalfields and the southern apex of Lorraine (fig. 4.4). The Ruhr rose to importance during the middle and late nineteenth century with large quantities of high-grade, easily

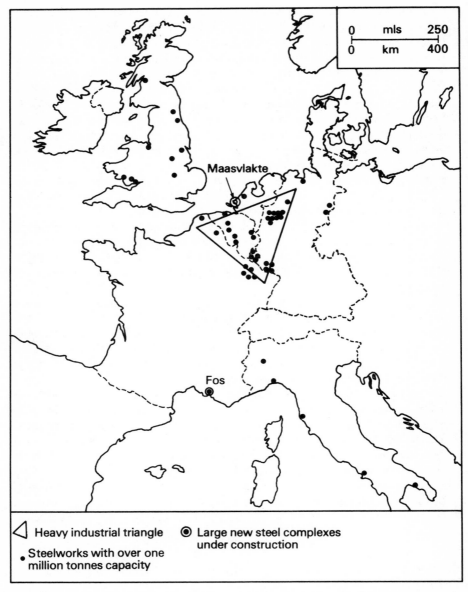

Figure 4.3 Major steel-producing centres in the EEC, 1974. *United Kingdom:* Ravenscraig*, Lackenby* and Consett, Scunthorpe*, Rotherham* and Corby, Port Talbot*, Ebbw Vale, Llanwern and Shotton; *Holland:* Ijmuiden; *France:* Dunkirk* and Denain, Gandrange*, Hagondange, Longwy, Seremange, Rombas; *Belgium:* Liège-Seraing*, Zelzate (Ghent)*, Clabecq-Sambre-La Louvière; *Italy:* Turin (Fiat), Bagnoli*, Cornigliano*, Taranto*, Piombino*; *W. Germany:* Saar (Neunkirchen-Volklingen), Bremen*, Ruhr (Duisburg*-Rheinhausen), Salzgitter; *Luxembourg:* Dudelange*, Differdange. (* = major development site)

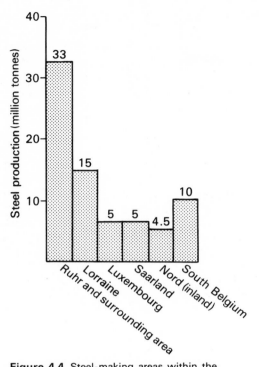

Figure 4.4 Steel-making areas within the 'Heavy Industrial Triangle', 1973. (Total 72·5 million tonnes)

extracted coking coal, and containing blackband iron-ore. The Siegerland iron-ore and limestone was close by. The river Rhine and its extensive canal system, including the Dortmund–Ems, were an excellent vehicle for cheap imports of iron-ore. Finally, the growth of the Ruhr as a major urban and industrial area helped generate its own market of numerous steel-using industries, manu-facturing locomotives, armaments, rolling stock, heavy engineering products and light engineering products such as cutlery. By 1938 Germany produced 22 million tonnes of steel, nearly 70 per cent of which came from the Ruhr. By 1964, in spite of a setback immediately after World War II, the Ruhr was producing 27 million tonnes of steel and by 1974 over 34 million tonnes, nearly 70 per cent of West Germany's total. Some idea of the concentrated nature of the German steel industry in the Ruhr is given by the fact that this great volume is produced in a conurbation of some 60 km × 16 km in extent, mainly in large integrated plants at Oberhausen, Rheinhausen, Duisburg and Dortmund. The Saarland coal-basin on the French border is responsible for another 10 per cent of West German production at Saarbrucken, Volklingen and Neunkirchen.

France: Nord/Pas de Calais

The French steel industry is much less concentrated, but one major area is the Nord/Pas de Calais coalfield. In 1967 it produced 5·2 million tonnes of steel,

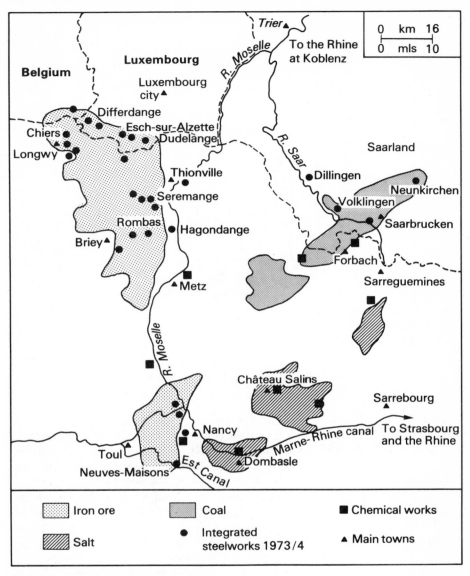

Figure 4.5 Lorraine, Luxembourg and the Saarland.

one-quarter of French production, and is located in three traditional districts: Denain–Valenciennes–Henin–Lietard, the centre of the heavy industry; at Boulogne and at Isbergues on the Aire canal; and the minor production centres of Maubeuge and Hautmont in the Sambre valley. These small-scale steelworks, often in the congested older areas of the coalfield, have become relatively insignificant in recent years when compared with the large new integrated works at Dunkerque, which now has 80 per cent of the region's steel-making capacity.

Belgium

Across the Belgian frontier lies the Sambre–Meuse coalfield. Both the coal and Devonian haematite iron-ores outcropping along the valley were the initial location factors for a very considerable heavy industrial zone. La Louvière–Charleroi–Namur and Liège–Seraing at the eastern end of the coalfield retain a large proportion of Belgium's steel industry, now in fewer, larger integrated works.

Lorraine and Luxembourg

Finally, the major home iron-ore producing region in the Community is Lorraine (fig. 4.5). This only developed just before the turn of the century because of the late exploitation of the Jurassic iron-ores. These lean ores (up to 30 per cent iron) with their high phosphorus content, became economic only with the invention of the Gilchrist–Thomas process. This stimulated the movement of steel manufacturing to the iron-ore field by the early twentieth century, similarly with that of the United Kingdom. Lorraine is now the principal French steel-making area with over 60 per cent of total production. Considerable rationalisation and modernisation of small factories has occurred and Lorraine will continue to be a very important primary steel-making area. Iron-ore output is 55 million tonnes (1974) per year and provides three-quarters of the needs of the French steel industry (fig. 4.6). The small but productive Lorraine coalfield

	Home production (million tonnes)	Iron content of home ores (%)	Imports (million tonnes)
West Germany	5·6	28	50·3
France	54·7	28	net exporter
Italy	0·8	32	14·6
Netherlands	0	–	7·0
Belgium	neg.	–	21·1
Luxembourg	2·6	27	12·1
United Kingdom	3·6	27	24·9
Eire	0	–	neg.
Denmark	neg.	–	neg.
Total Eur-9	67·6		130·0 (approx)

Figure 4.6 Supply of iron ore in the EEC, 1974.

means that Lorraine steel is unique in the EEC for having a complete range of locally based raw materials. However, the export of iron-ore to the rest of the community is increasingly difficult in competition with imported high-grade ores from Africa and Sweden. The Ruhr, Belgium and even the Nord no longer use Lorraine ore and its use is confined to its own region, the Saar and Luxembourg. The Lorraine steel-making area stretches from Nancy in the south through Hagondange and Thionville to Longwy. In Luxembourg, a large steel industry for such a small country is based upon the northern extension of the Lorraine ore-field. There are four steelworks near the southern border with France (fig. 4.5), but massive imports of coal are needed to sustain the industry, mainly from France and Belgium.

Steel centres away from the Rhinelands

The areas so far discussed in relation to continental Europe are the principal national steel-making regions of four countries: West Germany, France, Belgium and Luxembourg, which although apparently adjacent to one another, developed entirely separately. They are all based upon the highly centralised reserves of coal and iron-ore, but historical rivalries over the national frontiers which dissected this natural resource zone created fears during the nineteenth century that each steel industry was too close to the frontier for strategic safety. The best example of this geographical unity but historical separation, is the essential complementarity of the Ruhr and Lorraine, whose logical exchange of raw materials was for long prevented not only by transport problems but by national rivalry and high tariff barriers. The adjacent resources of Lorraine and the Saar have been a major factor in the enmity of France and Germany since 1870. One result of this has been the development of steel-making capacity, albeit small-scale, in regions away from the frontiers which were felt to be strategically safer, particularly in France and Germany. In France the Massif Central has scattered and small deposits of coal and iron-ore and had the added advantage of being within the heart of the country, safe from attack. Furthermore, the St. Etienne region (a small conurbation of some 400000 people) around the Loire coalfield, was the cradle of the industrial revolution in France and, until the end of the nineteenth century, was the leading area of steel production. To the north lies the small Blanzy coal basin with Le Creusot as another nineteenth century steel and engineering area. Other small coal basins with industrial pockets lying around the Massif Central are Commentry and Decazeville. An interesting example of these small, dispersed and often very specialised industrial pockets is the cutlery centre of Thiers, between St. Etienne and Clermont Ferrand. This pattern of inland dispersal was accentuated by the growth of such centres as Caen, where a steelworks was based upon local iron-ore, and Grand Quevilly below Rouen on the Seine, using imported iron-ore. In the Upper Isère and Arc valleys between Grenoble and Albertville, a specialised steel industry using hydro-electric power has developed. In West Germany the steelworks at Peine and Salzgitter in Saxony had been originally developed in 1938, partially upon the iron-ore and coal of the Harz foreland of Lower Saxony. These areas maintained their position during the inter-war years because of favourable government policies.

By the 1950s two new factors similar to those in the United Kingdom had emerged and were to play an increasingly important part in further development. These were the ECSC, and technological changes such as those in the UK which together have begun to change substantially patterns of location and structure.

The European Coal and Steel Community (ECSC)

This came into effect in July 1952 primarily as a common market in coal, steel, iron-ore, scrap, pig-iron and coke. Its effect upon the coal industry was referred to in the previous chapter, but in the steel industry it has helped on a European level to do what the British Steel Corporation has done at national level. It has lowered freight rates; ensured conditions of equal competition and a regular supply of raw materials; created a single market and price levels; led to modernisation, rationalisation and expansion of production; raised the living standards of workers; assisted new steelworks development projects with investment grants; and encouraged intra-national mergers.

The abolition of frontier tariffs, national subsidies, and transport-rate discrimination has greatly increased interdependence and intercommunity trade. Lorraine, for instance, had a natural geographical advantage for marketing its products in the adjacent parts of South Germany, and from 1956 to 1961 it increased its sale of rolled steel products there fourfold. The transport costs of Ruhr coke fell by 30 per cent in the ten years up to 1962. In 1952, just before the ECSC began, scrap cost 22 dollars per tonne in the Netherlands, but in Italy up to 55 dollars per tonne. The ECSC has been responsible for large reductions in transport charges across frontiers and for smoothing out cost variations between member states.

The stability and large home market within ECSC has encouraged long-term planning and an increased growth potential, and there has been a huge expansion of production since 1952. Between 1952 and 1964 the Community steel output more than doubled to 83 million tonnes and, by 1973, the enlarged EEC of nine produced 150 million tonnes, substantially more than USA or USSR. The investment loans, research activities and social policies of the ECSC have together been partially responsible for guiding the location of at least two new steel plants (fig. 4.7). The Sidmar steelworks on the Ghent–Terneuzen canal at Zelzate in East Flanders was built in 1962 in an area of economic depression. The Taranto steelworks in Southern Italy was constructed with a view to it becoming an initial growth point for metal fabricating industries, and for industrial employment in this depressed area.

The contemporary pattern of steel-making in the EEC

Raw materials

The attraction of the coalfields has diminished with better iron-ore sintering and preparation, and with improved fuel economy there has been a fall in the amount of coke needed per tonne of pig-iron. From the early 1960s it became progressively less economic to use home iron-ore, which has a low iron-content, and there was a great increase in imports of cheap, high-grade foreign ores of some 60 per cent iron purity (fig. 4.6). Seigerland production ceased in 1966 and Salzgitter ore is now used only locally. Lorraine is the only substantial home ore producer left with some 80 per cent of total Community production (fig. 4.5). West Germany finds it cheaper to import most of her iron-ore from Sweden, and supplies of cheap American coal via the Rhine waterway. The increasing use of

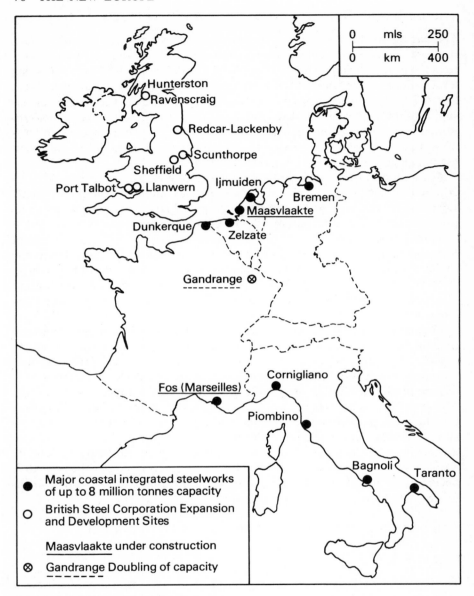

Figure 4.7 EEC coastal steelworks—current projects and expansion plans.

scrap, particularly in those heavy industrial districts which produce a surplus for re-using, is shown by the fact that it is used for a third of West Germany's and nearly 60 per cent of Italy's steel.

Coastal locations

The continuous wide-strip steel mill and the LD (Oxygen) process, were the two

Port Talbot iron and steel complex, showing the construction of the deep-water ore-terminal on the left.

other very significant developments which, alongside the need for large-scale imports, laid the necessary basis after 1960 for a cumulative movement to the large integrated coastal steelworks (fig. 4.7). These new locations have developed as a response to the increasing need for imports and deep-water ore-terminals, together with the need to eliminate transport costs to the interior. There are, including Port Talbot, Llanwern and Teesside in the UK, eleven coastal steelworks in Europe, producing over 40 million tonnes (fig. 4.8), and a further two are being built at Fos-sur-Mer, near Marseilles, and at Maasvlakte, downstream from Rotterdam. They are all large and many have a potential capacity of 5–10 million tonnes with berthing facilities for large ore-carriers. The first concentration of these is along the North Sea coast from Dunkerque to

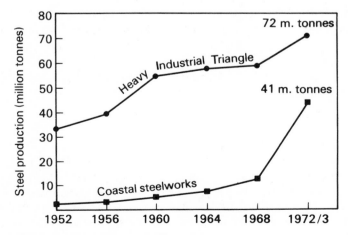

Figure 4.8 The growth in importance of the coastal steelworks, 1952–1973.

The Sidmar Zelzate steelworks, near Ghent,
showing a large converter in operation.

Bremen. Most of the Dutch steel production comes from the Ijmuiden works,
built at the end of the North Sea canal with a capacity for 4 million tonnes of
ingot steel, rolling mills and a tinplate factory. It has a dock capable of handling
80 000 tonne ore-carriers. The Sidmar plant at Ghent (Zelzate) currently produces 2 million tonnes of steel and is capable of expansion to treble that figure.
The only limitation here is that the Ghent–Terneuzen canal, by which it is
linked to the West Scheldt, can take only 60 000 tonne ore-carriers. The Bremen
works uses the Weserport facilities 55 km downstream for bulk ore-carriers, as
its own are limited to carriers of 28 000 tonnes. The Dunkerque works (4 million
tonnes of steel) has facilities for 100 000 tonne ore-carriers and, with Ijmuiden,
these two have the greatest potential in a situation where import handling
efficiency is critical.

Italy

It is the Italian steel industry which illustrates so vividly the dramatic growth
and locational changes of the past 20 years (fig. 4.9). Prior to 1945, with
negligible raw materials, steel-making was confined largely to northern Italy
near the sources of hydro-electric power and the steel-using industries for scrap.
Milan, Turin, Bergamo and Brescia had a number of small specialised steelworks producing quality steel in electric furnaces. Production was small-scale
and in 1953 was only 3·5 million tonnes. There was a small works at Piombino,
adjacent to Italy's only supplies of iron-ore, on the island of Elba. Since the early

	1913	1938	1956	1963	1971	1973	1974
France	4·7	6·2	13·4	19·0	22·8	25·3	27·0
West Germany	8·9	22·0	23·2	37·0	40·3	49·5	53·2
United Kingdom	7·8	13·2	16·5	23·7	24·2	26·6	22·4
Italy	n	2·1	3·5	9·0	17·5	20·9	23·8

n = negligible

Figure 4.9 The changing volume of steel production during the twentieth century.

1960s, however, production has increased at a phenomenal rate: in 1964 production had reached 9·8 million tonnes per year and by 1968 17 million tonnes. Production figures for 1974 rated Italian steel production slightly higher than that of the United Kingdom. Post-war reconstruction patterns have involved state participation and control. The state has taken a controlling interest through the holding company of Finsider, which now controls some 60 per cent of total production. The unemployment problem of Southern Italy was a major factor in the opening of the Taranto steelworks in 1964 and it was planned that this should be the nucleus for metal fabricating industries in Bari and Taranto. The whole programme of development has been based upon coastal steelworks which import iron-ore, scrap and coal very cheaply, and now four large integrated plants, Cornigliano, Piombino, Bagnoli and Taranto, produce 60 per cent of Italy's steel (fig. 4.7). Taranto, in particular, can handle ore-carriers of 100000 tonnes and it is planned to boost the present production of 4 million tonnes to 10 million tonnes per year.

The Heavy Industrial Triangle

Although the movement to the coast has been very substantial and will continue to grow, the northern Heavy Industrial Triangle still accounts for nearly 60 per cent of steel-making on the continent (fig. 4.8) and even higher proportions of West German, Belgian, Luxembourg and French national output (fig. 4.4). The tremendous concentration of steel-making capacity in the Ruhr has substantial advantages with its adjacent consumer markets, dense communications networks and local sources of scrap. Lorraine is a major factor in French expansion plans. A new steelworks has recently been built at Dillingen in the Saar. Enormous capital investment is required for the development of entirely new 'greenfield sites', and this is another reason for the maintenance and expansion of traditional steel-making regions. They have, in addition, a positive advantage which accrues directly from the establishment of the ECSC and Common Market. The triangle now has a new role. It is the most centrally placed industrial area within the community with good, short, internal lines of communication, the principal source of raw materials and a huge urban market and supply of labour. The canalisation of the Moselle has benefited Lorraine (fig. 4.5), particularly with its dependence upon Ruhr coke via a waterway from which frontier tariffs have now disappeared. The effective disappearance of the frontiers has given this region a new advantage: the natural unity which has always been prescribed by geography but denied by history. Its complementary resources can now be used in a coherent manner, focussed upon the major artery of the river Rhine and its tributaries. The advantages of this Rhineland region, with increasing integration, have encouraged its maintenance as the single most important steel-making region of the EEC (fig. 4.3).

State involvement

Considerable importance in decision-making still rests with the national governments and there is an increasing state involvement in both control and planning. Modernisation and rationalisation has involved re-location and amalgamations of companies, larger steelworks and an increasing domination by large corporations (fig. 4.10).

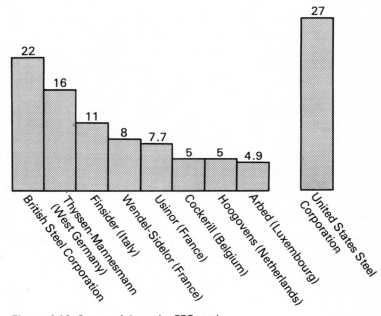

Figure 4.10 Output of the major EEC steel groups (million tonnes), 1973.

France

The French 'Plan Professionel' has three specific projects in hand:

(a) the doubling of the Gandrange works in Lorraine to 4 million tonnes capacity,
(b) the doubling of the capacity at Dunkerque to 8 million tonnes by 1974,
(c) the construction of a new plant at Fos-sur-Mer, near Marseilles, with 8 million tonnes capacity, based entirely upon imported raw materials.

This will completely alter the locational balance of the French steel industry. Its structure is also changing rapidly with rationalisation: it is now dominated by two large groups, Wendel-Sidelor and Usinor, which together account for 70 per cent of bulk steel output. There are still a larger number of small isolated companies as a legacy from the days when the small metallurgical centres of the Massif Central and sub-Alpine region flourished. Although many closures have been inevitable, survival has been based upon specialisation in special steels. Two major companies, Creusot-Loire and Chatillon-Commentry in the centre, and Ugine in the Isère valley now produce most of the French special and alloy steel.

Mergers and rationalisation

Italy, with the state-controlled Finsider controlling 60 per cent of production, bears the closest resemblance to the British Steel Corporation, but the other member countries have experienced reorganisational change in varying degrees. Luxembourg has five integrated plants near the French border producing 5 million tonnes of steel, 90 per cent of which is accounted for by Arbed. West Germany, the largest producer of steel in the community, had a number of major companies: Krupp, Hoechst, Stahlwerke and Klocknerwerke, although a recent merger has created a dominant group. Thyssen-Mannesmann, with 40 per cent of total capacity. In Belgium too, in 1970, Cockerill emerged as the largest group with 39 per cent of production.

The future

The Europe of the nine has a steel-making capacity of over 150 million tonnes. The increasing size of steelworks implies that there will be fewer, larger units. From no less than 113 companies in 1958, 60 per cent of production is now controlled by eight large companies (fig. 4.10). The Commission favours the eventual amalgamation of all bulk steel production into a new pattern, which would result in extensive cross-frontier mergers and a dozen major steel groups each producing up to 12 million tonnes per year. Their probable locations should suggest themselves.

5

Other industries:
automobiles, textiles and chemicals

The Automobile Industry

This industry has a central role in the complex industrial economies of the twentieth century. It is a major user of raw materials and a large-scale employer. In France it absorbs 50 per cent of the production of rubber, 50 per cent of the shaped aluminium, and 21 per cent of sheet steel production. One and a half million people gain their living from the industry. Its real growth has been since 1945 as a reflection of consumer demand. It is an assembly line and component industry with horizontal integration resulting in a few large companies dominating production. The geographical location of the industry is usually near large centres of population and does not often correspond to the older heavy-industry areas (fig. 5.1).

Development of the industry

The European motor industry originated in the 1890s with names such as Daimler, Lanchester and Panhard. In 1896 the Daimler Company began production in Coventry, but the industry had a slow undistinguished growth up to 1914, when it was primarily a small-scale producer of high-cost goods for a restricted market. Even until the slump of the 1930s it remained best known for a large number of specialist quality companies such as Lea Francis of UK and Ferrari of Italy.

But, during the 1930s, the character of the industry was changing. The economic depression had wiped out many firms and mergers had occurred on a large scale. In the UK the number of manufacturers declined from 88 in 1922 to 31 in 1931. By 1937 the UK produced 380000 cars and had become second world producer to USA. Mass production methods were introduced from America during the 1930s and the growth of real per capita income was another indication of the imminent development of the consumer and production boom which was to come after 1945. The importance of the consumer cannot be overestimated, as the main impetus to the development of the industry has been the growth of demand. The very rapid growth since 1945 corresponds to the initial development of the family car. Since then there has been replacement demand

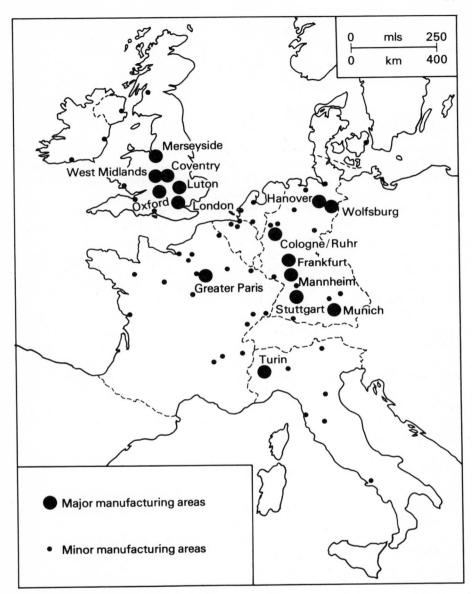

Figure 5.1 The motor vehicle industry—
principal locations.

with production lines depending upon planned obsolescence and the population requiring a replacement car at regular intervals. The third stage is just beginning to affect the European market, with the appearance of the second family car. There is now one vehicle for every six people in the EEC. The industry developed very rapidly between 1940 and 1970 and is consequently modern in characteristics. Factories are usually housed in one-storey modern buildings, and, with the large amount of space needed for storage and car parking, usually cover a wide area. They are often on 'greenfield sites', (e.g. Wolfsburg, West Germany) and some distance from city centres where space is readily available. Communications by road are invariably good and siting on by-pass roads is common. The car assembly factories on the A45 at Coventry are a good example of this.

Structure of the vehicle industry

The assembly line involves the concentration of vast amounts of supplies which come from subsidiary manufacturers. These provide basic materials such as pressed steel, rubber, glass, etc. and a host of manufactured components and accessories including electrical equipment and brakes. These specialist sub-contractors have traditionally been independent of the vehicle companies which are their main outlets and, therefore, vertical integration in the industry is almost non-existent. There are exceptions to this. British Leyland own Pressed Steel; Renault and Fiat have their own steel and metallurgy supplies; and Krupp, essentially a steel maker, also produces commercial vehicles. In general, however, the major component manufacturers are independent and exert a considerable monopoly. Solex supply two-thirds of the French, half the German and one-third of the United Kingdom market for carburettors. With a great number of independent suppliers there is therefore a real necessity for efficient distribution. This leads to a tendency for a number of vehicle industry zones to develop made up of linked component manufacturers and car assembly plants concentrated in and around city regions. This regional swarming has the advantages of short distances for the transport and distribution of components, a pool of skilled and semi-skilled labour, and easier technical cooperation. It is seen to best advantage in regions such as the West Midlands, Saxony, the Paris region and Milan–Turin.

Location

Each nation's vehicle-producing areas are usually the city regions, whose large populations provide the natural market (fig. 5.1). There is a distinct tendency for factories to be sited on the outer fringes of the city, away from the congested centres. In the Greater Paris region the three largest companies are all in the suburbs or satellite towns. Renault have their main works at Billancourt, but have other factories at Nanterre and Clichy to the north-west, at Rouen and Le Havre on the Lower Seine, and Orléans and Le Mans. There is also Citroen at Reims and Simca at Poissy. In Italy 90 per cent of vehicle production is around Turin and Milan and the United Kingdom has a traditional concentration in the West Midlands, particularly at Coventry and Birmingham. There are also anomalous situations: the Peugeot factories originated at Montbeliard and Sochaux in the Jura, and continue to operate successfully from there, high managerial and technical skills overcoming their apparent disadvantage of location.

West Germany illustrates a modification of this pattern: Daimler-Benz at Unterturkheim and Sindelfingen near Stuttgart, and at Mannheim and Gaggenau in the south Rhineland; General Motors (Opel) at Russelsheim (Frankfurt); BMW at Munich; Porsche at Stuttgart; and Ford at Cologne. All these indicate the importance of the cities of south Germany and the Rhineland. The largest single vehicle enterprise, however, Volkswagen, does not conform to this particular model. Wolfsburg was an early example of re-location of industry in 1933 to the then centre of Germany, partly for strategic reasons and partly as a policy of dispersing Ruhr industry. It was located next to the Mittelland canal, the main waterway from the Ruhr to Berlin. Now, however, since the post-1945 political division of Germany, Wolfsburg is very near the East German frontier and on the periphery of the EEC. The reputation and efficiency of the company have allowed it to expand its operations, the Volkswagen factory now employing over 70000 people. It has expanded to nearby Hanover, Brunswick and Kassel, and Saxony has become the country's second vehicle region with 40 per cent of output, equivalent to that of the south Rhineland.

To summarise, the EEC vehicle industry is principally located in the following areas: the Midlands and south-east of England; the Paris region; Milan and Turin; Saxony and the south Rhinelands. Nevertheless, the industry has been encouraged to move into areas of high unemployment in certain cases. In the UK this tendency is well established with factories on Merseyside, in South Wales, and at Linwood and Bathgate in Scotland. All British Leyland's commercial vehicle production is now at Bathgate. In France and Germany there is also a movement to the older coalfield areas which need a new industrial infrastructure. Peugeot have set up a factory near Lille and Opel at Bochum in the Ruhr.

The major vehicle companies

Horizontal integration has become almost complete. The assembly lines and mass production units are dominated by a few of the large companies, with the resulting economies of scale which have been achieved by the vehicle industry in the last thirty years. In the United Kingdom four groups produce practically all the motor vehicles including commercial vehicles. British Leyland (BLMC) is an excellent example of the process as it incorporates six famous car companies—Austin, Morris, Standard-Triumph, Jaguar, Daimler and Rover, as well as the commercial vehicle company, Leyland Motors. In 1974 it produced 45 per cent of the United Kingdom total, and is now the only British-controlled group. The rest are American subsidiaries: Ford Motor Company (UK), which produces 27 per cent; Vauxhall controlled by General Motors (15 per cent); and Chrysler UK, which incorporated the former Rootes Group (11 per cent). There are still several small, but significant, luxury manufacturers, including Rolls-Royce, Jensen and Morgan cars. On the continent there is a similar picture. In West Germany Volkswagen dominate the market, with nearly half of total production and a very considerable export market, followed again by Opel (General Motors), Ford and Daimler-Benz. France has three major companies: Renault (40 per cent), Citroen-Berliot (26 per cent) and Peugeot (20 per cent), whilst Simca (14 per cent) is a subsidiary of Chrysler. Italy, however, has the most marked concentration: one company, Fiat, produces 85 per cent of Italy's cars; Alfa Romeo produces 5 per cent. There are several minor producers in the luxury and sports car range: Maserati, Lancia and Ferrari. The Dutch company DAF, closely linked with Volvo, is a smaller-scale producer and the only significant representative of the Benelux group of countries.

The EEC and world competition

Motor vehicles are an important element in the EEC's trade. West Germany is the most successful exporter, with half her total production exported. France exports 40 per cent, Britain 35 per cent, and Italy 30 per cent of their total production. At the same time, the two-way pattern of trade has meant that there has been increasing import penetration, particularly from Japan. Imported cars now account for up to 40 per cent of UK passenger car sales. Within the Community there is much scope for increased trade in the future, and with the progressive abolition of tariffs, there have been spectacular increases in intra-community trade during the 1960s and 1970s. In 1958 only 51 000 passenger vehicles were sold amongst the 'original Six'; by 1963 there were 628 000 and by 1972, over 2 million. West Germany's imports of cars from the rest of the Community increased from 200 000 in 1966 to over 620 000 in 1973.

American involvement in the European vehicle industry is enormous but varies from 55 per cent control in the UK to 35 per cent in West Germany, and 20 per cent in France. In addition to this involvement, the American car industry itself operates on a very large scale and at very high efficiency. In 1967 General Motors of USA produced over 7 million vehicles, equivalent to total EEC production in that year (fig. 5.2). It is this American competition, and the more recent Japanese assault on the European market, which necessitates the existence of a few large EEC companies with the investment and research development capabilities which advantages of scale offer.

		Cars		Commercial vehicles	
	1967	1973	1974	1967	1974
West Germany	2296	3642	2840	187	265
France	1777	3202	3045	233	417
Italy	1439	1823	1631	103	141
Netherlands	49	94	86	7	13
Belgium*	164	260	756	25	30
Luxembourg	–	–	–	–	–
United Kingdom	1560	1747	1534	384	402
Ireland*	–	53	54	–	–
Denmark	–	–	7	–	–

* largely vehicle assembly by subsidiary companies.

Figure 5.2 EEC motor vehicle production and assembly (in thousand tonnes).

Much greater collaboration and increased integration within the EEC are both necessary and likely. Technical, commercial and marketing agreements are important. Another form of integration is the siting of assembly-lines in member countries. The UK vehicle industry has 14 assembly plants operating on the continent, largely in Belgium (7) and the Netherlands (4) which have only relatively small car industries, but there are also three around Paris. British Leyland have taken control of Innocenti of Milan, only to close the factory at the end of 1975.

In 1974 French Government approval was given to the merger between Citroen and Peugeot, to form a second large company, and to Berliet-Saviem which will dominate the French commercial vehicle industry. The trend towards larger units will probably continue until the EEC has car companies able to operate on the scale of the American companies such as General Motors and Ford.

The Textile Industry

The textile industry is an old staple industry, a major exporter and one of the most important single industries in the Community. It has a workforce of over 2 millions, representing about 7 per cent of total manufacturing employment. It is, however, beset by problems of declining production in the face of foreign competition, a relatively slow growth of domestic consumption, and an outmoded structure associated with its nineteenth century origins. Its precursor, the cottage industry, has retained a residual influence in the survival of subdivided processes and the tendency to small-scale factory units, with a poor degree of integration. It is often, therefore, described as a declining industry and has faced great problems of adjustment during the present century.

Location

There has been a tradition of heavy regionalisation and concentration in localities originally favoured with water-power, coal and the local availability or easy import facility of the raw material. On a European scale there are three major textile zones (fig. 5.3), all of which are based upon old industrial regions: Flanders and the Rhineland; Lombardy and Piedmont; and the sub-Pennine region of Lancashire and Yorkshire. Several smaller, though significant areas, often medieval in origin, have survived by specialising in high-quality fabrics or by developing a monopoly in a particular material or process.

Flanders—North Rhineland

Astride the Franco-Belgian border lies one of the leading textile areas in Europe, important since the Middle Ages. It stretches across the Plain of Flanders from

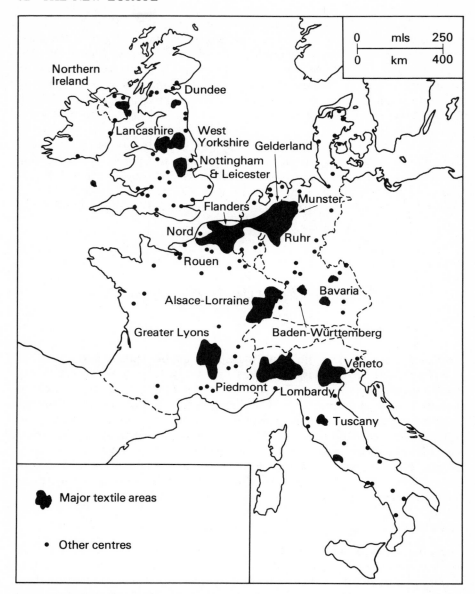

Figure 5.3 Principal textile manufacturing locations.

Lille into Belgium between Courtrai and Ghent. From its earlier concentration on local wool from the sheep grazed on chalk escarpments, and linen using flax from the Lys Valley, it has changed into a complex modern industry. Cotton, nylon and mixed fabrics are important at Lille, Roubaix-Tourcoing, Armentières and La Bassée, but fine linens, carpets, hosiery, clothing and furnishing fabrics are also manufactured, and outlying centres include Amiens, Abbeville and Cambrai. In Belgium about half of the total number of cotton spindles are in or around Ghent, but the Scheldt–Dendre Valley towns of Oudenaarde, Ranse, Tournai and Geerardsbergen are also important. Courtrai produces fine linen from Lys Valley flax though most flax is now imported from France and Poland. The industry has moved into Brabant and Brussels, producing carpets, blankets and fashionable clothing. The original woollen industry has now largely migrated to Verviers in the Ardennes to take advantage of the soft water and local wool.

The textile areas of the Netherlands and West Germany are a natural eastward extension. In the Netherlands the industry developed from the trading activities of the Hanseatic league along the Rhine, in the towns of Breda, Tilburg, Arnhem, Nijmegen and Rotterdam/Dordrecht. During the twentieth century there has been an eastward extension to the eastern heathland towns of Hengelo, Enschede, Emmen and Twente, where nylon and rayon production is most important. In adjacent West Germany lies the 'Baumwollstrasse' of North-Rhine/Westphalia, where a combination of Ruhr coal and the traditional crafts of towns such as Krefeld and München–Gladbach have produced a specialised textile industry which occupies towns around the fringes of the Ruhr. Krefeld's original speciality of silk and velvet has now been supplemented by nylon and terylene. The cotton industry is centred upon Wuppertal, München–Gladbach and Bocholt. Dusseldorf and Cologne are important too, and the area extends northwards to Munster and Bielefeld, which specialises in linen.

Lombardy and Upper Piedmont

There are over 500000 workers in the Italian textile industry, the bulk of which is concentrated along the northern Alpine fringe of the Po Valley, stretching from Biella through Milan, Bergamo and Vicenza to Padua. The principal concentration of cotton manufacturing is within a radius of 60 km from Milan, in the industrial satellite towns of Varese, Gallarate, Busto Arsizio and Legnano. There is quite intense regional specialisation, particularly in the silk manufacturing arc of towns, Como, Varese and Treviglio, and the concentration of woollens and worsteds in the Biellese and Bergamasque sub-Alpine valleys. Immediately to the south of Milan, the towns of Vercelli, Magenta and Pavia manufacture synthetic fibres. Another major woollen and knitwear area is based upon Padua, Vicenza, Schio and Valdegno, in Veneto Province.

The Lancashire/Yorkshire sub-Pennine region

The rise of the textile areas of northern England was caused by the coincidence of several factors in a unique situation, which led to the establishment of two areas which dominated world textile production in the nineteenth century. The natural factors were the suitability of the Pennines for sheep-rearing, abundant lime-free water, numerous sites for water-power, coupled with a high relative humidity, and power from the Lancashire coalfield. These were augmented by crucial human factors. These were the energy of pragmatic non-conformists and entrepreneurs, and their ability to accumulate capital, the inventions of textile machinery by Kay, Arkwright and Crompton, and the lack of guilds in this area.

The construction of port facilities, canals and railways as the expansion of these industrial areas got under way, and as imports of raw materials became necessary, was a further factor of concentration.

There was an extraordinary degree of specialisation in Lancashire, and in 1931 84 per cent of all cotton operatives in the United Kingdom were in East Lancashire and the adjoining part of Yorkshire. Manchester was the commercial centre, bank and warehouse. Spinning was localised in an arc of towns close to Manchester, and weaving more particularly in the group of towns north of the Rossendale Fells and in the Ribble Valley. The finishing trades (bleaching and dyeing) and clothing were not quite as localised, factories tending to be limited to one or other activity, which led to small production units and a lack of integration of any kind.

West Yorkshire developed an equally concentrated woollen textile region, based upon the Leeds/Bradford conurbation. Here the principal specialisation was in the type of product rather than, as in Lancashire, in processes. Long wools for worsteds predominate in Bradford and the north-west of the region, short wools for woollen products in the south-east, whilst carpets are made at Halifax, and Leeds is the ready-made clothing centre. Bradford is the financial and commercial centre of the industry.

Other areas

1. **Alsace-Lorraine:** This originated as a textile area in the medieval period. The Vosges mountains provided local wool, soft water and fast-flowing streams, and the industry has survived in factories around Epinal, Mulhouse, Belfort and Colmar, chiefly with cottons, thread, fine linen and hosiery.
2. **Greater Lyons:** Silk-making originated in the fifteenth century from exiled Italian merchants and is still so important that in 1968 80 per cent of French output came from this area. Rayon and nylon have developed to supplement the natural silk.
3. **Bavaria and Baden-Württemberg:** The cities of South Germany have a traditional textile industry with cottons at Stuttgart, Karlsruhe and Augsburg.
4. **Peninsula Italy:** There is a significant woollen area in Tuscany (Prato and Florence in the valley of the River Arno) and at Rome. Woollens have been supplemented with synthetics established by large companies like Snia–Viscosa. Local raw materials are an advantage, with mulberries supporting silkworms in the Marche and eucalypts being grown for rayon production. In the south large factories have been set up under the auspices of the Cassa del Mezzogiorno at Caserta and Frosinone (Naples) and Pisticci (Taranto).
5. **The East Midlands Hosiery Belt of England:** This is dominated by Leicester and Nottingham, but stretches south in the valley of the River Soar around Hinckley and north to Mansfield. This is certainly an area of textile expansion and owes its present prosperity to the expanding market for knitwear and the ease with which synthetic fibres can be utilised. Around Nottingham it is associated with the original lace industry and the early working of silk and cotton, and around Leicester with woollens.
6. **Northern Ireland:** Ulster is probably the greatest linen-manufacturing region

in the world. Belfast dominates the industry, but Lurgan, Lisburn, Portadown and Ballymena are also important. Although competition from cheaper goods and the decline in demand for high quality specialist linen has taken place, the industry still has a large export market and a large development of synthetics has taken place.

7. **Dundee, Scotland:** Linen and jute are the two products of this very specialised town. Dundee is only a little less important than Belfast for linen and its jute industry employs over 17 000 people. Dunfermline damasks and Paisley fabrics are other famous specialities.

8. **Kidderminster in Worcestershire, England:** This town is the largest single carpet centre in the world, with 17 carpet companies employing 10 000 people. one-third of the employed population.

9. **Rouen:** This is an isolated cotton-manufacturing town based upon raw cotton imported through Le Havre.

Decline and adjustment

It is the cotton industry, particularly that of Lancashire, which has shown the classic symptoms of decline and the need for restructuring an old industry. In the nineteenth century Europe dominated world textile production, and as late as 1900 Great Britain accounted for 50 per cent and the other EEC nations for 35 per cent of world textile exports. The huge fall in British exports this century was caused by the developing nations of Asia, formerly her export markets, beginning to build up their own textile industries. Lancashire felt the loss of markets most heavily because of its high degree of specialisation in cotton fabrics which were particularly oriented towards the export trade (fig. 5.4). By the 1920s the inherent disadvantages of Lancashire had become apparent: the lack of local raw materials; static home demand; the near impossibility of competing with the cheap labour of India, China, Japan and Hong-Kong; and an increasingly obsolete industrial structure with old machinery. Production dropped and unemployment rose. There has therefore been no option for Lancashire but to rationalise the structure of the industry, to improve efficiency, and to reduce capacity and the labour force at a socially acceptable rate.

	Employed (1000s)	*Output* (million yd²)	*Exports* (million yd²)
1912	622	8050	6913 (85 % of output)
1930	356	3500	2472
1938	288	3126	1449
1958	250	1294	327
1967	195	918	163
1973	80	496	

Figure 5.4 The decline of the United Kingdom cotton exports market.

In the rest of the Community there has been a similar pattern of events. The French and Belgian textile industry is still characterised by its small production units and long domestic traditions. In 1967 the Belgian industry had 700 cotton mills with an output equal to that of 100 mills in the Netherlands. In France about 5000 textile enterprises employed just over 400000 workers. Considerable rationalisation has taken place and employment in cotton has fallen markedly. Production, however, was not as dependent as that of the United Kingdom upon exports to the developing world and former colonial markets, and therefore contraction has not been so severe as in Lancashire. In Italy, production has even increased. However, the picture generally of the Community is one of marked adjustment to new conditions and a fall in textile employment generally (fig. 5.5).

	1958	1971
West Germany	607	499
France	518	425
Belgium/Luxembourg	172	121
Italy	481	542
Netherlands	103	76
United Kingdom	815	680
Eire	neg	42
Denmark	neg	20
Total	2696	2405

Figure 5.5 Changes in employment in the extile industry (in thousand). (EEC Regional Report, 1973)

There is now a definite trend towards larger companies and a greater integration of production to gain the economies of scale. In the United Kingdom in 1946 there were over 1300 registered companies, but now there are four large groups: Courtaulds, Coats/Patons, English Calico and Viyella. Courtaulds have accomplished a substantial amount of horizontal integration and now control 45 per cent of cotton spinning capacity. Of the 45 cotton mills they controlled in 1964, 13 have been closed and the remainder modernised. Viyella are represented in all processes of the industry from spinning through to clothing production, and are a good example of vertical integration. In the high-income European countries, the numerous fashion changes such as the advent of jeans and trouser suits which require rapid decisions and manufacturing changes are best taken by such large well-capitalised companies, although even they can be overtaken by very rapid changes. A case in point is the Courtauld closure of their Skelmersdale factory in late 1976.

Although the picture of textiles is one of overall decline, not all branches of the industry have experienced the same rapid decline as cotton. Production of woollens has remained virtually static whilst that of synthetic fibres has dramatically increased. Woollens have had a greater ability to specialise in high-quality fabrics and to concentrate on the high-value domestic market. The woollen industry was never quite so dependent upon the export market as cotton, and thus had fewer potential contraction problems. Wool can be blended easily with synthetic fibres and has benefited from the rapid rise of the carpet and hosiery industries. The volume of knitted goods doubled from 1958 to 1968.

Man-made fibres

Man-made or synthetic fibres have exercised a decisive influence upon the character of the textile industry during the twentieth century. Their principal role has been as a supplement to, or substitute for, natural fibres. They are lower in price and are much more versatile, capable of being blended to varying degrees with natural fibres. There is a great range of synthetic fibres of chemical origin, including in the United Kingdom Nylon, Terylene, Courtelle and Acrilan, and their variants in France (Crylon) and West Germany (Dralon). Rayon is a cellulose wood-pulp product, but this is of declining importance compared with the synthetic coal- and oil-based fibres.

	Woven wool fabric	Cotton fabric	Synthetic fibres
West Germany	38	250	767
France	65	196	238
Belgium/Luxembourg	12	68	153
Netherlands	14	67	
Italy	159	171	341
United Kingdom	72	65	396
Eire	2	3	8
Denmark	3	8	–
Total EEC	365	828	1903

Figure 5.6 EEC textile production (thousand tonnes), 1974. (EEC Industrial Statistics)

Production of synthetics has risen dramatically within the last twenty years. It is now greater than that of natural fibres (fig. 5.6) and this has partially masked the fall in production and manpower which has taken place in these natural fibres. The widespread introduction of man-made fibres has had a significant effect upon the traditional textile areas. The new ranges and qualities of the synthetics have helped resuscitate the industry and given a new lease of life to old manufacturing areas. The cotton towns of Lancashire are an example of the residual strength of the industry in the area where specialisation developed to its greatest extent. After 50 years of decline, it now looks as if the recent improvements in machinery, including the new ring loom and the new ranges of synthetic fabrics, have given the area new life. The industry has moved to new locations, often in the areas of petrochemical production as at Teesside (Billingham and Wilton), and into development areas as at Pontypool, but in the main, it has succeeded in maintaining its heavily regionalised character. Geographical inertia has played a large part in this as the textile regions have always been heavily capitalised in plant, machinery and skilled labour.

The widespread substitution of man-made fibres has had another important effect. Mixtures of fabrics such as polyester–cotton and wool–Terylene are increasingly rendering the traditional divisions within the industry obsolete. The influence of markets has become more important as half of the textile industry's output of cloth goes directly into consumer clothing. Rapid fashion changes have thus dictated a much closer identity of interests between the branches of the industry. The old processing distinctions are breaking down, and spinning, weaving, knitwear and clothing manufacture are increasingly part of one organism, the vertically integrated company. This has involved new capitalisation, rationalisation, amalgamations and the introduction of new production techniques. Most significant of all has been the growing association of textiles with the chemical industry, particularly petrochemicals and synthetic fibres.

The large chemical and petrochemical synthetic fibre groups have been forced to become financially involved because they produce raw materials on a large-scale for the textile industry. It is therefore natural that they should secure their outlets by controlling the means of production and marketing. This has led to the acquisition of textile companies. Imperial Chemical Industries, by incorporating British Nylon Spinners, and Courtaulds, who absorbed British Celanese in 1957, are now important components of the textile industry in the United Kingdom. In Italy Snia-Viscosa is in association with Montedison, the chemical group, and Hoechst of West Germany are entering into arrangements with textile companies. In the United Kingdom this trend has developed the furthest, because of the very steep decline of cotton and the urgent need for a rescue operation by the synthetic fibre groups. There is every sign that this interdependence will increase in the future throughout the EEC.

The Chemical Industry

The chemical industry is going through a period of rapid development and is one of the major growth industries in Europe. The West German chemical industry grew by 134 per cent between 1958 and 1967, twice the growth rate for German industry as a whole. It occupies a key place in the complex industrial economy largely because it supplies an ever-increasing number of raw materials upon which industry depends. In the United Kingdom, for example, only about 20 per cent of the products of the chemical industry enter the home consumer

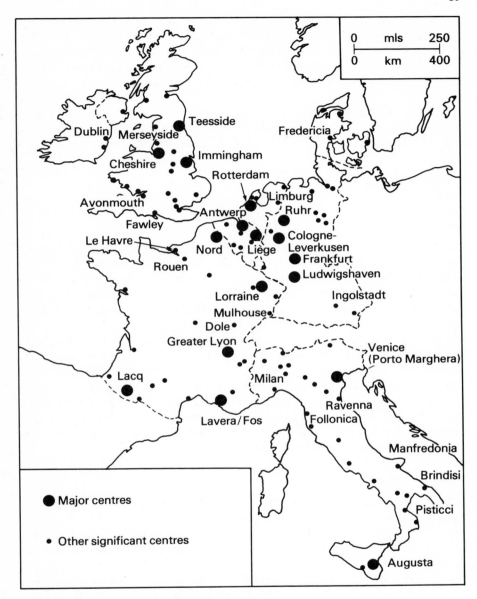

Figure 5.7 EEC chemical industry locations.

market directly, whereas at least 65 per cent are used by other sectors of industry. The textile industry has long depended upon chemical bleaches and dyestuffs, but more recently synthetic fibres from petrochemicals have partially replaced the traditional natural materials and have helped to resuscitate and transform the range and quality of textile products. The footwear industry depends on tanning materials, synthetic resins and rubber, and now increasingly, plastics. Fertilisers and crop protection chemicals are another rapidly developing sector of the industry. The heavy chemicals division produces acids and alkalis, and pharmaceuticals (drugs, medicines, cosmetics, photographic goods, soaps and toiletries) are manufactured as high-value specialist, lighter chemicals, more specifically for the consumer market.

This great complexity of products is matched by a variety of locations (fig. 5.7). There are three broad types of location: at a raw material and energy source; at the point of importation or trans-shipment of bulky raw materials; and near the market for the product. All three factors may operate at different periods of time.

Raw materials and energy

Coalfield locations

The coalfields provide a major concentration area as coal is both a raw material and was originally a source of energy. There are often other raw materials such as salt, anhydrite and potash. The major chemical manufacturing regions on the continent are the Ruhr, Saar, Sambre–Meuse, Limburg and Kempenland coalfields. The Heavy Industrial Triangle plays a significant part in the chemical industry. In the Ruhr, the main chemical centres are Duisburg, Dusseldorf and Leverkusen near Cologne. The coke-oven plants produce heavy chemicals, including coal tar, benzene, ammonia and sulphuric acid. There is also a new development in the north of the Ruhr at Marl-Huls, where natural gas is piped from the Ems gas-field. The Dutch South Limburg coalfield produces synthetic rubber, ammonia, and petrochemicals at the Maurits Colliery near Maastricht. In the Sambre–Meuse Valley, Liège is the centre for heavy chemicals, and in northern France the coalfield towns of Béthune, Lens and Douai have coke-ovens which produce aniline dyes, ammonia and acids.

Other mineral sources

A specific mineral resource may determine the location of a chemical industry, e.g., sulphur extraction from natural gas at Lacq and St. Marcet in the Pyrenees, the potash deposits at Mulhouse used for fertilisers, salt deposits in Lorraine (Dombasle and Sarralbe), and gas at Cortemaggiore in the Po Valley. Perhaps the largest area of this type is in Lower Saxony around Hanover, where oil, potash and salt account for the large-scale manufacture of fertilisers. Italy has many dispersed locations, including the processing of sulphur at Ragusa, in Sicily, and in Emilia-Romagna, and potash at Campo-Franco.

Hydro-electricity

The availability of hydroelectricity (HEP) is another localising factor. In Italy there are plants at Terni in the Appenines, Crotone in Calabria, and at Bolzano in the Alto-Adige for nitrate fertilisers. In France an electrochemical industry has developed in the Durance Valley (Argentière), at Grenoble in the Isère Valley, and in the Pyrenees, south of Lourdes.

Import and transhipment points

Oil refineries and petrochemicals

The influence of cheap transport has had a variety of effects. It often leads to the expansion and development of existing centres which were originally based upon raw materials. Oil refineries have become the principal locational factor for the petrochemical industry; cheap transport by inland waterway or pipeline is also important. The expansion of existing centres has occurred in the United Kingdom, where the original coal factor is complicated by others. The Merseyside chemical area stretches from St. Helens through Runcorn and Widnes into Cheshire at Northwich, and was originally based upon the saltfields of mid-Cheshire and the Lancashire coalfield. The oil refinery at Stanlow, the glass industry of St. Helens, the supplies of bleaches and dyes needed by the textile industry, the cheap import facilities of Liverpool and the Manchester Ship Canal for tropical vegetable oils, as well as limestone from Derbyshire, have compounded matters so that the industry now relates to a whole series of factors.

Teesside is a similar example where the main centres, Billingham and Wilton are linked by a pipeline under the Tees for movement of petroleum by-products. Anhydrite and salt from beneath the Tees estuary and also coal from Durham were the main raw materials at first. Much of the real impetus for the recent vast growth of the Wilton complex, making plastics, Terylene, and other synthetics, however, has been the development of Teesside as a major oil-refining and petrochemical centre.

In many cases transhipment points at deep-water estuaries or along large rivers, have become initial growth points. The oil refineries of the Rhine delta, particularly at Europoort and Antwerp, produce petrochemicals. The Dutch towns of Arnhem and Nijmegen along the Rhine have chemicals and rubber works. Similar developments have occurred at Marseilles, Avonmouth and Thameside, Humberside, Hamburg, Le Havre and Southampton Water. Italy has developed petrochemical locations at her major ports: Genoa, Naples, Augusta in Sicily, and Bari.

Inland areas

The best example of an inland transportation break-point is the mid-Rhineland, centred upon Frankfurt, Mannheim and Ludwigshaven. The Rhine axis reflects the ease of importation along a major waterway. At Ludwigshaven is the complex of Badische–Anilin/Soda–Fabrik AG (BASF) employing 45000 workers, the largest in Europe.

The oil and natural gas pipelines extending from Rotterdam to the Ruhr and Frankfurt, the South European pipeline from Trieste to Ingolstadt and that from Marseilles to the Rhine at Karlsruhe (fig. 2.7) are of increasing importance for the location of chemical factories.

Market locations

Branches of the chemical industry are widely distributed in the major cities. Here are found the lighter, less noxious chemical products which are manufactured on trading estates such as Slough, near London, with a good labour supply and market proximity. Paris, Brussels and London are the largest centres with pharmaceuticals and cosmetics. Lyons, Nottingham, Cologne and Manchester, are others. In Italy, the single most important area is the Milan–Turin axis. Milan employs one-third of the total chemical workers in Italy, manufacturing a very wide range of products for the very large consumer market in Northern Italy.

In addition to the consumer market, in many cases the market for associated products is an important factor. Examples are the crop-protection chemicals and fertilisers made at Hanover and Brunswick, close to the agriculture of the Börde of Saxony, and cities such as Ghent, Turin and Greater Lyons which produce dyestuffs for the textile industry.

Structure of the chemical industry

In this rapid growth industry there is scope for extensive research and development, automation, and capital investment. Certain characteristics therefore emerge. It tends to be organised in very large units, owned by a few giant companies. There has been a spectacular increase in the size of factory units, particularly in the field of petrochemicals. In 1960 the ethylene catalytic crackers had an average capacity of 50 000 tonnes, but by 1968 Imperial Chemical Industries of Teesside had a 450 000 tonne plant of this type.

Each EEC country has at least one major chemical group which exercises a partial monopoly, but the scale of operations does vary considerably. In West Germany the three largest firms (Hoechst, Bayer and BASF) share most of the industry; in France there is much less concentration with over 60 firms sharing at least half the market; in Italy, Montedison accounts for 75 per cent of the total sales. The United Kingdom is dominated by ICI which ranks by any standards as one of the largest companies in the western world and second behind the United States giant Du Pont (fig. 3.10). ICI may also be classed as a successful 'European' company (figs. 38, 3.9).

The chemical industry has benefited enormously by the dismantling of tariffs and the increase in intra-community trade. The vastly increased home market is evident from the sustained increase in demand each year for plastics, synthetic rubber and artificial fibres. European production of chemicals is now one-third of total world output. The importance of the industry can be measured by the fact that American investment is very high. Probably a quarter of the total United States investment in Western Europe is in the EEC chemical industry. Mergers at community level are now needed to reach the American size-level. Little has been accomplished so far, except in the field of photographic chemicals, by the merger of Agfa of West Germany and Gevaert of Belgium.

6

Agriculture:
the Common Agricultural Policy

A highly productive farming region

The Europe of the Nine is one of the most productive agricultural areas in the world and large parts of its landscape have become almost totally humanised after 2000 years of continuous cultivation. Sections in the regional chapters which follow are devoted to the variety of farming landscapes and products, for instance: the productivity and scale of the vast 'pays' of the Paris Basin; the efficiency of the dairy farming and specialised horticulture of Holland and Denmark; the rich crop lands of Northern Italy; the Rhineland vineyards; and the subsistence farming of the Mezzogiorno.

Scale and diversity

The largest single advantage of the EEC is its scale. The large market of over 250 million people is a tremendous incentive to farmers, but of even greater significance is latitudinal extent. The EEC stretches from latitude 37 to latitude 58 degrees north and covers an area capable of producing most foodstuffs apart from those which require tropical conditions. Italy can provide a large proportion of the community's rice and this is just one indication of the range of products which can be cultivated within these latitudinal limits.

	Agriculture as a % of gross domestic product	Food and agriculture imports as a % of total imports	Food and agriculture exports as a % of total exports	Net importer or exporter of food	% Contribution to Community budget (estimated)
West Germany	3·1	16·4	4·0	Importer	27
France	6·3	12·4	18·4	Exporter	22
Italy	8·1	20·1	8·1	Importer	17
Netherlands	5·9	14·2	22·1	Exporter	8
Belgium/Luxembourg	3·9	12·1	9·2	Importer	7
UK	2·2	19·5	7·0	Importer	16
Eire	17·0	12·7	43·0	Exporter	1
Denmark	7·9	10·5	35·3	Exporter	2

Figure 6.1 Agriculture: the importance to each member country, 1972–1973. (Source: CAP EEC)

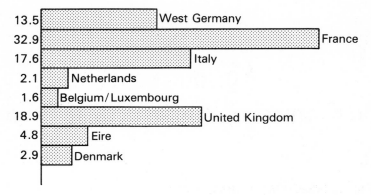

Figure 6.2 The total agricultural area
(million hectares).

There are, however, great variations between the member states in the importance attached to agriculture (fig. 6.1). In the UK agriculture occupies only 3 per cent of the working population and produces only 2·2 per cent of the gross domestic product, but UK farmers supply about 55 per cent of the country's food. Agriculture is therefore a valuable and very cost-effective part of the UK economy, playing a part out of all proportion to its manpower. In West Germany and Belgium agriculture provides only 3·1 and 3·9 per cent of gross domestic

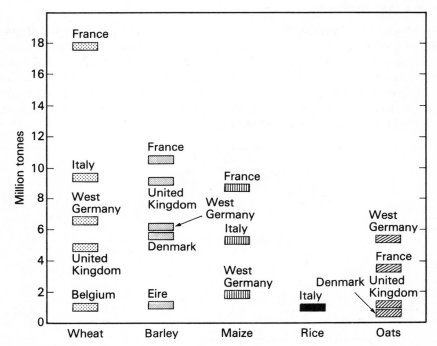

Figure 6.3 Cereals—average production
1971–1973.

Arable	Permanent pasture	
59.9	40.1	West Germany
57.9	42.1	France
70.3	29.7	Italy
90.1	9.9	Denmark
53.1	46.9	Belgium
48.2	51.8	Luxembourg
38.6	61.4	United Kingdom
23.9	76.1	Eire
40.2	59.8	Netherlands

Figure 6.4 Land use—percentage of agricultural area.

product respectively, for, like the UK, they are heavily industrialised, whereas in Italy the proportion is 8·1 per cent (1972) and in Denmark 7·9 per cent. Eire is even more agricultural in character, and has over 25 per cent of her total labour force on the land. France has the largest agricultural production in the community, emphasising her large areas of farmland (fig. 6.2) and position as 'The Granary of Europe' (fig. 6.3).

Land utilisation figures (fig. 6.4) show that Denmark and Italy have the largest proportions of arable land, followed by West Germany and France. In Belgium and Luxembourg there is an approximate balance between arable and pastoral land, whilst the United Kingdom, Eire and the Netherlands are predominantly pastoral. This adds yet another element to the scale, complexity and diversity of the agricultural scene, which will now be examined in greater detail.

Climate and agricultural regions

Climatic factors have the effect of creating four main agricultural zones (fig. 6.5).

1. **North-west Europe** is exposed to westerly winds from the Atlantic, and the normal climatic regime is therefore wet throughout the year, and variable with mild winters and cool summers. This maritime climate is characterised by a mixed farming regime with a bias towards a grassland and stock-rearing economy with specialised dairy farming. This is common on the coasts and lowlands of Eire and in the United Kingdom, Normandy, Brittany, the polders of the Netherlands, and Schleswig–Holstein in the North German lowlands. Denmark is a special case: only 10 per cent of the cultivable land is under grass, although it is within the coastal maritime belt; 45 per cent is under mixed cereals grown as stockfeed. This intensive method of feeding cattle indoors on grain is a more cost-effective way of producing dairy products.

2. **Towards the interior of the continent** the transitional continental climate has colder, though fairly short winters, but has sunny, hotter summers than the coastlands. With a lower overall rainfall, arable farming is much more important and cereals tend to dominate. This climate is combined with the

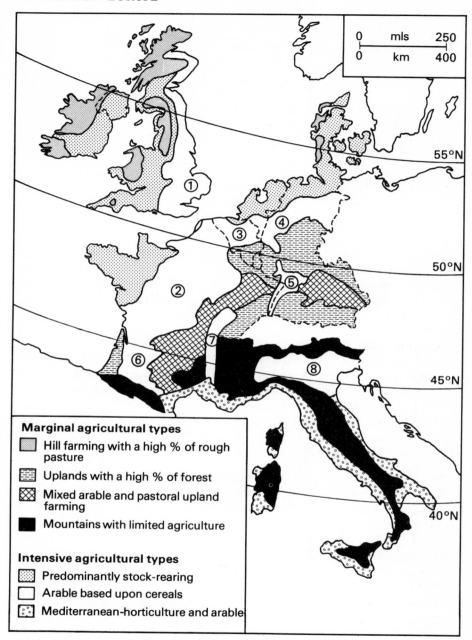

Figure 6.5 Principal agricultural regions (based upon macro-climatic and relief criteria). (1) East Anglia and the lowlands of eastern England; (2) Paris Basin and scarplands; (3) Flanders and High plain of Belgium; (4) Börde of Westphalia and Saxony; (5) Rhine–Main valley; (6) Basin of Aquitaine; (7) Rhône valley; (8) Plain of Lombardy.

presence of extensive lowlands, covered with fertile loess (limon), in areas such as the Paris Basin, Flanders, Picardy and the Börde of Westphalia and Saxony, giving rise to the community's major grain and sugar-beet producing area. East Anglia belongs to this agricultural type as it has the most extreme climate and the lowest rainfall in the United Kingdom. The additional advantage of an extensive chalky boulder-clay lowland has made it the United Kingdom's principal area of cereal cultivation. The Basin of Aquitaine has a long growing season and is climatically almost part of the French Midi. Likewise the plain of Lombardy is not truly mediterranean in climate, and both Aquitaine and Lombardy have a rich and varied pattern of agriculture with market gardens, orchards, vineyards and cattle pastures. More than half the land is, however, under cereals, particularly wheat and maize and, therefore, they merit inclusion as part of the community's major arable farming region.

3. **The dissected upland and mountain zones of the Hercynian plateaux** stretch across much of the interior of Europe. Agriculturally, these are marginal farming areas lying at an altitude of between 300 and 2000 metres and characterised by a cool damp climate, considerable rainfall and winter snow, together with exposed conditions and thin soils. There is the hill-farming and stock-breeding of the Pennines, Lake District and Welsh mountains, which is a valuable element in the UK stock-rearing economy. The Ardennes, Black Forest and Rhine Highlands have extensive forests which provide valuable timber. There are large areas of pasture and moorland with low rural population densities. The French Massif Central is more varied with areas of forest, interspersed with areas of rye, oats and buckwheat cultivation, whilst on the south-western margins are the limestone 'Causses' which traditionally have provided grazing for sheep, producing the famous Roquefort cheese.

The Alpine fold mountains provide yet another variation on this theme. The high western regions, with heavy precipitation, have fine stands of timber, but the main form of livelihood is usually stock-rearing based upon the alternate use of alpine and valley pastures in the classic transhumence system. In sheltered valleys, as for example north of Grenoble in the Isère valley (the Grésivaudan), are vineyards and orchards, whilst in more remote areas subsistence farming and depopulation is the usual pattern. A large part of the Italian Appenines are basically suited to tree crops such as the olive and vine, but 40 per cent of peninsular Italy is too steep for cultivation anyway, and soil erosion in the past has seriously damaged its capacity for agriculture of any kind.

4. **The southern coastal fringes of the community**, including the Midi of France and the Italian lowlands, have the traditional summer drought of the 'mediterranean' regime, but the agriculture varies so much with local conditions that the classic mediterranean complex of olive, vine and cereals is too simple a description of what occurs. The region of Northern Italy (chapter 16) which stretches from the Ligurian Riviera into Lombardy, illustrates this variation. Intensive horticulture, viticulture, fruit and floriculture is common on irrigated and terraced coastlands, with intensive crop and cereal production and cattle rearing in the interiors.

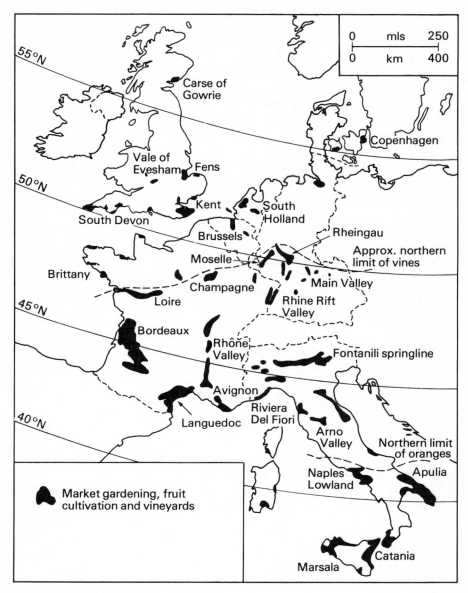

Figure 6.6 Specialised and intensive horticulture and viticulture.

Local variations due to micro-climatic effects, aspect and market demand

It will be apparent from the description of these four basic climatic divisions and their agricultural responses that, whilst climate is a useful factor in describing the latitudinal range of agricultural production available in the community, nevertheless there is a mosaic of localised farm types within this broad picture.

Vineyards and other crops in open fields
near Nuits St Georges in the Sâone valley.
The Cote D'Or is in the background.

Specialised agriculture depends upon locally favourable circumstances and is found in restricted areas (fig. 6.6).

Viticulture

The northern limit of the vine lies approximately from the river Loire to Koblenz on the mid-Rhine, and it is the sheltered slopes of the Rhine Gorge and Rift Valley, the warm soils and southward facing scarps of the Champagne Pouilleuse near Reims, and the southward-facing Cote D'Or, which allow the vine to flourish so far north of its natural habitat, the Mediterranean coast.

The Vale of Evesham

The Vale of Evesham and South Worcestershire experiences a warming effect with mild winters and early springs because of the funnelling effect of the Bristol channel upon the westerly winds. As a result it is an important area in the UK for the intensive cultivation of fruit, hops and vegetables.

Brittany

In Britanny the cultivation of primeurs (early vegetables) is made possible around the coast in sheltered bays such as St. Malo, Roscoff and Quimper. The mildness of the winters and early springs are associated with the Westerlies and North Atlantic Drift.

The Netherlands

Much of the intensive horticulture of Randstad, Holland, with its vegetables, glasshouses, and bulb cultivation, is on the mixed soils where sand has been blown inland from coastal dunes over the peat to create a fertile, easily worked soil.

Urban markets

In addition, economic factors have increasingly become predominant. The food requirements of the large city populations has created 'Von Thunen' type conditions, and land is intensively farmed immediately around the city. The perishable highly-priced fruit and vegetables are freed from transport costs of any magnitude and are in close proximity to their urban market. The environs of Paris, the Randstad and the Lea Valley in north London illustrate this.

Transport

A modification of this occurs where fast transport can provide an easy and inexpensive route to the market. The cultivation of primeurs near Avignon is not only due to the early springs of the southern Rhône valley, but also to the development of fast access routes to Paris.

Self-sufficiency

The differences in terms of land-use between the member countries show a picture of considerable strength. The Common Market has combined nine countries into one unit capable of producing the majority of its own food. These countries are together approaching self-sufficiency in food, adding great strength to each member country (fig. 6.7). Put another way, the grain-producing area of East Anglia is not sufficient to feed the UK's large industrial population, but the EEC as a whole can produce enough grain, given the right conditions. Alternatively, from northern Scotland to Sicily the product of the EEC is greater than the sum of its parts. The UK as a traditional grass and livestock region should benefit by becoming a major supplier of beef, pigmeat, and dairy produce. Italy and Southern France (fig. 6.8) have a climatic monopoly within the EEC in the production of sub-tropical crops such as vines, olive oil, rice and citrus fruits, and advantages in tomatoes and early vegetables. Denmark is a major supplier of dairy produce. The potential self-sufficiency of this large and productive area is the key to an understanding of the Common Agricultural Policy and is the reason for the early importance attached by the community to a policy for pooling and rationalising food production.

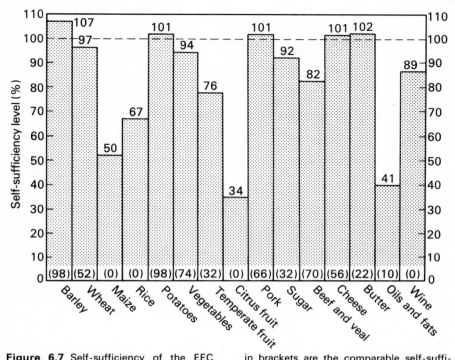

Figure 6.7 Self-sufficiency of the EEC Nine in food products, 1972–1973. (Figures in brackets are the comparable self-sufficiency levels for the United Kingdom alone.)

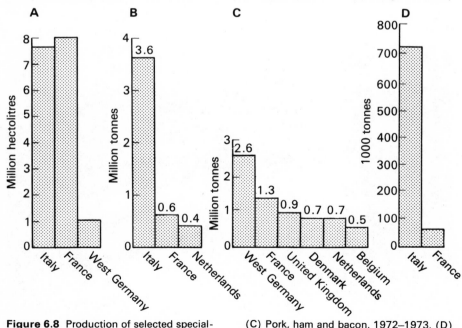

Figure 6.8 Production of selected specialist crops. (A) Wine production, 1973–1974. (B) Production of tomatoes, 1972–1973. (C) Pork, ham and bacon, 1972–1973. (D) Rice production, 1973.

Farm structure

There are very large differences in the social systems and farming techniques of the member states, and it is these variations which illustrate many of the problems inherent in the community's farm policy.

Land tenure and farm size varies considerably. At one end of the scale Tuscany, Emilia and the south of Italy have tiny peasant holdings (Minifundia) alternating with vast estates owned by absentee landlords (Latifundia). The underdeveloped Latifundia, with their typical extensive monoculture of wheat and day-labour system, exist alongside the peasant smallholdings of under 1 hectare and two or three widely separated patches of land. In 1950 over 70 per cent of holdings in the Mezzogiorno were under 3 hectares. It is only in the modernised and wealthier farming areas of Lombardy that a normal system of tenant occupation on farms nearer the average size occurs. France, on the other hand, has a tradition of owner-occupation and the average farm size is 18 hectares, but this figure disguises the real differences between regions. In the north-east most farms are over 25 hectares, whilst Brittany, Aquitaine and much of the Midi have a majority of farms under 11 hectares in size. The tendency to small farms, which are difficult to work for profit, is compounded by the system of widely scattered holdings which is a legacy of the Napoleonic code of equal inheritance. West Germany is also characterised by a high proportion of small farms, and in Bavaria and Swabia particularly these are often fragmented. In the Netherlands, however, many of the farms on the reclaimed polders are state-owned and rented out to the farmer in consolidated plots of land. By contrast, the UK has a more mature farm structure with the average farm size at 33 hectares and, more significantly, it has the greatest number of large farms over 400 hectares in the Community, often run by a bailiff or manager (fig. 6.9).

Reclaimed polders in South Flevoland.
Cereal harvesting by the Ijsellmeer Polders
Development Authority.

Glengesh, in County Donegal, with a remote mountainous environment and marginally economic farms restricted to stock-rearing with some hay and oats.

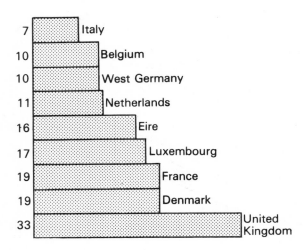

Figure 6.9 Average farm size (hectares).

| | *Percentage of labour force employed in agriculture* | | | | | |
	1950	1958	1965	1971	1972	1974
Belgium	11·3	9·0	6·1	4·4	4·2	3·7
France	28·3	23·0	17·0	13·2	12·9	12·0
West Germany	24·7	15·0	11·0	8·3	7·8	7·3
Italy	41·0	33·0	24·7	18·9	18·2	16·6
Luxembourg	24·0	17·0	13·5	10·1	9·3	6·6
Netherlands	14·1	12·0	8·0	6·9	6·9	6·6
United Kingdom	5·1	4·0	3·2	3·0	3·0	2·8
Denmark	–	22·0	–	10·9	9·8	9·6
Eire	–	38·0	–	26·9	25·7	24·3

Figure 6.10 Agricultural labour force, 1950–1974.

It follows, that with small and fragmented farms, many areas of the EEC have too large a farm population for efficiency. During the 1950s the 'original Six' had a very significant problem with Italy having 6·5 million people or 41 per cent of her labour force on the land (fig. 6.10). Even the Netherlands, a much more efficient agricultural country, had 14 per cent. By contrast the United Kingdom had 5 per cent of its working population employed in farming. French farmers are extremely important electorally because there are so many of them.

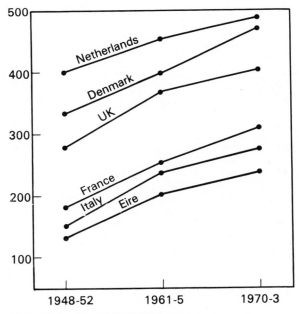

Figure 6.11 Milk yields (1000 kg per cow).

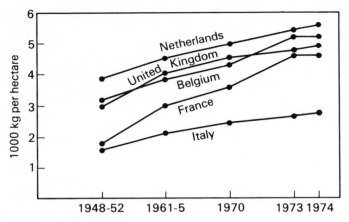

Figure 6.12 Wheat yields.

Many of the peasant farmers of France and Italy are over 50 years old and with this goes an innate conservatism and lack of enthusiasm for change. Production techniques illustrate the same picture, as the small-scale farmers often find it difficult to save and to invest the capital required to mechanise efficiently.

The tremendous variations in yields from one part of the EEC to another are a major problem (figs. 6.11 and 6.12). Even in the 1950s the Netherlands and Belgium had a consistently high yield of commodities such as wheat, a reflection of their intensive efficient farming, and of their orientation to the food requirements of large urban populations. Denmark has one of the most efficient farming systems in the world and the United Kingdom's yields, particularly in its favoured lowland areas, are very high. By contrast in the 1950s the yields for major crops in France and Italy reached only half the levels of those in the Netherlands. Perhaps the best indicators of productivity levels are seen in the simple comparison shown by the British farmer who produces food for twenty people; the Dane for seventeen; the French for eight and the German farmer for nine people. A model summarising these regional differences which also introduces the concept of the core and the periphery, is that taken from the ideas of Van Valkenburg (fig. 6.13). An index of high production is based on the following criteria: average production values for arable land; milk yields; and yields for eight selected crops. Figure 6.13 shows a high production area across the north European plain focused upon the Rhine delta and adjacent areas. Conversely, there are peripheral regions in which agriculture is much less favoured, including southern Italy, south-western France, south-eastern Germany and highland Britain.

The problems of size and fragmentation, together with an excessive farm labour force, inadequate mechanisation, backward farming techniques and low yields, are not universal throughout the market, but are widespread enough to cause considerable imbalance in the system. It was to take advantage of the benefits of scale to produce sufficient food and to improve the character of farming throughout the whole community, by removing these imbalances, that the Common Agricultural Policy was formulated.

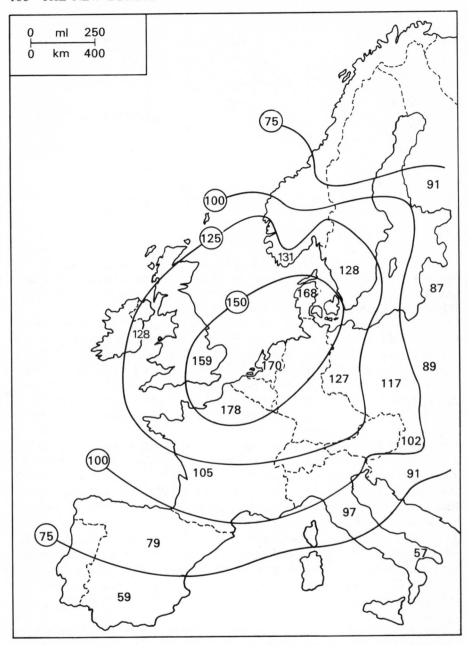

Figure 6.13 Intensity of agriculture in Europe. (Index of 100 = average European yield per acre of eight principal crops). (From Van Valkenburg)

The Danish Government Experimental Pig
Breeding Farm near Randers in Jutland.

The Common Agricultural Policy

One of the earliest examples of Community policy-making was the establishment of the Common Agricultural Policy in 1962. The policy is administered
by the European Agricultural Guidance and Guarantee Fund (EAGGF), the
words of which spell out its two major practical functions: the guidance and
improvement of farm production and the guarantee or protection of the farmer's
income. The central aim of the policy is to establish a single market for all farm
products. This means that national, fiscal and physical barriers to trade must
be abolished, with unrestricted intra-community free trade. There must be
stabilised and guaranteed prices at the same level throughout. Easy access to all
parts of the EEC by fast transport routes would thus eliminate or reduce to a
minimum the costs of transport. This ideally means that the most efficient producer will succeed and the effect of favourable environmental factors should
make itself increasingly felt. Ultimately this should mean that regional specialisation in agriculture will be the norm. United Kingdom farmers would specialise
in dairy products, lamb, beef, pork and poultry as well as cereals, because the
combination of arable and grassland and a livestock economy is particularly
fitted for the prevailing climatic and physical conditions. Conversely, Italy and
southern France have great climatic advantages in horticulture and a monopoly
in vines, olive oil and citrus fruits. Thus, each region produces what it is best

Intensive cultivation of 'primeurs' near
Remy, Provence, in the Bouches Du Rhône.
Notice the windbreaks of cypress trees and
the amphitheatre of the Alpes Maritimes at
the rear.

suited for and national independence becomes regional interdependence. The
potential self-sufficiency which has already been mentioned for the nine
countries is enormously strengthened by this specialisation in each region.

The protection of the farmers income

This is one of the major purposes of the Common Agricultural Policy. It is
recognised that in an industrial society it is more difficult to maintain farm incomes at a level comparable with those of industrial workers and the policy sets
out to give this guarantee. Why protect the farmers? The answer lies partially
with the composition of the original Six and the fact that France and Italy in
particular have always had a large and electorally powerful farming section in
their population (fig. 6.10). France and Italy always relied upon the Agricultural
Policy to act as a compensatory factor in return for opening their markets to
West German industrial products. The protection of the farmer's income, the
guarantee policy, works in the following way. A common pricing system is applied to each product and a target price is fixed each year which estimates a fair
return for an efficient farmer in open competition. Every farmer can therefore
sell on the open market for a price related to the target price, but if the price
slumps there is an intervention price at which the local intervention organisation, run by the community, will step in and buy up the product. This intervention price is about 8 per cent below market price and is a type of 'floor' or
reserve price. In addition, if a foreign producer wishes to sell food within the
market, he has to pay a levy at the frontier which raises his prices to the level of

the target price, thus excluding any low cost imports from undercutting the community farmers' products. So the farmers' incomes are protected at an artificial level, the target price, but there is one safeguard for the consumer. If the market price for a product goes over the target price competition from imports will bring it down to the target level again, thus providing a measure of price regulation.

To pay for this price support, the member countries pay to the Fund the levies which they have received from food imports, customs duty receipts and a proportion of their receipts from value added tax. In effect, the indirect taxes paid by the consumer are the source of the farmers' guaranteed protection.

The biggest problems to emerge through protection have been surpluses. During periods of glut, to which dairy products in particular are prone, the community buys up and stores vast quantities of the product at the support or intervention price. Butter is a good example of this and the 'butter mountain' of the early 1970s illustrates the point that protection, if not associated with reform, creates surpluses and is very inefficient in the long term. Essentially, the problem is that the regulated price which protects an elderly smallholder in the Massif Central from financial ruin, encourages the efficient farmers in the Paris Basin to produce more and more, thus creating periodic surpluses.

Agricultural guidance and reform

The other positive function of the Common Agricultural Policy is guidance and reform. This is a long-term aim and has been embodied in the Mansholt ten year plan for rationalisation and improvement by 1980. Specifically, two-thirds of EEC farmers are over the age of 50 (71 per cent of Italian farmers); four-fifths of the farms have less than 10 cattle; and the average farm is 10 hectares in size. The typical farm in the United Kingdom is three times this size and is about the ideal size for which the community is aiming (fig. 6.9).

In the period since 1950 there has been a dramatic general improvement in the agricultural structure. Three factors are involved and it is difficult to identify relative importance. Initially, there can be no doubt that the stimulating effects of the large internal market of over 200 million people has had an effect, particularly upon France, whose export of agricultural produce doubled between 1966 and 1971. Two-thirds of these exports are to member countries. Equally, the policies of national governments have had a considerable effect. The 'Cassa Del Mezzogiorno' is a comprehensive plan designed to aid the Italian south with industrial development and growth points, but it has also carried out substantial measures of farm improvement and labour force education. The French 'Remembrement' policy was officially introduced in 1941 and official agencies were set up in 1960 and 1962. These buy land which is used to consolidate fragmented holdings and to enlarge smallholdings into viable units. They also encourage farmers in western France to retire at age 60, and retrain men leaving the land for other employment. In addition to the work of these agencies, France is also experiencing a massive rural exodus as a result of economic forces and the attraction of urban life, which are creating a rural out-migration at the rate of 150000 people per year. Some mountain areas of marginal farming like the

A Danish dairy-farming landscape with a mixture of heathland, pasture, hay and fodder crops, and woodland.

Jura, Vosges and Massif Central are becoming depopulated whilst the main lines of French government policy are that a balanced agriculture is necessary with different stimuli depending on the area. Hill farmers are now given bonuses to increase their cattle herds, and grants are made to young farmers who will settle in areas with population below the minimum desirable level (11 people per square kilometre). On the other hand, in areas like Brittany where there are too many farmers, there are inducements to retire or amalgamate. There is room for the small family farm giving a living to three or four people. The large, highly mechanised grain farm of the Paris Basin needs entirely different conditions from those required by the smaller, highly efficient dairy farm of 50 cattle, typical of Holland and Denmark. It is difficult to say, however, whether the money allocated by the European Investment Bank and the EAGGF for dairy processing, seeds, irrigation channels, fruit and vegetable processing plant, and retirement pensions for farmers at age 45 has been responsible for the general improvements. The combined effects of economic forces, national policies and the guidance policies of the Common Agricultural Policy are clearly working in conjunction, and the result is a sustained improvement in the farming structure over the past twenty years.

The percentage of the population employed on the land has been substantially reduced (fig. 6.10). In the original Six the total labour force fell from 16 million in 1950 to 11·5 million in 1966, and again, to 9·9 million in 1969. The differences emerge sharply in the 1972–4 situation. The United Kingdom, Belgium and West Germany, with 3 per cent, 4 per cent and 8 per cent respectively of their population on the land, are heavily industrialised, whereas Italy, Eire and, to a lesser extent, France still have a very high proportion of their working population on the land. In terms of productivity, yields of all important crops have im-

Mechanised harvesting of fruit in Apulia,
southern Italy.

proved, often by very large amounts, and, in France particularly, cereal yields
have doubled (fig. 6.12). Large increases in mechanisation and the use of
fertilisers are also recorded (fig. 6.14).

In spite of the continuous improvement over a long period, there are remaining problems of inefficiency, over production of some foodstuffs and scarcity of
others. The Mansholt plan was published by the then Commissioner for Agriculture in 1969 and attempts to solve these problems. It recommended that by
1980 another 5 million workers should be withdrawn from farming; half of these
were to receive pensions and half were to be retrained for industrial jobs. As a

	Use of fertilisers (kg per hectare)			Tractors per 100 hectares	Use of fertilisers: regional variations
	1965	1970	1974	1974	
France	91	128	170	4·1	Over 200 kg per hectare in the Paris Basin
Netherlands	239	278	307	7·0	Over 450 kg per hectare in the market gardening areas.
Italy	49	63	81	4·5	

Figure 6.14 Use of fertilisers and machinery.

La Roche in the Ardennes. Agriculture and settlement is limited to the river valleys, and the wealth of this region lies in its timber and tourism.

corollary, 5 million hectares of marginal land were to be taken out of agricultural production and used for afforestation and parkland. Although controversial, the principles behind this scheme were accepted: the initial stages of this far-reaching reform have begun. Its ultimate aim is to eliminate the marginal high cost producer, thus raising efficiency, lowering target prices and eliminating surpluses.

Self-sufficiency and the associated States

The community is substantially self-sufficient in many major foodstuffs and even where imports are necessary, home production can often supply from 80 to 95 per cent of demand (fig. 6.7). Nevertheless, imports of food are increasing considerably owing to growth in demand and a considerable rise in living standards. Maize, citrus fruits and vegetable oils are the main deficiencies. Cereal imports, particularly, have soared since 1958 because of their use as feed-stocks for animals. The position is complicated further by the export of soft wheat, of which the EEC has a surplus, and the larger quantity of imports of hard wheat. The surpluses previously mentioned such as butter and beef, and in 1976 wine, need to be regulated more finely, without lurching from a position of surplus into one of shortage. The EEC has attained a high degree of self-sufficiency. The

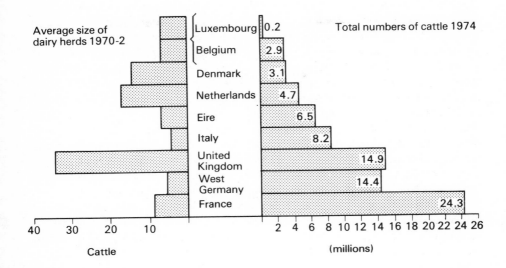

Figure 6.15 Cattle in the EEC.

central problem is to smooth out deficiencies and surpluses, and the price control mechanisms are not entirely adequate to do this, without a system of targets or production limits.

A logical extension of the Common Agricultural Policy is the augmentation of the Community's temperate products with those tropical foodstuffs which it cannot produce for climatic reasons. Many ex-colonies, particularly in Africa, are associated with the EEC. In 1963 eighteen African states, most of them ex-colonies of France, became associates at the Yaounde Convention. Since then, however, many of Great Britain's former colonies have become associated, culminating in the Lomé Agreement in 1975. The associates obtain tariff-free entry into the Community for one or more of their staple and export commodities, thus assuring them of an expanding market, and they also obtain aid for development projects through the European Development Fund. The Community gains because it has an assured supply of primary products and tropical foodstuffs, and a preferential market for its manufactured goods.

The position of the United Kingdom

Within the Community there is a clash of interests with regard to the agricultural policy and there are many underlying tensions. West Germany and the United Kingdom are heavily industrialised and urbanised, so that population has outstripped food production since the early nineteenth century. They are thus large-scale importers and negligible exporters of food. Their propensity to imports (and the levies paid upon these) means that they both make large contributions to the Common Agricultural Policy funds. The United Kingdom, in particular, because of her very efficient farming system, will obtain very little from the Common Agricultural Policy for structural reforms and development projects. France and Italy on the other hand are large-scale food producers and France is a large food exporter. Eire, though a small volume producer, has a small population and is therefore a major exporter of dairy produce. These last three members have the most acute structural problems and gain immensely from the guaranteed prices, export subsidies, large internal market and grant aid implicit in the Common Agricultural Policy. The Netherlands and Denmark are two members whose agricultural exports exceed imports and this reflects their traditional specialisation and efficiency in dairying and horticulture, combined with a small population. Denmark lost a substantial proportion of her traditional market in West Germany when the original Six adopted the agricultural policy, but her membership now gives her unrestricted access to the large industrial markets of the United Kingdom and West Germany.

The United Kingdom, in particular, finds the Common Agricultural Policy unfavourable to her own interests. It was the circumstances of her unique position with her early industrialisation, limited land resources and a large urbanised population that led to the adoption of a cheap food policy from the 1840s onwards. Under a policy of free trade, cheap imports from anywhere in the world were allowed to enter the country and most of these were from territories largely under United Kingdom control until a decade or so ago. United Kingdom farmers (high cost producers, relative to those of Canada and New Zealand) were compensated with deficiency payments which made up the difference between their high costs and prices, and the price levels of the lower cost imports. The farmer stayed in business with a subsidy, the imports entered freely at a low price level, the tax-payer paid the difference, but the consumer enjoyed very low retail prices for food. This was a fine arrangement for a country with a small farming population, needing essential food imports and also controlling economically, if not always administratively, vast agricultural areas of the world. This situation was transformed during the Second World War and since. The need to increase production and self-sufficiency during the period 1939 to 1945, the current 'agricultural revolution', and the acceptance that governments have an obligation to manage and maintain an efficient national food production machine, had led to a much greater contribution by British farmers to an overall national self-sufficiency rate of 55 to 60 per cent and to virtual self-sufficiency in eggs, milk, potatoes, barley, pork and poultry.

As part of the EEC the United Kingdom has abandoned her former position as a free-trade importer from the Commonwealth and the rest of the world, and entered one of European protection. Two points emerge. The United Kingdom farmer is generally in a very good position. With a system of guaranteed high prices, his efficiency should mean a great stimulation of production upon integration into the large European market which is aiming for substantial self-sufficiency. Specialised groups such as the horticulturalist may have problems because of climatic disadvantages, but in general the United Kingdom farmer is now entering a period where there should be great demand for his cereals and livestock products. However, there is the problem of late entry to a system designed for different needs. The ultimate aim of the Common Agricultural Policy cannot be questioned. In the long term its aim is that the agricultural strength of the whole shall be the basis for the specialisation and reform of all the parts, and that the integration of nine countries will create a strong food and agriculture system which can supply all the needs of 250 million people. However, for the United Kingdom at present, the advantages are very doubtful. The consumer has lost the protection of subsidies and is within a system of high prices. The United Kingdom has to pay a large contribution to the agricultural fund because she is a major importer of food. Finally, she obtains little or nothing from the fund because her agriculture, with the possible exception of hill farming, needs little aid or restructuring.

Conclusion

In the initial urgency of its establishment, the Common Agricultural Policy would appear to have created a somewhat crude control mechanism which needs considerable refinement. Change is needed to correct the problem of surpluses and a penalty for over-production beyond agreed levels seems necessary. In a managed system of farming, the consumer must be considered as well as the farmer and this means that prices ought not to be completely free to rise because of the need for self-sufficiency at all costs. Low cost imports can play at least a part in keeping prices down, as can subsidies in cases of urgency and for specific products. The operation of the Common Agricultural Policy has been questioned recently by both the UK and West Germany and a major review is being undertaken.

One major difficulty in the establishment of an equilibrium situation in farming is the time factor. It takes time to produce a dairy herd, and there is a lag between investment and production. This is essentially the reason for the periodic surpluses with which the CAP, has had to cope.

The second problem relates to the accounting mechanism of the CAP. All pricing and calculations take place in a 'green (agricultural) currency', which is a variant of each member states own currency. Thus we have the 'Green Pound' and 'Green Franc'. One of the difficulties which has arisen in the 1970s is the periodic devaluation of currencies such as the Pound. As the 'Green Pound' has not been adjusted, its value is therefore now (1977) higher than it should be. This has given the United Kingdom an advantage in that its food prices are lower and subsidised because they are paid for in a currency which is higher in value than the real pound. During 1975 and 1976 the UK therefore gained financially by the operation of this system. For the future stable operation of the CAP the system of 'Green currencies' must be part of a stabilised currency exchange rate which can be adjusted easily and gradually.

There is need for greater flexibility based upon all the member countries' needs. Perhaps the right answer is to look at the community's aid policy as a whole, and to give it an enlarged role as an agricultural, regional, industrial and social fund, which will allow for a system of coherent financial and economic planning over the whole community.

7

Trade:
the World's largest trading group

The EEC is now the world's most significant trading group, and in 1971 the original Six contributed approximately 30 per cent of the world's total by value, with the UK separately adding another 6 per cent. The combined totals for 1973 show that the enlarged community is responsible for over 42 per cent by value of world trade (fig. 7.1).

There are considerable variations in the relative importance of trade to each country. In 1973 the Netherlands and Belgium/Luxembourg, with their commercial traditions, had an export trade which is equal to 40 per cent and 48 per cent respectively of gross domestic product (GDP). This is far higher than the equivalent figure of 19 per cent for the UK and 17 per cent for West Germany, usually considered as essentially exporting countries (fig. 7.1). France has the lowest proportions with trade accounting for 14 per cent of GDP, partially reflecting her greater self-sufficiency in food production.

	Imports (million dollars)	Exports (million dollars)	Exports as approximate percentage of GDP
West Germany	43421	53552	17·6
France	29574	28453	14·5
Italy	22259	17794	18·2
Netherlands	19539	19255	40·7
Belgium/Luxembourg	17492	17854	47·5
EEC (Six)	132285	136908	20·1
United Kingdom	31026	24374	19·6
Eire	2225	1697	38·4
Denmark	6161	4951	25·3
EEC (Nine)	171798	167931	20·3
World	411920	395440	

Figure 7.1 EEC and world trade, 1973.

Why such a large involvement?

The reasons for this large involvement in foreign trade are complex, but may be identified under three headings:

1. **Widespread, intensive industrialisation** was based in the eighteenth and nineteenth centuries upon mineral resources which have become depleted to the point of exhaustion. The mineral resources of the Community, though extensive in some commodities such as coal, are incomplete, with major deficiencies at present in certain crucial areas, such as petroleum, high-grade iron ores and non-ferrous metals (fig. 7.2). Many of the more accessible coal-seams have

	West Germany	France	Belgium/ Luxembourg	Netherlands	Italy	UK	Eire	Denmark	EEC9	Percentage of world production
Coal	108·7	29·7	9·9	2·9	0·2	119·5	0·9	–	271·6	13·0
Crude Oil	7·1	1·5	–	1·6	1·2	0·3	0	–	12·4	0·1
Copper*	n	n	n	n	n	n	13·6*	n	16·4*	0·2
Iron-ore	6·4	54·7	3·8	n	0·3	7·1	n	n	72·8	9·0
Bauxite	n	3·2	n	n	n	n	n	n	3·3	5·0
Salt	10·5	5·5	n	2·9	4·4	9·2	n	n	29·0	22·0
Potash	2·4	1·6	n	n	0·1	n	n	n	4·1	22·0

n = negligible
* 1000 tonnes

Figure 7.2 Selected resources of the EEC Nine, 1972–1973. (million tonnes)

been worked out, so the coal is now difficult to exploit and is high-cost, and the remaining British and French Jurassic iron-ores have an iron content of only 28 per cent. Although there are adequate reserves of salt, and the recent discoveries of natural gas and petroleum in the North Sea will redress the balance considerably, nevertheless the basic picture is one of deficiency in raw materials, with a corresponding reliance on large-scale imports (32 per cent of total imports in 1973) (fig. 7.3).

Commodity group	Imports (percentage)					Exports (percentage)				
	EEC 6			UK	EEC 9	EEC 6			UK	EEC 9
	1958	1966	1972	1973	1974	1958	1966	1972	1973	1974
Foodstuffs	25	21	16	30	12	10	8	7	7	10
Fuel and raw materials	47	39	37	35	32	10	8	3	8	10
Manufactured products	28	40	45	45	56	80	84	90	85	80

Figure 7.3 External trade—main commodity groups (by value).

2. **A heavily-urbanised population with a high standard of living.** Resources are used at an ever-increasing rate in industrialised societies, and there is an underlying propensity to import semi-finished materials for further process- ing, together with finished manufactures which simply add to the range and choice open to the consumer (fig. 7.3). Wealth generates imports and the richer the society the greater is the reliance upon a complex movement of imports and exports of all categories.

3. **Food is an important element in the community's import trade**, despite a poten- tial self-sufficiency in temperate foods. Sixteen per cent of imports in 1973 were of foodstuffs, including temperate foods from USA and Australia, and tropical foods from Africa and Asia (fig. 7.4). This illustrates the importance of the former colonial territories, and explains their status as associate trading partners of the EEC. The 1962 Yaounde Agreement, and the Lomé Conven- tion of 1975, were both preferential trade and aid treaties.

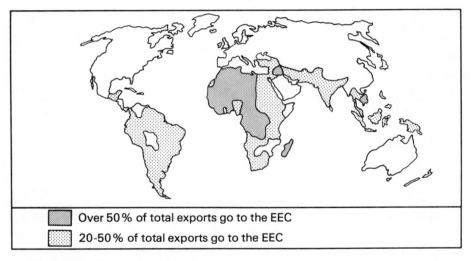

Over 50% of total exports go to the EEC

20-50% of total exports go to the EEC

Figure 7.4 The Community's share in the exports of the developing world.

Free Trade and trading blocks

A major trading area such as the EEC depends on a substantial and uninter- rupted flow of goods and services, and it is therefore in the common interest that the barriers to international trade are as low as possible. One of the main barriers is the range of protective duties levied on imports by all major countries to pro- tect their own productive capacity. In the nineteenth century, largely under the influence of Great Britain, there was an extension of 'free trade' throughout the world. This meant that food supplies from the large-scale producers in the newly discovered continents could be purchased at low cost, largely for the benefit of the rapidly industrialising Western World. At the same time, manufactured goods from Europe were exported on a massive scale. During the twentieth century there has been a move towards protectionism as all the newly inde-

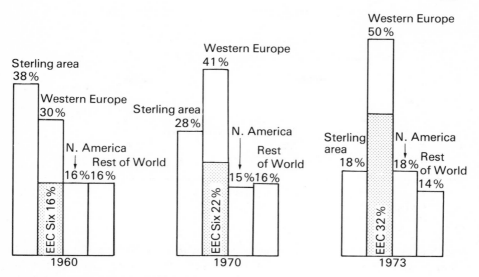

Figure 7.5 Direction of British exports.

pendent countries have sought to protect their own industries by placing tariffs on industrial goods formerly bought in Europe. Equally, they have looked elsewhere when freed from the necessity of trade with the former colonial power. This is shown in the decline in the proportion of United Kingdom exports going to the 'sterling area' (largely synonymous with the former British Empire) (fig. 7.5). As high as 80 per cent during the nineteenth century, these exports declined to 38 per cent (1960), 28 per cent (1970) and by 1973 to 18 per cent.

Here is the essential need for combining the resources of the small, highly industrialised nations of Europe on a continental scale. The EEC gives them a guaranteed home market of over 250 million people which is a huge internal trading unit, with ample potential to replace the lost colonial markets. The combined industrial base and export strength is capable of much more vigorous competition with such countries as the United States. This combination has developed essentially through two structures: the Common Market and the Customs Union.

The Common Market and intra-community trade

The Common Market allows goods, services, people and capital to circulate freely throughout the nine member countries, the basic pre-requisite for this being free-trade, the abolition of all customs duties, tariffs and quotas between the member countries. This has effected a very rapid expansion of trade within the single market. The original Six completed the abolition of all internal tariffs by 1969, but the three new members are still adjusting to the Community levels via a transition period, scheduled to be completed in 1978. Upon completion of this period, a single market of 250 million people will stretch from Scotland to Sicily. The real expansion of trade relating to this is an internal or intra-community trade, and the period from 1958 to 1971 saw a substantial increase in

	1957	1970	1971	1973
Belgium/Luxembourg	44	59	63	71
France	21	49	50	55
West Germany	24	44	47	52
Italy	21	41	42	48
Netherlands	41	56	55	61
United Kingdom	16 (1960)	–	22	32
Eire	–	–	69	71
Denmark	–	–	32	50

Figure 7.6 Intra-Community trade. Percentage of total imports coming from other member countries.

volume between the member states, together with a redirection of trade which had previously been external to the community. Mutual trade between the Six rose during this period from \$6790 million to \$48 117 million, a seven-fold rise. The individual members raised their proportion of trade with each other from 25 per cent to 52 per cent (fig. 7.6). All have benefited: Italy has become an exporter of fashion clothing and consumer durables; France and the Netherlands have greatly expanded their exports of agricultural produce; and West Germany's persistently favourable balance of trade is due principally to the opening of EEC markets to her efficient industry. The UK hopes to gain similar benefits through a vastly increased market for the products of the specialised engineering, chemical, vehicle, electronics, telecommunication and aerospace industries. Intra-community trade is the means by which the special expertise and advantages of each member country may be used with greater efficiency to achieve interdependence.

The Customs Union and external trade

At the same time as the Common Market Treaty provided for the reduction to zero of internal tariffs, it also required all members to conform to a common external tariff. This is a Customs Union and is the distinguishing feature of the EEC. This may be compared with the purpose of EFTA, which was simply to promote free trade between its members, with each country keeping its trade relations with third countries quite separate. The EEC has formed a single trading unit without internal barriers and with a common external tariff wall. Essentially, therefore, it is creating one single economic unit from nine separate ones. The common external tariff deals with external trade relationships, that is, with the rest of the world.

The character and direction of external trade is summed up as follows. Over 44 per cent of imports are of raw materials and foodstuffs, whilst 56 per cent are manufactured goods. Eighty per cent of exports are of manufactures, and 20 per cent are primary products (fig. 7.3). There is thus a large, complex, and increasing movement of manufactured goods throughout the developed world.

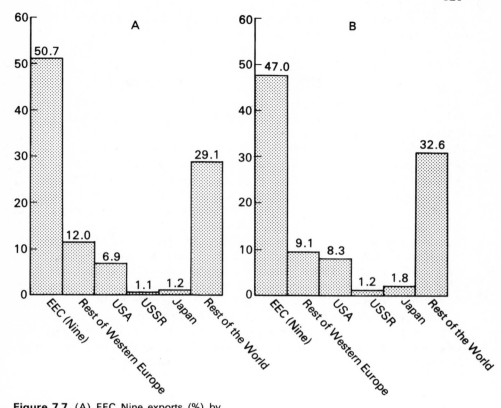

Figure 7.7 (A) EEC Nine exports (%) by area of destination, 1974. (B) EEC Nine imports (%) by area of origin, 1974.

Over 62 per cent of total trade by value is with the industrialised and wealthy countries such as the rest of Europe, North America and Japan (fig. 7.7). Trade with the underdeveloped countries overall accounts for a third of the total, but is more significant in terms of the balance of imports and exports. The EEC's exports to the underdeveloped world are substantially exceeded by imports from that quarter. If there is an economic weakness in the EEC, it is over-reliance upon imports of foodstuffs, petroleum and other raw materials from the underdeveloped world.

Viewed in a somewhat different light, the underdeveloped world needs the trade of the richer countries, and the major value of a trading bloc such as the EEC is that, by its high rate of growth, it has the ability to create and sustain a larger volume of world trade, and so help the poorer countries. It is readily assumed that the outward-looking trade policies of the UK, and her traditional involvement in world affairs, will help the enlarged community, which has hitherto been rather protectionist, to adopt more outward-looking policies on future trade. There is a continuing movement internationally to reduce tariffs and increase the volume of world trade, and the 'Kennedy Round' was one of the attempts to achieve this. There have been substantial signs since 1974 of greater flexibility in the Community's external trade policy, the cane-sugar agreement being one of these.

Other barriers to trade

Although the Customs Union and the dismantling of all internal duties and quotas has been the most significant single act in the formation of the Common Market, nevertheless there are many technical and physical barriers to trade which must be eliminated before a unified economic system comes into being. Industrial standards, metrication, and public health and safety regulations are areas where harmonisation is needed. Monopolies are another problem. The Commission has to approve monopolistic trading agreements, but generally these are not discouraged as they have to be seen in a world context rather than a national one. Cross-frontier community mergers are actively encouraged, but the harmonisation of company law, financial liability, tax laws and mercantile practice is necessary before long-term intra-community mergers are feasible. Public purchasing policy is another area for agreement, as in a single market each government should purchase the cheapest and best quality product available, even if this involves a cross-frontier product. As yet, each country tends to purchase from within its own industries, quite naturally, but this is an indication that economic union is still far from complete. Finally, perhaps most important of all, is transport. A swift integrated transport system is the best way of ensuring unrestricted movement of goods throughout the community, either inside its common market, or outside its common tariff wall.

8

Transport:
movement on a continental scale

Speed and complexity

The signing of the Treaty of Rome, and the subsequent enlargement of the Community to nine, has increased to a continental scale the planning of transport operations. Increased speeds have reduced the time needed to cross Europe and it is often better to think of travel in terms of time rather than distance. The Italian Riviera is two hours away from London by air or twenty-four hours by road or rail and sea.

At the same time there is a growing complexity of transport systems and an associated need for efficient linkage and integration. Canals and railways, for long dominant in long-distance movement, are now supplemented and at times supplanted by motorways. Air travel is taking over long-distance passenger transport, and the hovercraft is adding to cross-channel and other short-distance sea routes. The integration of all these is made possible by the container revolution, and by technological feats like the Channel tunnel project, the trans-Alpine tunnels and the development of the Euro-route system of motorways.

There are also other specialised transportation methods which are part of the totality of movement in an economic context. Movement of capital (chapter 3, Industry), goods (chapter 7, Trade), liquid fuel (chapter 2, Energy), and labour (chapter 9, Population) are considered in other chapters.

Railways

Railways, despite substantial competition from other forms of transport, still play a major role, although there are wide variations between the nine member states (fig. 8.1). France has a very comprehensive network of railways and they carry the highest number of passengers and greatest tonnage of freight. The relatively large area of France and the long distances benefit rail haulage. Government support has been substantial since the railways were completely rebuilt after 1945. French Railways (SNCF) is a public service with competition from road haulage reduced by restrictive licensing. West Germany's railways carry similar amounts of freight and passengers, and have a very dense network relative to area, but are less important relative to other forms of transport, specifically waterways. Italy has a small network of railways compared to her area, partially a result of the retarded growth of the system up to the 1930s. The great length (1000 km) of peninsular Italy, the rugged nature of the relief and the

	Inland waterways		Railways		Merchant fleet	Civil aviation
	Length in use (km)	Tonne-kilometres (millions)	Length of line operated (km)	Tonne-kilometres (millions)	1000 tonnes gross	Passenger-kilometres (millions)
West Germany	4506	50972	28926	70723	7980	11106
France	8568	13738	34382	78386	8835	17846
Italy	2237	391	16072	18145	9322	9783
Netherlands	4787	33197	2832	3370	5501	9071
Belgium/ Luxembourg	1570	6853	4309	10209	1215	3710
United Kingdom	569	–	18187	30499	31566	25167
Eire	–	–	2189	603	209	1756
Denmark	–	–	1999	2093	4460	na

na = not applicable

Figure 8.1 Comparative transport data, 1974.

inability of much of the area south of Lombardy to sustain a high level of traffic were all factors in this retardation. Although the railways are now state-operated they still constitute a minimal system compared with much of the rest of the Community.

The United Kingdom railway system has experienced a high rate of decline. The high rate of urban sprawl, a population equal to that of France on half of the area, and a well-developed network of roads have combined to emphasise the disadvantage of the railways as a relatively inflexible form of transport. The railways, although state-owned since 1948, have had to operate in open competition with, and have lost ground to, the roads both in passengers and haulage. The United Kingdom was over-endowed with railways due to the railway mania of the nineteenth century, when much duplication of railway lines and services occurred. This very dense network has been pruned considerably during three periods of rationalisation. The first took place when the system was brought under the control of four large companies: London, Midland and Scottish; London and North Eastern Railway; Great Western Railway; and Southern Railway. In 1948 the system was nationalised as British Rail, and during the 1960s the Beeching Report and subsequent pruning reduced the mileage by about one-third to 19000km. The United Kingdom network has the same density as that of France, relative to area, but is considerably less used, particularly for freight.

The smaller EEC countries have well-developed rail systems, although their use varies according to other factors. Belgian railways are particularly well used for freight, indicative of the general level of industrialisation; by contrast that of the Netherlands is under-used pro-rata because of the competition from its extensive waterway system. Eire has a low-density network relative to its area, indicative of a small population and the lack of major industrial and urban areas.

The railway system in the EEC is a useful indicator of the economics of development. There is the minimal system of the rural underdeveloped stage and the extensive well-utilised network over large areas. Finally, there is the post-railway era in which substantial competition from other forms of transport has created a situation where the high cost capital intensive railway system requires subsidisation and state-control.

Inland waterways

The importance of inland waterways is related to the occurrence of large navigable rivers and the lack of physical barriers. Denmark and Eire have no commercial waterways of any significance. In Italy only the River Po and its tributaries are of any value for freight as the rest of the peninsula has rugged terrain with short mountain torrents and few rivers of any size. The UK depends even less upon inland water transport for a variety of reasons, perhaps the most important of which is the limited size of barges characteristic of the early narrow canal system and the disuse into which it fell after its virtual destruction by railway and road competition.

The Rhine Gorge, with both passenger and barge traffic.

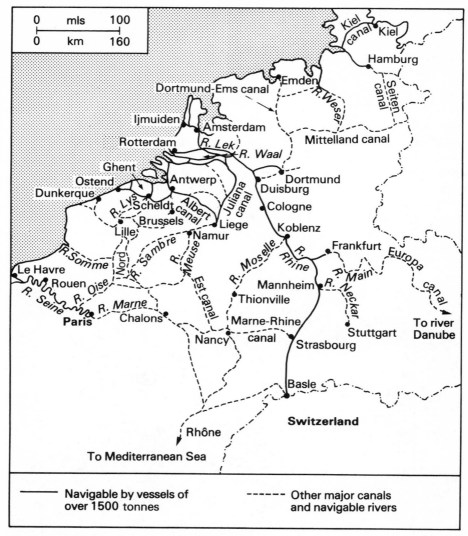

Figure 8.2 Inland waterways associated
with the Rhinelands.

Those countries of the North European plain drained by the Rhine and its
tributaries, however, have the natural basis for an extensive canal system (fig.
8.2). Eastern France, Belgium, the Netherlands and West Germany depend to a
large extent upon inland waterways. West Germany's economic axis trends
north–south along the length of the Rhine and movement is primarily between
the industrial areas along its banks. The importance of the Rhine can be seen in
the total West German tonnage carried by waterways, actually more than in the
Netherlands (fig. 8.1). In the Netherlands over half of all freight is carried by
water (fig. 8.3), reflecting the traditional character of the country, but also

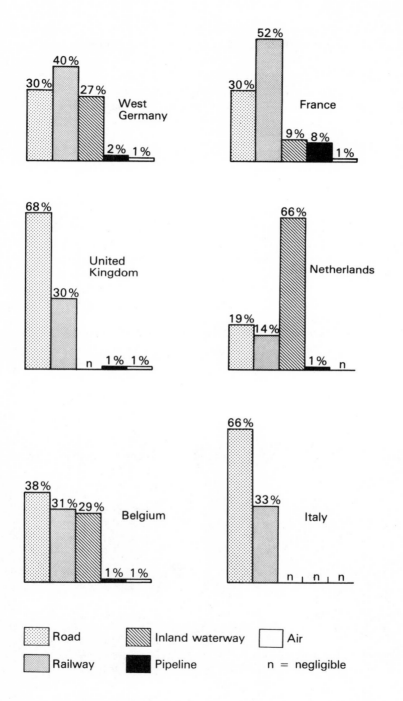

Figure 8.3 Percentage of inland freight carried by each type of transport, 1972–1973.

underlining its position at the mouth of the Rhine with Rotterdam as the great entrepôt of Europe. Belgian freight is carried by water almost as much as by rail. The Scheldt and Meuse rivers and the Albert and Juliana Canals form a very important link with north-eastern France, Antwerp and the Rhine. To France the main value of inland waterways is the linkage of the Paris basin via the Seine to the coast, via the Oise/Nord Canal to Lille, and via the Marne and Moselle system with Lorraine, Strasbourg and the Rhine.

Road transport

All countries of the EEC have a well-developed network of roads and it is difficult and perhaps irrelevant to compare total mileages owing to the different methods of classification. The French Route Nationales are similar to the British 'A' roads, but the similarities cannot be pressed to the extent that they provide any significant comparison. Two points are important: the relative values nationally of road transport compared with the other forms of bulk transport; and the development of the motorway networks as a reflection of current geographical relationships.

West Germany and Belgium possess the nearest approach to a balanced transport system with the three major forms of inland transport: road, rail,

The new bridge across the Little Belt linking
the Danish island of Funen with Jutland.

and waterway, each carrying approximately one-third of inland freight (fig. 8.3). The United Kingdom and Italy emerge as the greatest users of road transport, two-thirds of all freight being carried by road in these two countries. In Italy the reasons are largely historical, since until the 1930s there was a very poorly integrated system of railways, with no through routes over the 1000 km from north to south, and very great difficulties east–west across the Apennines. This minimal network was associated with the late unification and weak industrialisation of Italy up to the 1930s. To cope with her rapidly expanding economy since 1945, and aided by modern technology, the Italians have constructed an excellent Autostrada system with some superb feats of engineering. Perhaps the most famous is the Autostrada Del Sole, which links Milan to Naples over 750 km, with many bridges, tunnels and dramatic views. The long north–south distances have been mastered by motorways, but even more significant is the construction of motorways and tunnels through the Alps which have done much to end the relative isolation of Italy from the trunk of Europe (fig. 8.4). Along the Riviera to France from Genoa, from Turin up the Val D'Aosta and through the Mont Blanc tunnel, from Milan northwards to the

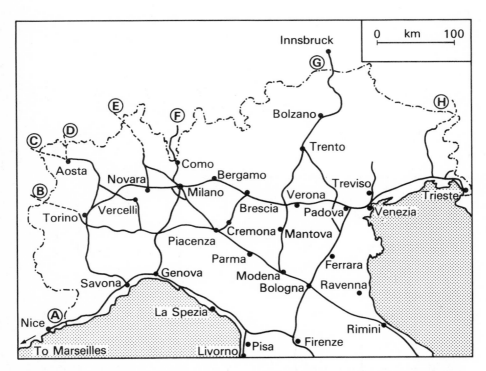

Figure 8.4 Autostrada in northern Italy and the principal links across the alpine mountain system. (A) Riviera coastal motorway to Marseilles and Rhône valley; (B) Mt. Cenis Pass to Chambery and Lyon; (C) Mt. Blanc tunnel to Chamaix and Upper Rhône valley; (D) Grand St. Bernard Pass to Lake Geneva; (E) Simplon Pass to Switzerland; (F) St. Gotthard Pass to Zurich, Basle and Rhine valley; (G) Brenner Pass motorway to Innsbruck and Munich; (H) Villach (Austria); Salzburg–Munich route.

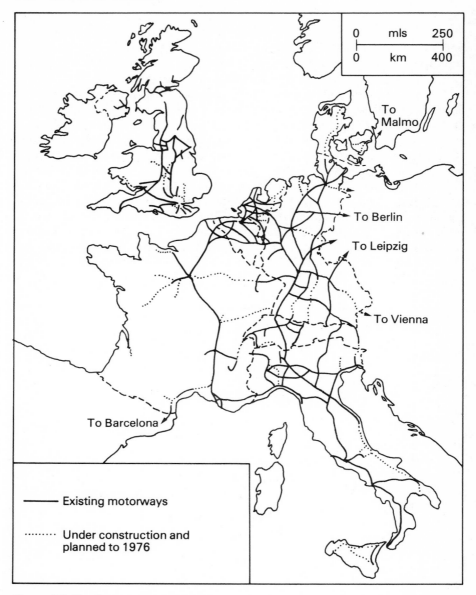

Figure 8.5 The E-route motorway system.

Simplon and St. Gotthard passes, and from Verona northwards to the Brenner Pass, the Italian Autostrada are linked by fast routes to the rest of the EEC.

Although Italy's network is very extensive and a critical element in her economy, the West German Autobahn system has a greater mileage and was originally constructed as part of the National Socialist programme before 1939

Autobahn through the Spessart Uplands
near Frankfurt-on-Main.

(fig. 8.5). Following the post-war division of Germany, the main trend has become north–south based essentially upon two lines of movement. The Rhineland is the primary artery, linking the Ruhr with Bonn, the Saar, Frankfurt,
Mannheim and Stuttgart. A second line runs from the North Sea ports of Hamburg and Bremen south to Hanover, Brunswick and Kassel, and thence to
Nuremburg and Munich. East–west routes link up these two axes at major
urban nodes.

The other EEC countries have rapidly developing motorway systems which
reflect their axes of greater activity. The importance of London and Paris is
illustrated by the concentration of roads and motorways upon these two cities.
In the United Kingdom the radial pattern based upon London is supplemented
by a figure 'H' which is centred upon the industrial Midlands and links the
industrial areas of Northern England and Scotland with London, South Wales
and the Bristol area. The French system is based essentially upon links from
Paris to the Lower Seine, Lille, Dunkerque and the Nord, and south to Lyons,
the Rhône Valley, Marseilles and the Côte D'Azur (fig. 8.5).

Belgium and the Netherlands have a greater milage of motorways in proportion to area than any other part of the EEC. This reflects three significant
geographical facts: a high level of economic activity; a high density of population; and their position as the focal zone of the Community (fig. 8.6).

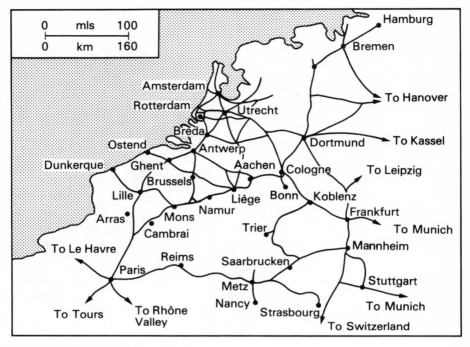

Figure 8.6 Motorway links within the Triangle.

Air and sea transport

The economic effects of air and sea transport are concerned principally with the movement of passengers and materials in international trade, but at the same time there is considerable national and intra-community movement. Civil aviation is primarily important for passenger traffic and some indication is given (figs. 8.1 and 8.7) of the relative importance of national air-fleets, passenger density and principal airports. The significance of London is related to the United Kingdom's traditional international relationships, whilst Paris, Frankfurt and Rome reflect a combination of the nodality of capital cities and core regions, together with their position as transit points between Europe and the rest of the world. One of the most important and fast-growing airline functions is holiday traffic charters, largely to the Mediterranean.

Shipping is related mainly to trade, and here, although the original Six had a substantial merchant shipping fleet, with the Netherlands proportionately the most important, the accession of Great Britain to the community has completely changed its character. The United Kingdom's fleet was almost as large as the original Six put together (fig. 8.1), and the Nine now have easily the largest merchant shipping fleet in the world. It is a function of the international trading traditions of the UK that this significance is so marked, and it contrasts with the mainly continental character of the original Six. In addition the accession of the United Kingdom, Denmark and Ireland has meant that intra-community sea

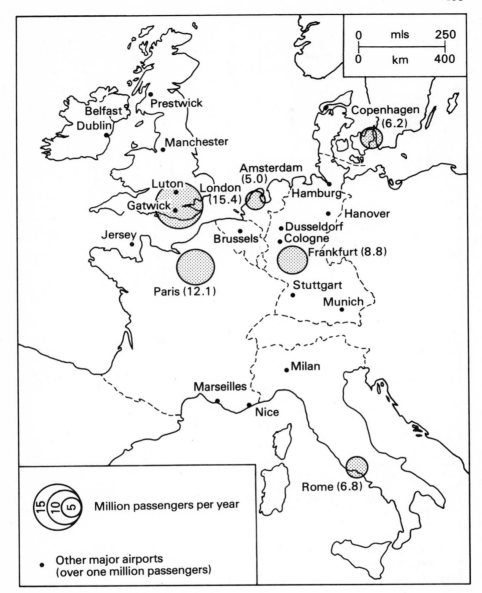

Figure 8.7 Major EEC airports. (Average
numbers of passengers 1970–1972).

traffic, hitherto largely coastal, is now an essential part of movement between
two island and seven continental member states. The map of ports and sea
traffic (fig. 8.8) shows the area of greatest significance. The North Sea coast and
English Channel, from the Tyne to Southampton and from Le Havre to Hamburg, have the greatest number of large ports and carry most passengers and
freight. These are amongst the busiest sea-lanes in the world, and are another

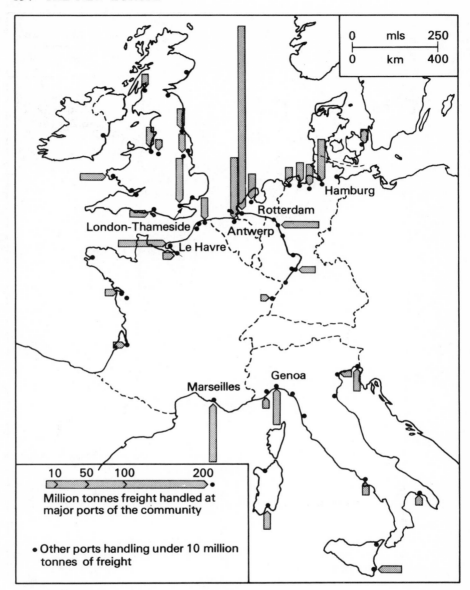

Figure 8.8 Seaports and inland ports of the
EEC. (Average amounts of freight handled
1970–1972).

significant reflection of the high level of economic activity in the northern part
of the community. In addition, there are major ports on the Atlantic coast of the
United Kingdom and France, and the Mediterranean ports act as input points
to the community from the south.

There are a number of 'Euroports' which handle a large tonnage and serve a
substantial part of the whole community. Rotterdam is by far the largest,

Schiphol Airport, Amsterdam, one of the
busiest airports in Europe.

although its tonnage figures are relatively distorted by the very large amounts of
petroleum which it receives. Other major Euroports are Antwerp, London,
Merseyside, Le Havre, Hamburg, Marseilles and Genoa. The other ports are
smaller, often specialised and serve a more limited region.

Principal lines of movement

The transport system as a whole within the community is dominated by several
corridors in which the rate and density of movement is at an extremely high
level (fig. 8.9). There are two primary north–south axes: from Le Havre to Paris
via the Seine, and thence to Lyons and Marseilles via the Rhône Valley; and
from Rotterdam via the River Rhine to south Germany. These are supplemented
by the Stuttgart–Munich, Frankfurt–Main Valley and Hamburg–Bremen–
Ruhr axes, and are linked to each other via the Belfort corridor and the Nord–
Brussels Sambre–Meuse Valley. To the north the main UK axis from Lancashire
to the south-east region is linked to the continent by the Channel sea lanes,
whilst to the south the Italian line from Milan–Turin–Genoa is increasingly
joined to the main stream by means of trans-Alpine routes. The concept of a
community core will be developed subsequently, but nevertheless, it is apparent
that the main stream of movement is encompassed within a zone delimited by
joining Manchester, Southampton, Paris, the Rhône Valley, Milan, Frankfurt,
the Ruhr, Rotterdam and Leeds.

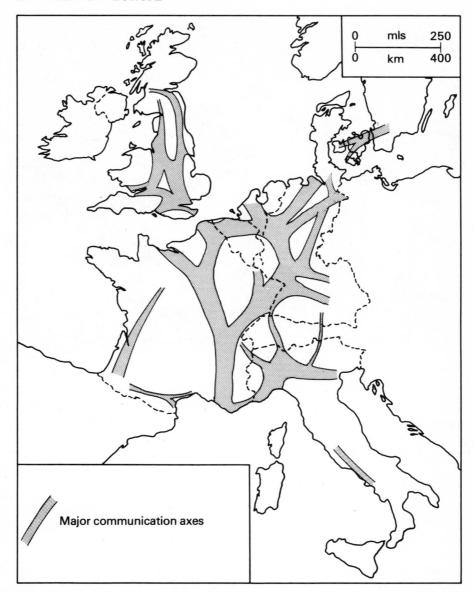

Figure 8.9 Principal lines of movement within the EEC (diagrammatised). (From G. Parker)

The Treaty of Rome and transport policy

The divergences that have emerged in the transport systems of the Nine indicate the need for Community action in the formulation of a coherent transport policy. It is set out in the Treaty of Rome that 'the community should establish a common transport policy to enable the free movement of people and goods over national boundaries'. By 1965 it had been accepted in principle that the two most important objectives were the establishment of fair competition and a regulated transport market. To promote fair competition there is the need to formulate a uniform system of transport taxation, with licensing rules which will allow lorries to make journeys throughout all member countries, and a standardisation of working hours and conditions. One of the most difficult problems has been standardisation of overall lorry weights, as they vary from 32 to 50 tonnes. The commission has proposed 40 tonnes as a compromise, but there are considerable fears that this is unacceptable environmentally in the UK and Eire, where the maximum is 32 tonnes. It is intended to achieve a regulated transport market by controlling freight rates; by maintenance and stabilisation of the railway system; and by a common system of containerised freight to integrate the road, rail, inland waterway and sea transport network. It is likely that future policies will also attempt to look at the co-ordination of air and sea transport, because the enlarged community is no longer linked by a continuous land surface and distances are much greater. In addition, Rhine shipping is such a major feature in the economy of five of the member states that some form of integration will be necessary.

The most important practical step, however, towards fast, uninterrupted movement and the completion of the customs union amongst the nine member countries, is the development of the 'E' road system (fig. 8.5) which links the major trunk roads and motorways across national frontiers. Some intra-national routes have already been carefully coordinated, for example, the Dutch motorway from Rotterdam to Utrecht and Arnhem which connects with the German autobahn system in the Ruhr and Rhineland (fig. 8.6). The South Belgian motorway from Liège to Namur, Charleroi and Mons connects directly with the French system either south to Paris or north to Lille and Dunkerque. The Antwerp–Liège motorway joins the German system at Aachen. The EEC Commission encourages consultation procedures which allow for this cross-frontier integration. The European Investment Bank has also contributed to many projects of this type such as the Brussels–Paris motorway, the Val d'Aosta–Mont Blanc and Grand St. Bernard tunnels and motorways, and the Brenner Pass route linking the Italian Autostrada Del Sole with the German system south of Munich.

9

Population:
the axis of city development

Diversity

The enlarged EEC has a combined population of 253 million people, and includes four large countries each with populations of over 50 millions, four smaller states, and the tiny Grand Duchy of Luxembourg with 300000 people (fig. 9.1).

	Population	Percentage in agriculture	Percentage in industry	Percentage in services	Percentage of population urbanised
Belgium	9673000	4·4	43·4	50·3	66
France	51250000	12·9	39·3	47·7	63
West Germany	61284000	7·8	49·1	43·1	78
Italy	53899000	18·2	44·3	37·5	45
Luxembourg	342000	9·3	48·3	42·4	62
Netherlands	13190000	6·9	36·6	56·5	80
United Kingdom	55668000	2·7	43·7	53·5	80
Denmark	4963000	9·8	34·2	56·0	74
Eire	2978000	25·7	30·3	44·0	44
USA (for comparison)	–	4·2	30·7	60·2	75

Figure 9.1 Population, employment and urbanisation (1972–1973).

This economic grouping, stretching from northern Scotland to Sicily, also includes a great number of ethnic and linguistic types. The peoples of Italy and France, traditionally known as Latin or Mediterranean, speak languages belonging to the Romance group, whilst the northern part of the community is dominated by the Teutonic group of languages (German, English, Scandinavian and Dutch). It is also relevant to associated broadly the predominance of the Roman Catholic Church in the south with the Romance language groups and more specifically with France and Italy, whilst making a similar association between Protestantism and the areas around the North Sea. There is, therefore, a broad distinction between the northern and southern sections of the community on the basis of religion, language and culture.

In general, the language divisions are those of national frontiers, but there are several complicating factors. The Celtic language is represented by minority

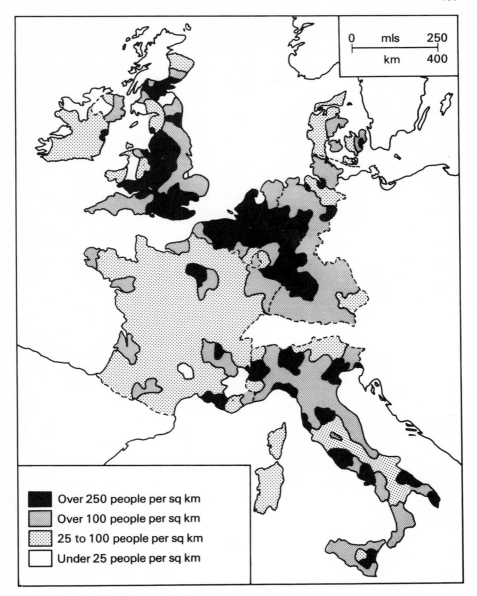

Figure 9.2 Density of population, 1971–1972.

groups and usually exists alongside the major national language, as in the case of the Welsh, Gaelic, Breton and Basque areas. Along the Franco-German frontier zone in Alsace and Lorraine is a German-speaking minority, and the whole Rhineland area in the past has been a zone of contention between the two major groups, French and Germanic. In Belgium there is a complete division along linguistic lines between the French-speaking Walloons in the south and the Dutch-speaking Flemings in the north. However, these distinctions have rapidly begun to lose their former psychological importance, and the economic pressures of the twentieth century, combined with political maturity and a desire for peaceful cooperation and federation, have created 'unity within diversity'. There is of necessity a system of official languages in the community: French, English, German, Italian, Dutch and Danish, the first two being in most common use.

Distribution and density of population

This tends to reflect relative regional advantages, and indicates the countries with the highest degrees of population concentration and urbanisation (fig. 9.2).

Using national statistics, the member states may be divided into four groups (fig. 9.3). The Netherlands and Belgium have a very high population density with over 300 people per square kilometre. The Netherlands has the highest density of all and half its population is concentrated in the Randstad conurbation. Belgium's population is highest around the Brussels–Antwerp area, with similar concentrations throughout the commercial cities of Flanders, and the Sambre–Meuse coalfield.

Country	Population per square kilometre
Netherlands	366
Belgium	319
West Germany	249
United Kingdom	220
Italy	182
Luxembourg	137
Denmark	117
France	96
Eire	43

Figure 9.3 Density of population, 1973.

High densities of population, over 180 per square kilometre, are recorded in the UK, West Germany, and Italy, but these figures hide considerable variations from one part of the country to another. The Italian population concentrations in the Lombardy lowlands, Ligurian coast, and the Rome–Naples area contrast with the sparsely populated Alps and Central Appenines. West Germany and the UK have major concentrations in their industrial zones and city regions. These favoured zones of population concentration, the German Rhinelands and the English lowland (fig. 9.2), contrast again significantly with many upland areas in both countries which have extremely low densities.

France, Denmark and Luxembourg have relatively low overall densities of under 140 people per square kilometre, reflecting their largely agricultural and rural character. France has a remarkably even distribution of population, and apart from Paris there are few concentrations of any great extent. Even the Nord and Lorraine heavy industrial areas have not attained the same degree of population density as comparable areas in West Germany or the UK, Luxembourg City and the steel-making district of Esch-sur-Alzette in the south of Luxembourg have a moderately high density (250 per square kilometre), whilst Copenhagen is a significant exception to the rule in Denmark.

Eire has the lowest density of all, with an average of 43 people per square kilometre. This is associated with a long tradition of rural depopulation, lack of mineral resources, and a peripheral position in relation to Europe as a whole. The only centre of any size is the capital, Dublin.

Economic structure and population patterns

Population density is one indication of the rate and scale of economic activity, but equally valid indices are employment characteristics and the degree of urbanisation. The proportions of the population employed in agriculture, industry and services measure fairly accurately the stage of evolution which any country has reached (fig. 9.1). The percentage of the population which is urbanised indicates a sophisticated life-style associated with a mature economy. The relative proportions for each sector of the economy in the EEC countries are compared with those for the USA which has great productivity and a high proportion of employment in the tertiary sector. The UK shows the nearest approach to the American situation, with a well-developed tertiary sector, efficient agriculture, large industrial sector and high degree of urbanisation. The Netherlands, Belgium, Denmark and West Germany have largely similar characteristics. West Germany has a larger and less efficient agricultural sector, but it has a large industrial sector and a high degree of urbanisation. Denmark has a large agricultural sector. In all these countries there is an advanced social and economic superstructure, associated with a high standard of living and

	Total population	Percentage in agriculture	Percentage in industry	Percentage in services
Greater Paris	9 962 000	0·8	37·5	61·7
Piedmont	4 477 000	11·1	56·8	32·1
Basilicata	608 000	35·3	27·1	37·6
Liguria	1 866 000	7·3	38·3	54·4
Normandy (Lower)	1 305 000	24·9	33·6	41·5
N. Rhine/Westphalia	17 221 000	3·1	51·5	45·3
Brabant (Brussels)	2 202 000	2·7	33·4	63·8
Limousin	643 000	33·6	30·1	36·3
North Holland	2 283 000	3·6	33·2	63·2
Lower Bavaria	993 000	20·9	44·2	34·9

Figure 9.4 Regional population characteristics, 1973.

urban life-style. There is a different emphasis when interpreting figures for France, Italy, Luxembourg and Eire, which have an enlarged agricultural sector and a lower degree of urbanisation, Italy and Eire being the most extreme examples.

National averages tend to blur the differences between contrasting regions of economic sophistication or underdevelopment, and some idea of these extremes may be gathered from the figures which compare sample EEC regions (fig. 9.4). Concentrations of population in Greater Paris, North-Rhine Westphalia and Piedmont contrast with the very low populations of Limousin and Basilicata, but of equal significance is the difference in service employment levels which exist between Paris, Brabant (Brussels) and Liguria on the one hand and Basilicata and Limousin on the other. There are also other characteristic types, for example, the agricultural regions of Lower Normandy and Lower Bavaria, and the heavy industrialised North-Rhine Westphalia. It is in these figures that the essential contrasts between regions can be seen: wealthy urganised regions with a high level of service-sector employment; industrial conurba-

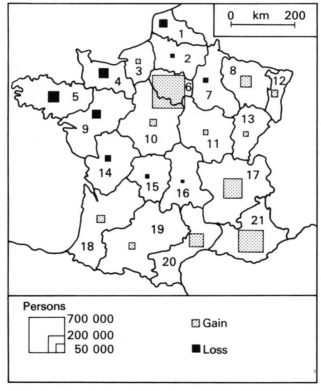

Figure 9.5 France: population change by migration 1954–1962. Planning regions: 1. Nord; 2. Picardie; 3. Haut Normandie; 4. Basse Normandie; 5. Bretagne; 6. Region Parisienne; 7. Champagne; 8. Lorraine; 9. Pays de la Loire; 10. Centre; 11. Bourgogne; 12. Alsace; 13. Franche-Comte; 14. Poitou-Charentes; 15. Limousin; 16. Auvergne; 17. Rhône–Alpes; 18. Aquitaine; 19. Midi–Pyrenees; 20. Languedoc; 21. Provence–Cote D'Azur. (From J. Clarke)

tions with a high percentage of employment in industry; rich farming areas with high rural populations; and marginal farming areas finding it difficult to sustain even low population levels.

Population mobility

The patterns of population distribution which have been illustrated are best explained by the economic pressures which have been operating since the sixteenth century. The movement towards more efficient farms, enclosures and the intensive production of food has been associated with the rise of manufacturing and mass production. The movement away from isolated, rural mountain or upland environments towards the more favoured industrial regions is known as urban concentration and rural depopulation. Consumer wealth and a complex transport system have vastly increased population mobility and intensified this trend.

Both population density and rates of internal migration are indicators of population change, France being a good example (fig. 9.5). Only three regions have persistently gained population on a large scale, Paris, Provence–Côte D'Azur, and Rhône–Alpes (fig. 9.6). These three absorbed half the total popula-

Region	Net migration flow	
1960–1969		
North-Rhine Westphalia	+	525 893
Baden-Württemberg (South Rhineland)	+	425 426
Hessen (Middle Rhineland)	+	473 153
Piedmont	+	493 846
Lombardy	+	640 531
Liguria	+	145 158
Brabant	+	148 323
Lower Saxony (Nieder Sachsen)	+	46 023
Limburg (Holland)	−	9 237
Campania	−	307 708
Calabria	−	331 194
Mezzogiorno (total)	−	1 894 245
1954–1968		
Paris Region	+	1 075 700
Provence Cote D'Azur	+	733 800
Rhône-Alpes	+	443 900
Nord	−	68 500
Bretagne	−	79 900

Figure 9.6 Net migration flows in sample regions.

tion increase from 1954–68. Net migration losses were recorded in the Massif Central, an impoverished and isolated upland region; in western France, which is basically an area of contracting agricultural employment with few alternative manufacturing sources of employment; and in the old industrial area of the north-east where contracting employment in coal-mining, heavy metallurgy and textiles is combined with slow replacement by new industries. Finally, in inner Paris the urban renewal of the city central area is causing the 'volcano effect', that is the reduction of the city centre population together with an associated replacement growth in the outer suburbs and in the wider Paris region.

Areas of population decline

The rate of decline of rural, peripheral, or upland regions varies considerably. In the UK rural depopulation has been going on since the sixteenth century and has produced a farming population which is less than 3 per cent of the total labour force, as well as a high level of urban concentration. There are, however, large peripheral and mountainous areas which are still losing people in spite of Government schemes to introduce employment and improve facilities. Since the 1930s the principal losses have been in the Scottish Highlands, and the uplands of the Cheviots, Pennines, the Lake District and Wales. Smaller losses are also recorded in the remoter rural parts of East Anglia, Lincolnshire, Devon, Cornwall and the Welsh border counties of Shropshire and Hereford.

In France the movement has been much slower, and as late as 1945 over 33 per cent of the population was classed as rural and agricultural. Recently, however, the pace has quickened as farmers and their families have been leaving the land at the rate of 150000 per annum. Regions like the Ardennes and Massif Central have a complex internal population movement. Although population is lost from the central areas, there is often a concentration into lowland fringes and valleys within the zone as a whole. The Massif Central (fig. 9.7) is still losing people from its mountainous spine, particularly the départements of Haute-Loire, Cantal, Aveyron, Lozère, Corrèze and Creuse, but the valley of the Allier in the north, containing Moulins and Clermont Ferrand, has seen considerable growth. Clermont Ferrand is practically a 'company town' of the Michelin Tyre Group, and also gains by being in easy communication with Paris. Limoges and St. Etienne are other old industrial towns on the margin which are minor growth areas. The Ardennes are within commuting range of the Liège conurbation to the north, and towns such as Aywaille have experienced growth in a new dormitory role. In addition, there is the development of 'second homes' in the Ourthe Valley, and upland regions like the Ardennes may well become re-populated, as they are becoming a major leisure area.

There are great differences in opportunity and wealth between northern and southern Italy (fig. 9.6). The out-migration from the Mezzogiorno is a sustained response to the overpopulation, low standards of living and poor employment opportunities. Much of the movement is to Piedmont, Lombardy and Liguria, but in addition there has been a major movement into West Germany and other EEC countries, an important feature of the free movement of labour allowed

Figure 9.7 Départements of the Massif Central. (From H. Clout)

within the Community. In 1969 182 000 Italian nationals emigrated, over 70 per cent to nearby West European countries, and most of these came from Southern Italy.

Old and exhausted coal-mining areas are also responsible for pockets of either population decline, relative stagnation, or unemployment and dislocation. Commuting is a partial answer. The Belgian Borinage is an example where many ex-miners travel daily to Charleroi and Brussels. The small high-cost coalfields of the margins of the Massif Central, Montluçon Decazeville and Commentry are now under a complete closure plan which will intensify migration from the whole area. In the north-east of England there is heavy migration from the old Durham mining villages to new towns such as Washington and Peterlee. The Nord region of France has similar problems, losing 68 000 people during the period 1954–68 (fig. 9.6).

Areas of population growth

Twentieth century population growth areas lie around the major nodes of industry and transport, the city regions, and in new residential and leisure areas.

Low-cost assembly points on major estuaries and transport nodes such as Rotterdam, Antwerp, Hamburg, Marseilles and Teesside have become the growth points for such industries as oil refining, petrochemicals and other basic processing of raw materials. The West Midlands conurbation, at the central point of convergence of the UK motorway system, possesses a varied and sophisticated vehicle and engineering industry.

The capital cities or core regions of the member states have experienced continuous population growth since the mid-nineteenth century. Their attraction lies in their functions as administrative, cultural, service and prestige centres. They lie at the focal point of the national transport network, and have two significant resources—a pool of skilled labour and a huge market. They are examples of the ultimate factor behind multi-million city growth: the non-basic or self sustaining capability of the large population concentration. London, the Randstad, Brussels and Paris are good examples.

The Rhine Valley of West Germany has experienced sustained population growth (fig. 9.6) but illustrates a variation on the capital city concentration theme. West Germany has a political history of many independent states each with its capital city, and with the loss of Berlin resulting from the division of Germany, is a country with a large number of almost equal regional centres. No one city dominates completely. Thus various cities in the Rhine valley enjoy specialised, yet inter-related, functions: Bonn as administrative centre; Frankfurt and Düsseldorf as financial centres; Duisburg as the major port; Cologne and Mannheim as major commercial and industrial cities. In South Germany Munich, Stuttgart, and Nuremberg enjoy extensive regional status. In Italy, the principal manufacturing and core region lies in the northern triangle of Milan, Turin and Genoa. Nevertheless, the historic, cultural and administrative functions of Rome, and the regional importance of Naples, ensure their continuing growth.

Population growth in coastal and other environmentally attractive areas is associated with wealth, holidays, retirement, mobility and the phenomenon of the 'second home'. Large areas of the English south coast have become continuous suburban development as towns like Bournemouth and Poole, and the Bognor Regis and Brighton group, coalesce. They are the new leisure service centres. On a much larger scale is the pattern of linear growth along the Côte D'Azur from Cannes to Monte Carlo and along the coast of the Ligurian Riviera (fig. 9.6).

The conurbation and city region

The most characteristic feature of contemporary Europe is the extent and scale of city growth (figs 9.8 and 9.9). The percentage of the population which is urbanised is very high in all EEC countries except Eire and Italy. The pattern of small and nucleated cities of the medieval period was succeeded in the nineteenth

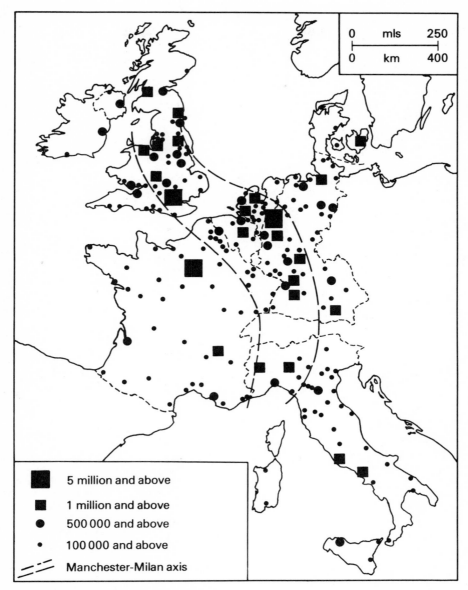

Figure 9.8 Major cities and the axis of city development.

century by the conurbation, a sprawling structure composed of a number of coalescing industrial towns. The city of Stoke-on-Trent, comprises six towns based upon the North Staffordshire coalfield and the pottery industry, and is perhaps the best structural example of an agglomeration of industrial towns. The Ruhr, Lille–Roubaix–Tourcoing agglomeration and the Greater Man-

City	Population (1000s) 1970–72	EEC rank
London	12762	1
Rhine–Ruhr	10419	2
Paris	8714	3
Randstad	4353	4
West Midlands	2981	5
Rome	2920	6
Greater Manchester	2541	7
Hamburg	2407	8
West Berlin	2240	9
Glasgow (Clydeside)	2008	10
Leeds–Bradford (W. Yorkshire)	1945	11
Stuttgart	1935	12
Liverpool (Merseyside)	1823	13
Milan	1750	14
Mannheim–Ludwigshaven	1578	15
Frankfurt-on-Main	1520	16
Munich	1502	17
Copenhagen	1380	18
Naples	1233	19
Torino	1178	20
Lyon	1075	21
Brussels	1075	22
Marseilles	964	23
Lille	881	24
Genova	842	25
Newcastle-on-Tyne	804	26
Antwerp	663	27
Palermo	659	28
Bremen	606	29
Dublin	566	30
Hanover	554	31
Nuremberg	515	32
Sheffield	513	33
Bologna	500	34

Figure 9.9 Rank-size of EEC cities. (After K. Davis and P. Hall)

chester region (fig. 9.10) are much larger examples. The twentieth century has witnessed such an increase in mobility that people often now live up to 60 km out of the city and commute daily to work. The life-style of the city is a great attraction, and its retail, commercial, administrative and cultural services ex-

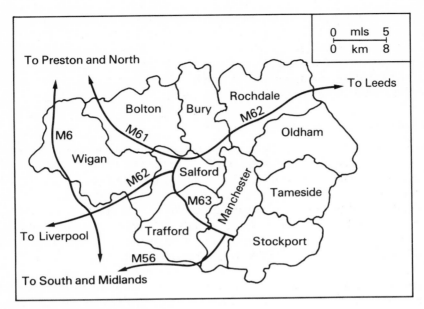

Figure 9.10 The Greater Manchester city region.

pand so that congestion becomes the great problem in the city centre. Replacement of obsolescent property means that displacement of people to the city margins, and the mushrooming of new housing estates has meant a vast expansion in the area of the city.

The term 'city' is no longer enough, as in the case of Paris. Paris city has 2·6 million people; the Région Parisienne includes the city and four départements (chapter 19). It extends over nearly 2000 km² and has a population of over 8 million. The London planning region, bounded approximately by a radius of 60 km from Charing Cross station, has a population of 12·5 million people, and is really three concentric zones. The Greater London conurbation, with nearly 8 million people, forms the core and is surrounded by the green belt, a successful device which has substantially arrested continuous growth. The outer ring consists of old centres such as Aylesbury and Guildford and eight new towns such as Stevenage and Crawley, established after the 1944 Act of Parliament. The rapid suburbanisation of this outer ring has proceeded apace, so that this is now a part of London's 'commuter belt'. The effects of city growth now reach far beyond the London planning region, however. The whole of south-east England from the Wash to the Solent is now affected by plans for new cities such as Milton Keynes and major town expansion plans such as Basingstoke, Peterborough and Ashford. Some are as far as 125 km from London.

Such regions of dynamic growth are 'city regions' dominated by the central city and surrounded by industry and housing, leisure areas and open space. On the fringe there are old-established towns, metropolitan villages and non-contiguous residential areas and new towns. These are all linked to the employment facilities and life style of the city by fast suburban communications. The four largest city regions in the EEC are Greater London, The Ruhr, Greater Paris and Randstad. These are followed by a group each with populations around the 2·5 million mark: Rome, Greater Manchester (fig. 9.10), the West Midlands and Hamburg. Finally however, it is the very great number of medium sized cities with populations of over 500000 which demonstrates fully the substantial degree of urbanisation which now exists.

The axis of population concentration

There is a withdrawal of population from rural and peripheral areas towards two central areas of concentration (fig. 9.2). In the UK there is a quadrilateral based upon Manchester, Leeds, Gravesend and Southampton. On the continent there is a triangle best described by joining lines from Stuttgart to the coast at Dunkirk and Hamburg. These are not exclusive, and areas external to these such as Greater Paris, Lyons, Northern Italy and Rome are important subsidiary nodes. If a high rate of migration is taken as the most significant factor, the Rhône Valley and Côte D'Azur of France show sustained growth over a long period.

The main axis of city development thus stretches from South Lancashire to Northern Italy, often referred to as the Manchester–Milan axis (fig. 9.8). This is a wide belt which essentially crosses the English lowland and thence to the heavily urbanised North Sea coastlands stretching from Lille through Belgium to the Randstad. The River Rhine has three great city agglomerations, Rhine–Ruhr, Rhine–Main, and Rhine–Neckar, which embrace the great regional and industrial centres of West Germany. Though broken by the Alpine mountain chain, the theme re-emerges in the Plain of Lombardy with its traditions of city life and its position as the core area of Italy.

This great axis of urbanisation, and the population contrasts which it shows with other areas in the community, becomes of key importance in the next chapter. This will consider the question of the existence within the community of a dynamic core and problem periphery.

10

Regional disparities: core and periphery

Areas of growth and decline

Much of Western Europe has experienced substantial economic growth and greatly increased prosperity since 1954. More varied energy sources, increased farm production, greater industrial efficiency, greater mobility, a larger volume of trade, greater purchasing power and a wide variety of consumer goods, all create an impression of prosperity. But the principal problem within this wealthy society is that of 'dualism'. This is the propensity to uneven growth and the emergence of marked contrasts between natural growth areas and problem regions. Calabria in Southern Italy has less than 40 per cent and Northern Ireland 50 per cent of the average income per head in the EEC, whilst the Brussels region has 150 per cent. The basic reason for these disparities, in part at least, is the operation of the Common Market itself. The increased cross-frontier competition, and operation of the large free market amongst 250 million people, means that the strongest competitors gain whilst the weakest lose. Industry tends to move to the area which will allow it to operate at maximum efficiency and with the highest profit. There is increasing recognition that the free market has to be distorted to a certain extent to aid the weaker regions, and that, as an obvious case, Italy's Mezzogiorno needs financial assistance to enable it to compete with the factories of Milan and Turin. The establishment of the principle that intensive regions of activity need no help, and that less intensive, inactive or declining areas require considerable aid or reconstruction, is one of the very significant innovations in the modern industrial state. It has become an important policy-making area in the EEC.

The economic heartland

The preceding chapters have attempted to illustrate a major theme: the contrasts between the economic heartland and the peripheral regions of the EEC.

1. In **agriculture**, the area of large-scale, intensive and efficient food production centres upon the polders, boulder clays and loess lowlands of the North European Plain and south-eastern England.

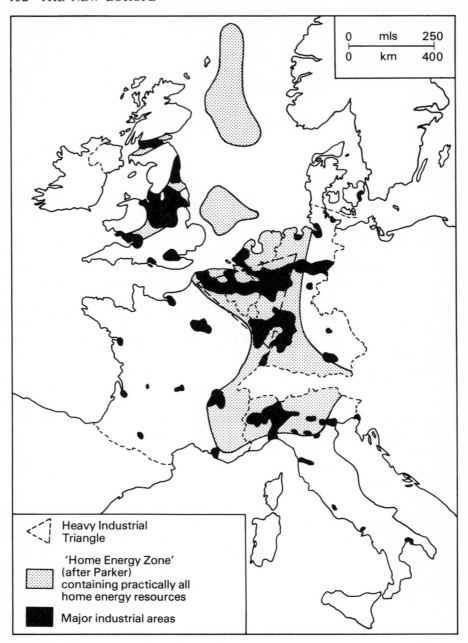

Figure 10.1 Home energy and industrial zones of the EEC.

2. The **Home Energy Zone** (fig. 10.1) includes the coalfields of the United Kingdom and the Heavy Industrial Triangle which produce 95 per cent of the
Community's coal and lignite. Ninety per cent of the EEC hydro-electricity
comes from the Alpine zone of south-eastern France and Italy, which forms
the southern portion of the Home Energy Zone. If the large reserves of gas
and oil in the North Sea are added, then the vast bulk of the Community's
home energy supplies will continue to be found along a north–south axis
which includes the North Sea littoral and the Rhinelands. This is the 'Home
Energy Production Zone' of G. Parker.
3. **Manufacturing industry** (fig. 10.1) is concentrated in the German Rhinelands,
Eastern France, Central Belgium and the Rhine Delta, with a very large
proportion of the community's coal, iron-ore, steel, refined oil, engineering,
chemicals, textiles and vehicle production. To this industrial triangle must be
added the Manchester–London axis, Greater Paris and the Milan–Turin core,
for, although physically separate, they form a logical extension of the central
industrial axis. In addition they complete the picture of national core areas,
most of which lie within this central zone.
4. **Mobility** is at its height along the Rhineland routeways (figs 8.2, 8.5 and 8.6)
and the waterway system of the Rhine and its tributaries is both physically and
psychologically the central artery of the community, containing its greatest
seaport.
5. **The demographic heart of the community** (fig. 10.2) lies within an area delimited by Boulogne–Nancy–Stuttgart–Hanover–Amsterdam (Kormoss,
1959). Related to the original six-member community, it was found that this
area had 20 per cent of the land area but 40 per cent of the population, and
contained some 80 million people. The map of population density (fig. 9.2)
confirms this picture of a heavily populated core. If the UK 'coffin' or quadrilateral (fig. 10.2) is added, the existence of a population heartland in the
Rhineland stretching across the North Sea into England is a reality.
6. **Wealth**, as measured by gross domestic product per capita, is another index
which illustrates the relative wealth of much of the central part of the EEC.
The contrast here is more significant when approached from the other side of
the coin, for it is here that the relative poverty of southern Italy and Eire and
the other peripheral regions is illustrated (fig. 10.3). The estimates of gross
domestic product, however, must be treated with some reserve as national
figures are not exactly comparable.

The Rhineland

Geographically perhaps the most significant part of this heartland is the Rhineland, partly because of its centrality, but also because it illustrates the profound
consequences of political change upon economic strength. The Rhineland was
for long denied the unifying forces from which most of the European nation-
states emerged. The states were either grouped around a cultural heartland as in
France, or sheltered behind natural physical frontiers as in England. Even
Germany and Italy, which emerged late as nations, had a cohesive culture and
were brought to nationhood by the political cores of Prussia and Piedmont

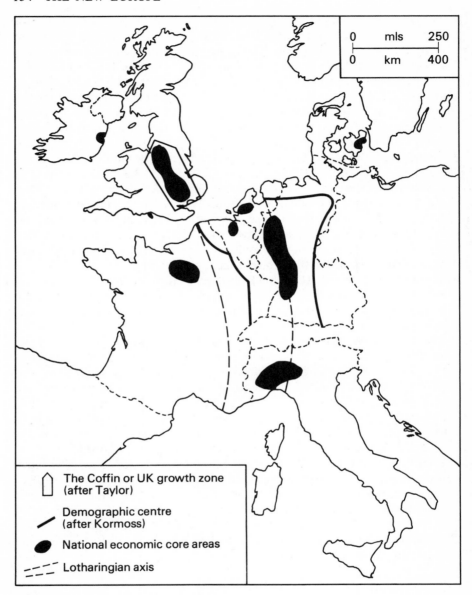

Figure 10.2 The 'Manchester to Milan growth axis' of the EEC.

respectively. Moreover, Italy had the advantage of natural frontiers, and Germany a political and military force of great strength in the Hohenzollern kings of Prussia.

By contrast the Rhineland was denied any political cohesion and natural frontiers and became a buffer state between two strong cultural heartlands. By The Treaty of Verdun, 843 A.D., Charlemagne's Empire was dismembered into

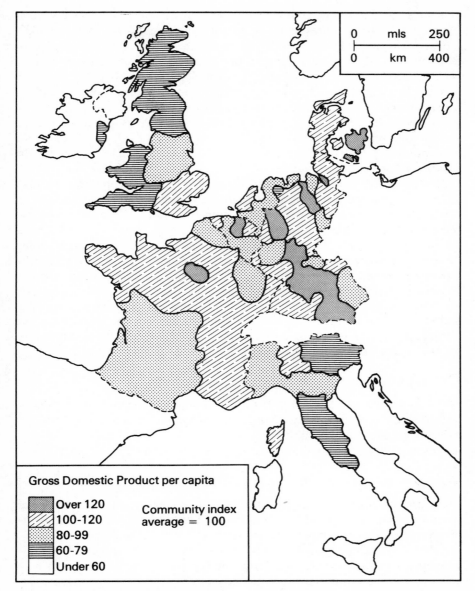

Figure 10.3 Relative wealth in the EEC. These figures have been taken on a regional basis for 1971–1972, partially modified and updated, but must be treated with reserve as national data are not exactly comparable. (Source: EEC Commission)

three parts: the Western Kingdom evolved into modern France; the Eastern Kingdom of the Saxons became the Holy Roman Empire and later Germany; and the Middle Kingdom or Lotharingia (fig. 10.2) was a narrow corridor or buffer zone in between. It covered the present area of Belgium, Holland, Luxembourg, the German Rhinelands and the Saarland, Alsace-Lorraine, Switzerland, Burgundy, and Northern Italy. These emerged at various periods as smaller and less powerful states. Belgium was under Spanish and later Austrian rule for centuries and was a late developer into statehood in 1832. Holland was born in revolution in the sixteenth century. Switzerland, a confederation with four official languages, but with a majority of German-speaking people, debated whether to join the German Zollverein during the nineteenth century, as also did the Grand Duchy of Luxembourg. Alsace-Lorraine and the Saarland, and specifically their mineral resources, have been a major source of friction between Germany and France over the last 150 years, and have changed hands on a number of occasions. The Rhinelands have been a contentious zone for centuries; a zone of convergence and political change and instability; the cockpit of Europe.

The locational advantages of the Rhineland have now become real. Its large industrial zones, mineral resources, the great urban centres, the water-ways and network of other communications have been allowed to realise their potential because of the development of the Community. From being an unstable frontier zone, its economic unity 'always prescribed by geography, always prevented by history'[1] has become real. The frontier image and the restrictions of politically separate economies have been removed by the EEC. The cohesion provided by an intricate system of converging transport links, the proximity of the majority of home energy and heavy industry production and the possession of three national core areas (fig. 10.2), has made the Rhinelands the keystone of the Community's economy. In place of the unstable Rhinelands of nineteenth century Europe, a 'super-core' region on a continental scale has emerged.

The economic regions of the EEC

The consideration of the economic heartland on the one hand, and peripheral regions on the other, leads into a more accurate analysis of four types of regions: dynamic growth centres; stable rural areas; older industrial regions with varying degrees of maladjustment; remote peripheral areas with harsh environments.

Regions of dynamic growth

These are regions with a high level of economic activity, having experienced sustained population growth, a rapid industrialisation rate, and a high degree of urbanisation. The Rhinelands and three other national economic cores— Greater Paris, the upper plain of Lombardy and the Manchester–London axis— together constitute this economic heartland (fig. 10.2). There is even a case for adding others of more recent rapid economic growth, such as Hanover– Brunswick, Marseilles and Greater Lyons, which form extensions not too far removed from the central axis. Economic life revolves around the 'city region' and, as illustrated in the previous chapter (fig. 9.8), the principal great cities of the community lie within a broad arcuate axis stretching between Manchester, Paris, the Rhineland and Milan. However, the very nature of rapid growth is associated with the questions of pollution and congestion. Rotterdam and the Lower Rhine have considerable pollution problems, whilst the growth of

[1] The Schumann Declaration.

Metropolitan areas such as the Randstad and Paris poses enormous planning problems.

Stable rural regions

These are balanced rural communities which have few economic problems because of slower growth which can be absorbed more easily. They have an air of permanence and stability, and a dominantly agricultural base with efficient farming. Moderate urban growth is based upon the rural service centre or market town, often with the cathedral city as its principal focal point. East Anglia and the lower Severn Valley of Worcestershire and Gloucestershire are good examples in the U.K. Amiens, Reims, Troyes and Orleans act as centres of rich agricultural hinterlands in France. Würzburg and Bamberg in West Germany, and Piacenza and Verona in Northern Italy, have the same characteristics.

Older industrial regions

Regional difficulties are not always the result of remoteness, or a harsh environment. Many industrial areas of Europe can be found close to the 'axial growth belt' which runs from Greater Manchester to Milan. These areas such as the Nord, Saar and Sambre–Meuse coalfields, and even the Ruhr, have problems related to the decline of industries of nineteenth century origin like coal and textiles. There is also often an unattractive environment of man-made dereliction and obsolescent buildings. Central Scotland and north-eastern England are two of the earliest locations of the industrial revolution. They are more remote from the main areas of growth in the UK, and face similar problems, contracting industries and exhausted resources.

The maladjustment stems from a loss of economic vitality, but with injections of capital, new industries can be brought into these areas. These are usually labour-intensive light and consumer-goods industries which use the existing abundant labour supply. Retraining of the labour force and the provision of new houses, roads and services, is necessary to replace the obsolete and unattractive environment. There is great potential but industrial restructuring and adjustment to the twentieth century is needed.

The periphery: remote regions and harsh environments

Easily the most serious problem areas are those relatively backward regions which have a marginal agricultural base and lack of industrial employment. Occasionally there are small pockets of mineral resources which have stimulated development such as the small coalfields of the Massif Central and tin-mining in Cornwall, but after a short period contraction and the resulting unemployment have only aggravated the local situation. Persistent out-migration from these regions is the most common reflection of their problems (fig. 10.4).

(a) Southern Italy is the most extreme example. It is remote from the mainstream of economic activity, and has a desiccated environment, inefficient agriculture, over-population, inadequate transport, and a limited local market owing to the low living standards.

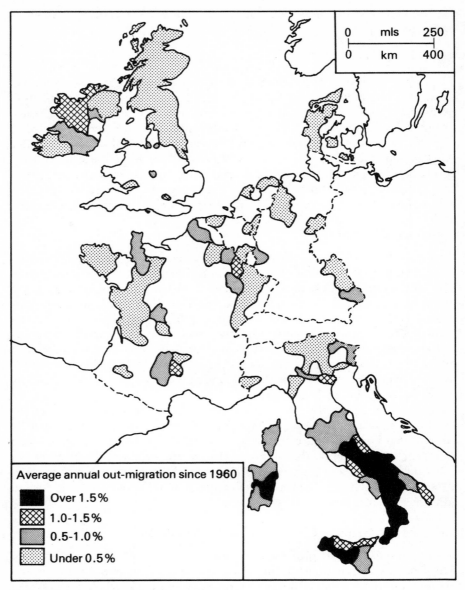

Figure 10.4 Areas of persistent out-migration. (Source: EEC Commission)

(b) The Massif Central, the Highlands of Scotland, Eire, and much of Atlantic Britain generally, are within the category of upland, remote and harsh environments. Moorland and marginal farming is the norm. The Central Hercynian uplands, the Ardennes, Eifel and Vosges, are of the same general type, though more heavily forested.

(c) The Dutch and North German heathlands of Groningen, Oldenburg and Luneberg have the infertile acidic soils of the glacial outwash plain.

(d) In Lower Bavaria and the Thuringia-Wald the upland environment has combined with the debilitating effects of being close to the East German and Czech frontier zone across which there is very little movement.

(e) Western France, west of a line from Normandy to Marseilles, is characterised by an over-dependence upon agricultural employment. In 1962 in Brittany 45 per cent, in Aquitaine 34 per cent, and in Limousin 44 per cent of the labour force were employed on the land. As structural reform and improved techniques of farming are introduced, agricultural employment is now declining quite steeply and there is no compensating rate of growth in industrial and tertiary employment. Income levels are lower than the national average, and industrial activity is limited to a few centres, including Toulouse, Bordeaux, Nantes and Le Mans. Net out-migration is a severe problem over large areas including Brittany, and the Loire–Poitou region.

National policies

The revitalisation of these regions of difficulty, retardation or maladjustment, has been accepted as a necessary policy in the last few decades, and various regional classifications have been carried out at national level.

British development areas

The British classification is a detailed three-fold division into special development areas, development areas and intermediate areas. Originating in the 1930s with the establishment of trading estates, government policy was coordinated in 1966 by the Industrial Development Act which placed 40 per cent of the land area and 20 per cent of the population of the United Kingdom under development schedules. These development areas are designated usually on the basis of a 4·5 per cent rate of unemployment of the insured population. Industrial companies are encouraged to move into the area by receiving grants for building factories, working capital, and machinery installation. The special development areas are severely declining coalfields and new factories receive extra priorities including a rent-free period of five years. The intermediate areas include the North-West, Yorkshire and Humberside, which have a vulnerable economy partially dependent on declining industries like coal and textiles, and which were also characterised by a poor environment with much dereliction. The essence of the British problem is industrial maladjustment, although two areas, the Highlands and Islands of Scotland and Northern Ireland, are special cases and their problems must be seen in a rather different context.

France

France has a dual problem. There is not only the division between the eastern zone of industry, urbanisation and wealth and the western rural retarded zone, but also the imbalance posed by the traditional dominance of Paris. The excessive centralisation of administration, educational opportunity, commerce

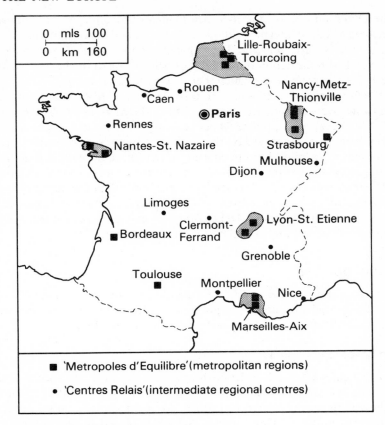

Figure 10.5 France: city regions and development poles. (From I. B. Thompson)

and wealth in the capital city has created a serious gap between Paris and what has been called 'le desert français'. French planning has therefore concentrated upon two themes:

(i) to develop the under-industrialised areas, state assistance being given to industries particularly in the section of the country west of a line from Cherbourg to Marseilles.
(ii) to create eight 'metropoles d'equilibre' to act as commercial, industrial and cultural centres as a counterbalance to Paris, and to act as poles of development (fig. 10.5).

Southern Italy

The most typically peripheral under-developed region in the EEC is the Italian Mezzogiorno (see chapter 17). The problem is so intractable here because of the extent of the area, its history and the dramatic contrasts with the wealthy northern half of Italy. The 'Cassa Del Mezzogiorno' was set up in 1951 and has had some remarkable successes. There have been key projects like the steelworks at Taranto, petrochemical works in Sicily and at Brindisi, and the construction of the Autostrada Del Sole, south to Naples and Reggio. The problem was to channel the investments on a scale sufficient to be effective and it has been realised that this could be done only by concentrating attention on development poles, of which the Bari–Taranto axis is the most important.

Other problem regions

The other members of the community do not have such large-scale problem areas primarily because of their position closer to the European growth axis. However, the Belgian coalfields and the old textile areas of West Flanders are development areas for similar reasons to those of the United Kingdom. Most of the efforts of West Germany and the Netherlands have gone into their land reclamation schemes for the northern coastlands and heathlands from the Yssel Lake to the Elbe.

Community Regional Policy

The early Community Funds

Much has already been done at national level in giving help to problem regions, and one of the articles in the Treaty of Rome was concerned with 'aid to promote the economic development of regions where the standard of living is abnormally low or where there is serious unemployment'. The Common Agricultural Policy, through the 'European Agricultural Guarantee and Guidance Fund' (EAGGF), gives specific aid to backward farming regions. The ECSC is concerned with the retraining of workers who have become unemployed because of closures of coal-mines, and uses its funds to attract new industry into the declining areas. Similarly the Social Fund is concerned with other problem industries. Perhaps most important is the European Investment Bank.

The European Investment Bank (EIB)

The EIB has a separate identity, but works closely with the Commission and the member governments. Its aims, as laid down in the Treaty of Rome, are:

1. to grant loans for projects in under-developed regions of the community such as the Mezzogiorno.
2. to grant loans and assistance for the modernisation, extension and reorganisation of particular industries. Loans to the British Steel Corporation at Scunthorpe come into this category.
3. to finance projects of joint interest to member states, which may be difficult to finance by one member country alone. The cross-frontier motorways (Nice to Genoa or Paris to Brussels) are such an example, or the trans-Alpine Mont Blanc tunnel between Italy and France. The improvement of communications between member states is of key interest to the Community. By 1972 the EIB had made loans for 300 projects worth 1500 million dollars.

	Number of projects	Percentage of total value
West Germany	44	12·5
France	56	20
Italy	196	50
Netherlands	5	1·5
Belgium	6	2·5
Luxembourg	3	0·5
Associated countries		13·0

Figure 10.6 EIB loans up to 1972.

As can be seen from fig. 10.6, half the investment has gone to Italy and most of this to the Mezzogiorno. Irrigation projects in the Metapontino of Apulia, the Naples to Reggio railway, the Taranto steelworks and a thermal power station at Salerno are examples of this very important activity (fig. 17.3).

Regional policy

It has become widely accepted that regional policy should be a major area of community activity. Since the 1973 enlargement of the community to nine, pressure for regional aid increased because of the serious regional imbalances in countries like the United Kingdom and the peripheral nature of member states like Eire. It was not surprising that immediately after the enlargement in 1973, the new Commission member for regional development, George Thomson, introduced a proposal for a Regional Fund. There was great difficulty over the total amount of aid to be given, but eventually the Regional Development Fund became operative on 1st January 1975, with an initial grant of 600 million pounds over three years. The criteria upon which regions were to receive aid were as follows:

(a) A lower gross domestic product than the community average.
(b) Heavy dependence on employment in declining industries with at least 20 per cent of local employment in such a category.
(c) A persistently high rate of unemployment over a number of years, at least 3·5 per cent (this includes agricultural under-employment regions, such as Eire and Southern Italy).
(d) A high and sustained rate of emigration (10 per 1000 each year averaged over a long period).

It can be seen from these criteria that those areas qualifying for regional aid (fig. 10.7) are essentially the community's upland and remote rural regions. But the complexity of the situation is shown by the inclusion of problem areas of industrial maladjustment including those which exist closer to the community's growth axis, amongst them the coalfields of south Belgium. The concept of the 'dynamic core' and 'problem periphery' is valid, but it is not a simple division, and must be analysed carefully.

The Regional Fund limits total aid to 15 per cent of the cost of any industrial

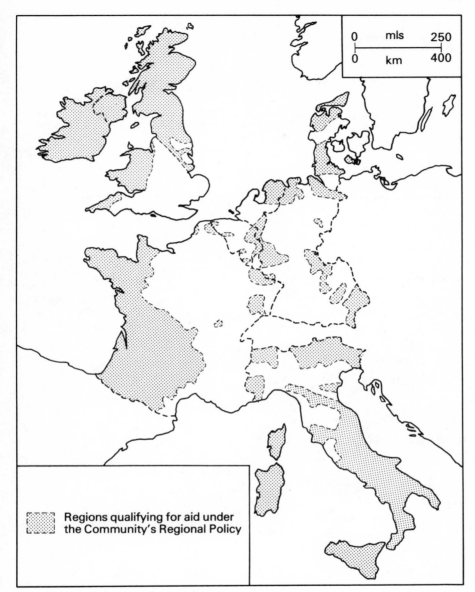

0   mls   250

0   km   400

Regions qualifying for aid under
the Community's Regional Policy

Figure 10.7 EEC Regional Development
Fund.

project, or 30 per cent of that of an infrastructure project. The Fund is in its
infancy and will need considerable expansion if it is to be effective. Nevertheless,
an important principle is established: namely that agriculture is not the only
deserving cause. The Regional Fund is a recognition of the fact that in a wealthy
mature society the less-favoured regions of remoteness and difficulty, of a contracting industrial base, or with an obsolescent environment, require a portion
of the accrued wealth to be set aside for their development or resuscitation.

11

North-Rhine Westphalia: crossroads of Europe

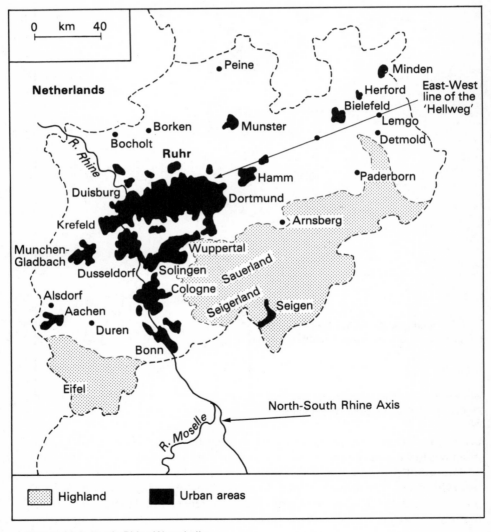

Figure 11.1 North-Rhine Westphalia.

North-Rhine-Westphalia is the administrative region (fig. 11.1) which contains both major growth elements and problems of industrial restructuring, and is situated along the principal growth axis of the EEC.

The Ruhr coalfield: development

This is one of the world's best examples of a heavy industrial region based upon coal. It produces one-third of the coal and half the coking coal, one-fifth of the steel, and it makes a significant contribution to the oil-refining, petrochemicals and heavy engineering industries of the enlarged EEC. It lies close to the centre

The old industrial landscape of the Ruhr is shown by this steelworks in Oberhausen.

of the so-called 'growth zone' of the EEC. Its development began from the eleventh century onwards when the medieval cities of Cologne, Duisburg, Essen and Dortmund originated as market and trade centres along the 'Hellweg', the ancient east–west line of migration through Europe. With the increasing importance of the Rhine routeway, the Ruhr has been a major route focus for hundreds of years. In addition, iron-making was practised immediately to the south in the forested Sauerland. Although coal was mined from very early times, it was in the 1830s that the first shafts were bored in the concealed coalfield areas to the north of the river Ruhr, and since that time the mining has been moving steadily northwards into the Emscher and Lippe valleys.

The 'take-off' period was the 1870s when the 'Fettkohle' or coking coal in the Ruhr was found to be of extremely good quality and suitable for the improved iron-furnaces. The unification of Germany in 1871 was responsible for a great burst of confidence and industrial expansion, with coal-mining increasing from 5 million tonnes in 1870 to 60 million tonnes in 1900. With the construction of the Dortmund–Ems and Rhine–Herne canals, the advantages of the Rhine were improved considerably for heavy industry based on local coal and waterborne raw materials. By 1913 coal output had reached 115 million tonnes and iron and steel production 7 million tonnes. The Ruhr's great industrial significance is shown by its resilience in twice recovering after a great deal of its capacity has been either destroyed or dismantled. After the first World War coal output reached 127 million tonnes and iron and steel 13 million tonnes in 1938, and after the second World War coal reached the peak post-war production level of 125 million tonnes in 1956.

A distinctive feature of the Ruhr is its great density of settlement. It is an amalgamation of over 20 towns and cities, a complex conurbation or polycentric city stretching east–west from Hamm to Geldern and north–south from the river Ruhr to the Lippe (fig. 11.2). The Ruhr Planning Region (SVR) contains over 6 million people, great cities like Dortmund, Essen and Duisburg, and 18 'free cities' in all. In addition, Cologne, Dusseldorf, Bonn and many other associated towns make up the Rhine/Ruhr Conurbation of some 10 million people.

The decline of coal

The extent of the coalfield can be seen in fig. 11.2. The real problem has become the increasing depth at which mining has to be carried out. The coal seams dip to the north and the nineteenth century 'adit' mines are exhausted, whilst the average depth of mines today is nearly 1000 metres in the northern concealed part of the coalfield. The progressive migration northwards into the deeper mines has resulted in an increase in costs at a time of unequal competition from cheap Middle Eastern oil. The Ruhr is in a much better position than most established coalfields in Western Europe, because its coal is by no means exhausted. There are proven reserves of 65000 million tonnes. There are two other circumstances in which it is much superior to other coalfields. The first is in the great variety of types of coal, over 50 varieties, including the famous 'Fettkohle', and the second is the extremely high level of productivity achieved by

167

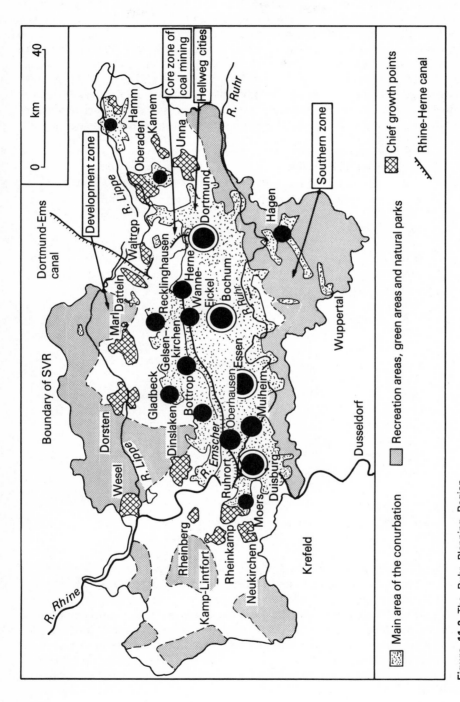

Figure 11.2 The Ruhr Planning Region (SVR) with four major planning zones. (From P. Hall)

large-scale mechanisation. However, the Ruhr has been affected by the same factors as the other major coalfields in the trend during the 1960s to diversify sources of energy, and especially in the cheap competition from oil. Coal production had fallen to below 110 million tonnes by 1967. The mining force has fallen from 400 000 in 1956, to 240 000 in 1967, and 150 000 in 1974; the number of pits has fallen from 99 in 1964 to 57 in 1969 and 45 in 1973 (fig. 11.3). Associated with this has been a remarkable rise in productivity as inefficient mines were closed or amalgamated and the larger mines remained, with production rising since 1964 from 3060 tonnes to 4770 tonnes per mine per day.

Year	Coal Production Million tonnes produced	Year	Steel Production Thousand tonnes produced
1850	1·5	1860	130 000
1870	5	1913	7000
1900	60	1938	13 000
1913	115	1957	18 000
1938	127	1965	23 000
1956	125	1970	28 000
1965	116	1974	30 000
1970	96		
1974	84		

Year	Operative coal mines	Year	No. of coal miners
1850	200	1950	500 000
1890	175	1956	494 000
1950	150	1964	325 000
1961	120	1969	183 000
1964	99	1974	150 000
1969	57		
1974	45		

Figure 11.3 Ruhr coal and steel production.

There has been an accompanying structural reorganisation. Twenty-six of the coal companies amalgamated in 1969 to form Ruhrkole AG, which now controls 94 per cent of total hard coal production in the Ruhr basin.

A real social problem was that the mine closures affected employment patterns tremendously, with over 200 000 coal miners being made redundant since 1956. More significantly, the Emscher valley (fig. 11.2) has suffered more than the other areas. The impact has been concentrated by the nature of the coalfield. The area south of the river Ruhr has long lost its mining capability as the shallow 'adit' mines of the nineteenth century ceased to be used; the area north of Dinslaken and Recklinghausen contains the newer, deeper, and more modern mines. The central Ruhr towns of the Emscher valley such as Gelsenkirchen and Bottrop have been affected most, as their employment and economy was based upon coal-mining to a far greater extent than in the other parts of the conurbation.

However, since 1973 the position has changed again. The decline of coal mining has been arrested, and coal production has been stabilised at 84 million tonnes (1974) (fig. 11.3). The energy crisis has led to a reappraisal of the position of coal. West German law requires that the electricity industry uses 40 million tonnes of coal per annum and the steel industry 30 million tonnes. The coal industry in the Ruhr is therefore protected to a high degree, has stabilised, and will probably see increased production again in the future.

Industrial change

Structural problems facing the Ruhr are not confined to the coal industry, although that is the most seriously affected. The steel industry is affected by the relatively high cost of Ruhr coal as compared with oil and American coal, and the competition from the new coastal steelworks which rely entirely on imported materials. However, the steel industry has demonstrated its remarkable resilience by actually growing in total output (30 million tonnes in 1974) (fig. 11.3). The Ruhr has maintained and improved its steel capability by adjusting in two ways. Firstly, steel-making has migrated heavily to the points of greatest cost-effectiveness, that is, the Rhine water frontage on the west, and to the Dortmund–Ems and Rhine–Herne canals in the east. Steel-making has all but

The new Opel car assembly plant at Bochum in the Ruhr.

ceased in the central parts of the Ruhr, at Bochum and Essen. The Rhine front-age at Duisburg–Ruhrort and Rheinhausen now produces 19 million tonnes of steel and Dortmund nearly 7 million tonnes.

The comparative advantages of water-front locations, owing to the very sub-stantial imports of Swedish iron-ore via the Rhine (25 million tonnes in 1974) and Lorraine iron-ore (5 million tonnes in 1974) has affected the present-day location of the Ruhr steel industry. In addition, there has been considerable reinvestment in new steel plant and reorganisation into larger units such as Thyssen-Mannesmann. Companies like Dortmund Hoechst are now associated with the Ijmuiden works on the Dutch coast, thereby gaining the advantages of scale. The central area has become a steel-using area with motor cars produced at Bochum, electrical equipment, substitute metal-industries such as aluminium- and zinc-smelting at Essen, and consumer goods industries including textiles and clothing, to employ the female labour force.

The heavy chemical industry has had remarkable success in adapting to changed circumstances. The loss of the chemical industries on the Middle Elbe after the partition of Germany has given a considerable fillip to the Ruhr. The industry has abandoned its traditional dependence upon coal and coke by-products, and since 1950, oil has been the major raw material transported by pipeline and by the Rhine routeway into the Ruhr from Rotterdam. The growth of oil refineries and petrochemicals at Marl-Huls and Gelsenkirchen are as-sociated with this. Lighter chemical industries such as pharmaceuticals have also developed.

Settlement and planning

The other main problem is the unplanned, high density and obsolescent en-vironment. The stages of development of the coalfield are largely responsible for the nature of urban development. The Ruhr maybe divided into four main zones: the southern zone; the Hellweg; the core coal-mining zone; and northern development zone (fig. 11.2). The regional planning authority for the Ruhr (Seidlungsverband Ruhrkohlenbezirk) has been active in promoting schemes for balanced industrial development, new housing schemes, new town re-development, green areas, leisure parks and reclamation of tips and spoil heaps. Its activities vary, however, according to the needs of the four zones.

The southern zone coincides essentially with much of the valley of the river Ruhr and the low hills to the south. Here very few coal mines and little heavy industry remain, and population is much less dense than in other parts of the Ruhr. The area consists of the southern residential suburbs of Essen, Bochum and Dortmund, reservoirs on the Ruhr river for water supply, and four large leisure parks, which have already been laid out to serve the cities to the north.

The Hellweg cities of Duisburg, Essen, Bochum and Dortmund are large, well-developed urban areas with good shopping facilities, cultural and historic cores, and with important commercial interests, company head offices and a high proportion of professional people. They are therefore balanced and wealthy urban communities, although surrounded by extensive housing areas of monotonous design or obsolescence and by heavy industrial areas. Their prob-

The Western Hellweg shopping precinct in Dortmund. This street, carrying the name of the ancient east—west routeway across Germany, symbolises the nodality of the cities of the Rhine—Ruhr conurbation.

lems, therefore, involve planning for high density living, but they present much less of a problem than the area immediately to the north.

The core coal-mining zone along the Emscher valley exhibits the greatest problems. Rapid nineteenth century growth meant that villages such as Gelsenkirchen grew into monofunctional mining towns with heavy industry. Others

The Königsallee, along the line of the old
town moat. This is now one of the most
elegant and expensive streets in Dusseldorf.

such as Oberhausen, Recklinghausen, Herne and Bottrop had proportions as
high as 50 and 60 per cent in mining employment. Both air and water pollution
are problems and the Emscher is one of the worst polluted rivers in Western
Europe. As much as 40 per cent of the land is old mining land and is often dere-
lict. Obsolescent housing, unsightly heavy industry and the absence of green
space are the principal features of the area, quite apart from the economic problem of redeployment of its labour and considerable migration into the outer
areas of the Ruhr.

To the north lies the development zone. This is the most recent coal-mining
area and although the mines are deep, the pits are large, modern and efficient.
This is the newer concealed coalfield, lying at a depth of up to 1300 metres, and
the coal is often converted at the pithead into electricity for the industries
further south. Heavy industry has not developed here to any large extent but
instead there are many light and consumer industry factories. The zone's share
of the Ruhr total population is only about 12 to 15 per cent, and so there is
considerable space for development. Major growth points for both new towns
and industrial complexes are planned at Wesel, Dinslaken, Dorsten, Marl-
Huls and Datteln (fig. 11.2).

Other manufacturing towns

There are a number of important sub-zones and groups of towns which are
outside the Ruhr Planning Authority area, yet which have close associations with
it (fig. 11.1).

1. The first group comprises the textile towns on the west bank of the Rhine. Krefeld is a traditional centre for silk and velvets, and Munchen–Gladbach and Rheydt have textile machinery works, wool and cotton mills, and clothing factories.
2. To the south-west lies the city of Aachen with its small coalfield and the huge brown coal deposit on the Ville ridge west of Bonn and Cologne, which is open-cast mined. The Ruhr coal seams themselves are being mined farther northwards and the northern extensions are worked near Munster.
3. To the south lies the Sauerland and Seigerland and the deep valleys of the Seig and Wupper cut out of the Rhine plateaux. Here are towns related to the early importance of local raw materials and power, and the later specialisation and inertia which has led to two highly complex manufacturing concentrations. Both the manufacture of high quality cutlery at Remscheid and Solingen, and the manufacture of locks and keys at Velbert can be traced to the smelting of local iron-ore deposits worked with charcoal from the forests, and these industries survive now because of accumulated skills and specialisation. The old-established textile manufacturing towns of Elberfeld and Barmen were based upon the abundance of water power in the Wupper valley, urban growth having now merged them into the conurbation of Wuppertal.

The cities along the Rhine valley

It is along the Rhine valley, however, that the greatest growth area is found. That part of the Rhineland which lies immediately to the south of the Ruhr is dominated by three cities—Dusseldorf, Cologne and Bonn (fig. 11.1). Dusseldorf is referred to in West Germany as the 'Rhinegold', a term which indicated its wealth and reflects its image as an example of the German economic miracle. It was not a medieval city and developed only during the seventeenth century as a minor principality, from which it has grown into the modern banking, financial and commercial centre of North-Rhine Westphalia. As a financial centre it has a remarkable expertise amongst its 'prominenz' or establishment, and it is also the administrative capital of North-Rhine Westphalia. Its wealth is typified by the enormous amount of rebuilding which has taken place since 1945 to create one of the most modern cities in Europe. The 'Königsallee', an expensive shopping street set in park-like boulevard surroundings, exemplifies the city's wealth. There are also impressive skyscraper offices and headquarter buildings of the major Ruhr companies, Krupp and Thyssen, as well as those of international companies such as IBM and the Chase Manhattan Bank. Not only does the city act as the financial capital of the Ruhr but it also has its own industries, principally engineering, and the huge chemical complex at Leverkusen is just to the south.

Cologne is an ancient settlement founded in Roman times, which flourished as a medieval trade centre of the Hanseatic League, based upon its position where the river route from Flanders into the Rhinelands crossed the fertile loess embayment and the Hellweg. It was the railway development of the nineteenth century, however, which gave the city its modern importance. It is still both an important railway junction and an inland port. As a commercial and business centre it is a rival to Dusseldorf, but in addition it has a very varied industrial base, ranging from iron and steel, oil and petrochemical production, to engineering and car manufacture. It also has a wide range of consumer goods including leather, cosmetics, clothing and chocolate, which are an unusual feature in the region and which originated in the traditions of medieval crafts of the old city.

Farther south again is the city of Bonn, capital of West Germany. It is situated at the point where the Rhine emerges from its gorge, and is a relatively small city of medieval origins. Its bishopric, university and medieval prosperity were based largely upon its function as the historic seat of the Principality of Cologne. Although the Federal capital since 1949, it has remained relatively small with light industries, including machine tools, paper and furniture. Its population is now 300000.

North-Rhine Westphalia: the advantages of centrality

Here, then, is the 'Land' of North-Rhine Westphalia, the richest and most populous part of West Germany with a total population of 17 million within which is the Rhine–Ruhr Conurbation with over ten million people. The Ruhr Planning Region has over 6 million people, whilst the Dusseldorf and Cologne city regions have one and a half million people each. The state as a whole has increased its population steadily, and between 1950 and 1960 there was a dramatic 25 per cent increase. There is, however, a distinction to be made between the growth of the long-established cities and outer suburban and commuter areas, and the structural problems which have caused a slackening of growth and even decline of population in the central coalfield areas. The central core of the Ruhr coalfield, the Emscher valley, has in fact lost some 300000 people from towns like Gelsenkirchen, Bottrop and Bochum, but these have been involved in a sub-regional movement to the cities of Dusseldorf and Cologne, and to the new towns and suburbs on the edge of the coalfield. Any loss of population in the centre has therefore been compensated within the region.

The Ruhr coalfield has had several major advantages in its structural and economic reconstruction.

(a) It is part of the Land of North-Rhine Westphalia, the single most populous, wealthy, and industrious region in West Germany, and it has benefited by its association with the state government in Dusseldorf. For instance, since 1945, four new universities have been established in the Ruhr where none existed before, all part of the changing image of this heavy industry region.
(b) The influence of the Planning Authority (SVR) can be seen in the changing quality of the environment. Although much remains to be done, the green areas, nature parks, reclaimed spoil-heaps and new urban motorways are a witness to its effect since it was set up in 1920. Of the total area of the Ruhr Planning Region, only 24 per cent is urbanised; 53 per cent is open land and farmland; over 20 per cent is woodland and leisure areas. There is plenty of

room available for gradual, planned and comprehensive redevelopment within the whole area (fig. 11.2).

(c) The nature of the coalfield is of great significance. It has few of the problems of thin seams and low productivity associated with many of the other EEC coalfields, and has traditionally been the most productive in Western Europe. There has been a steady reduction in the number of coal-mines, rather than the massive reductions which have been seen elsewhere. In the light of the new energy situation, with coal regaining a competitive position, many Ruhr coal-mines are likely candidates for reopening.

(d) The regional distinctiveness of the Ruhr owes much to the intensive interdependence of its industry and transport system. The steel and chemicals complex has been strengthened by new steel-using industries, by petrochemicals and oil-refining, and by light engineering and consumer-products industry.

(e) The Rhine waterway has remained central to West Germany's economy and has also become the growth-axis of the EEC (chapter 10) underlining the position of centrality which the Ruhr possesses.

(f) Finally, the Ruhr lies on the great historic lateral axis of the city development, the Hellweg (fig. 11.1), and is associated within North-Rhine Westphalia with great cities like Cologne, Dortmund and Dusseldorf. The long established structures of these cities, with their commercial wealth, financial services and shopping facilities, enables them to withstand change and their growing industries are able to absorb the excess population from the Ruhr coal-mining areas. In addition, the large consumer market of 17 million people is a major factor in the development of new industries. North-Rhine Westphalia is effectively at the crossroads of Europe and any problems of industrial adjustment must necessarily be made that much easier.

The Middle Rhinelands:
three city regions

Varied resources

The Middle Rhine valley of West Germany stretches from Weisbaden and Frankfurt-on-Main in the north to Karlsruhe in the south, and is not complete without some consideration of the right-bank tributary valley of the Neckar, in which is the city of Stuttgart (fig. 12.1). Thus defined, it is a most important economic area lying within the EEC core. It has been a traditional zone of urbanisation from Roman times, and throughout the Middle Ages towns like Worms, Mainz, Speyer and Heidelberg were associated with bishoprics or universities, and later there were royal residences and planned cities such as Karlsruhe. There is an abundance of resources, and four principal factors may be identified as contributing at various stages to its development.

A rich and diverse farming region

This is a most productive agricultural area, a fact reflected in the densely popu-lated countryside, with large and numerous villages. Particularly along the foothills, on the loess lands and on the sheltered terraces there is a wide variety of agriculture. The Rhine–Main plain to the north of Frankfurt, the Wetterau, is extremely fertile and is 70 per cent arable, whilst to the west of Frankfurt is the Rheingau with its orchards and vineyards. The Kraichgau between the Rhine and Neckar is a loess-loam with arable lands, orchards and vineyards. By contrast the alluvial plains along the rivers are heavy clays liable to flooding, with damp water meadows. The advantages of the region are not only the wide variety of landscape and terrain, but also the occurrence of loess, which is easily cultivated and has a relatively high fertility, together with a greater amount of sunshine and hotter summers, than the more northerly parts of Germany. In particular, the cultivation of the vine depends to a great extent upon south-facing slopes, and these are found at the point where the Rhine makes its west-ward turn to enter the gorge. As a result, the south-facing slopes of the Taunus ridge overlooking the Rhine have an almost continuous covering of vineyards for some twenty miles from Wiesbaden to the gorge, giving one of the most famous wine-producing areas in West Germany—the Rheingau. Here originate the most famous names in German wines, such as Johannisberg and Rudesheim.

Farther south, another intensive area of cultivation is the Bergstrasse, the loess-loam foothill of the Odenwald between Darmstadt and Heidelberg. This

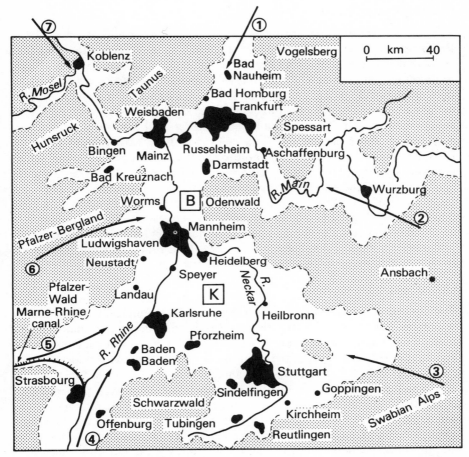

Figure 12.1 The Middle Rhinelands: zone of convergence. Major routeways into the Middle Rhinelands: 1. The Hessian Corridor; 2. Main Valley from Nuremburg; 3. Foreland route from Augsburg and Munich; 4. Upper Rhine route from Basle; 5. Saverne Gap from Lorraine; 6. Route from the Saarland; 7. Rhine route from Rotterdam and the Ruhr. K = Kraichgau; B = Bergstrasse.

area on the eastern side of the Rift valley cultivates vines, tobacco and fruit, and almost opposite on the western side are the Worms–Neirstein–Oppenheim vineyards on the Haupterrasse, backed by the Pfalzer Bergland.

The Kraichgau between the Rhine and Neckar is limestone covered with loess and is one of the most intensively farmed areas in south Germany. Cereals are more in evidence because of the gently undulating or even nature of the land above level-bedded limestones. In addition there are fodder crops, sugar-beet, fruit, hops and the vine. The landscape is completely cleared and farming is very intensive, with large prosperous villages and a high rural density of population. It is upon this prosperous countryside that the initial wealth of the Middle Rhinelands is based.

Convergence of routes

The convergence of routes is a second advantage. Since medieval times the valley corridor has become an area of convergence as a link between the North Sea and Alpine passes, and between France and Austria. The position of the Rhine–Main valley, surrounded by the Hercynian mountain blocks yet with major gaps from north, south, east and west, has created the greatest junction in middle Europe. The traditional trade routes of the Middle Ages have been superseded by the railways and autobahnen. Fig. 12.1 illustrates the passageways, the Hessian Corridor, the Main valley from Wurzburg, routes from Munich via Stuttgart, the Upper Rhine route from Basle and the Alps, the Belfort gap from Lyons and the Rhône, the Saverne gap from Paris, Lorraine and the Saar, and the Rhine waterway route from the Ruhr and Benelux countries. The importance of the Rhine corridor has been increased immeasurably by the development of the EEC, as the whole effect of the convergence of routes has to be looked upon on a European scale rather than as hitherto on a German scale. The Rhine valley is now the central axis of the EEC rather than being a frontier zone, a change which has been stressed in chapter 10.

Flourishing cities

The concentration of human resources is the most significant reason for the importance of the Middle Rhinelands. Rather than depending upon mineral resources, it has developed around the numerous medieval cities and bishoprics, and has flourished because of the cultural and economic activity associated with a continual inflow of trade, expertise and new ideas. The earliest development of towns was during the Roman period, when the Rhine was the frontier of civilisation, and later the medieval bishoprics, such as Worms, Speyer and Mainz, developed on the west bank of the river. Heidelberg is the chief east-bank medieval and university town which has developed at the junction of plain and foothills. There is a line of small towns from Freiburg up to Frankfurt, in particular along the Bergstrasse north of Heidelberg. Baroque towns are usually associated with the numerous principalities and minor states which existed up to the nineteenth century. Karlsruhe is the best example of a planned city, founded in 1715 by the Margrave of Baden, and has a well-preserved radial pattern of roads leading to the Royal palace. Darmstadt was the seat of the Elector of Hesse, while Mannheim was originally founded as a capital city by the ruler of the Palatinate, and its rectilinear pattern of streets reflects the original planned town. The trade, culture and economic activity of this river region have been developed over a thousand years, and they have depended to a great extent upon the traffic carried by the river Rhine, although the effects of this have been seen to a much greater extent during the present century.

The Rhine

The importance of the river Rhine as a trading artery cannot be over-estimated. Long-distance commerce between Basle and the Netherlands has been considerable since the Middle Ages. It declined later largely because of the considerable sums of money required by the strategically positioned toll-enforcing castles along the line of the river, but there was a revival in trade during the nineteenth century. The river was first freed from tolls during the French Revolutionary wars, and in 1868 was made an international navigation channel. Navigation was vastly improved during the nineteenth century by deepening, bedrock blasting and straightening of the channel. The next step was to improve the tributaries as the converging arteries of the river. The Rhine–Marne canal was built from Paris via Strasbourg, the Main itself was improved up to Frankfurt, and with the advent of Ruhr coal and industrial products the trade south into the Middle Rhine region rapidly increased in volume. The growth of industry and cities has been directly affected by the Rhine acting as a factor of convergence. This is an industrial region far from the coast and the river has played a particularly relevant part in bringing the advantages of low-cost water transport. Since 1960 enormous strides have been made. The Main is now navigable for 1500-tonne barges as far as Bamberg, and the new Rhine–Main–Danube canal goes as far as Regensburg. The Neckar is navigable (1350 tonnes) as far as Stuttgart. On the west bank the advent of the EEC has done much to emphasise the centrality of the Middle Rhine and the Rhine–Marne canal is to be supplemented by a link southwards to the Rhône via Belfort. The Rhine itself is navigable up to Basle for 1500-tonne barges, but the major river ports are Mannheim and Ludwigshaven, which handle 9·1 and 9·2 million tonnes per annum respectively. Frankfurt-on-Main handles nearly 8 million tonnes per annum, Mainz 4 million and Karlsruhe 6·6 million. The other smaller ports, such as Weisbaden and Speyer, have a handling capacity of just over one million tonnes. Aschaffenburg, at the point where the Main emerges from the Odenwald–Spessart uplands, deals with one million tonnes annually. The effective limit of all-year-round navigation is Strasbourg; between here and Basle only a three-

Major inland ports	Traffic volume (million tonnes)
Mannheim	9·1
Ludwigshaven	9·2
Frankfurt	7·6
Karlsruhe	6·6
Mainz	4·0
Neckar Heilbronn	5·6
Stuttgart	3·1
Main Offenbach	1·2
Aschaffenburg	1·0
Wurzburg	1·6
For comparison	
Duisburg Ruhrort	20·1
Duisburg Works	20·3

Figure 12.2 Middle Rhine inland ports—traffic volume, 1969–1970.

month navigable period during the high-water period is possible. Thus, some comparison may be made from the following progression: The limit for ocean-going craft is Cologne; barges of 7000 tonnes reach Duisburg, 5000 tonnes Mannheim, and 2500 tonnes Strasbourg. If the total traffic by river to the ports in the Middle Rhine region (fig. 12.2) are added together, they are roughly comparable to the trade of Duisburg. Although such figures highlight the importance of Duisburg to the Ruhr, the Middle Rhine region nevertheless emerges as a very substantial focus of water transport.

There are three city regions of special note: Greater Frankfurt; Ludwigshaven–Mannheim; and Stuttgart. Each of these illustrates different characteristics and deserves separate consideration.

The Rhine–Main complex—Frankfurt-on-Main

The area under consideration lies in a triangular zone located by Frankfurt-on-Main, Weisbaden–Mainz and Darmstadt (fig. 12.3). Throughout history there

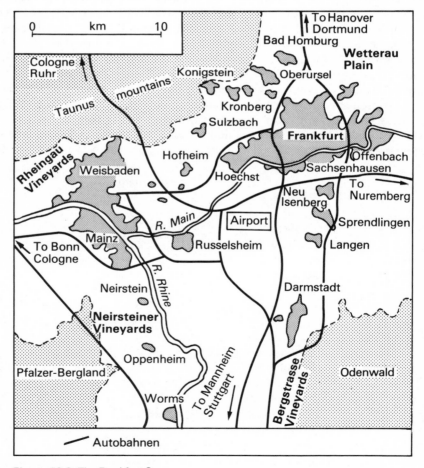

Figure 12.2 The Frankfurt Cross.

have been continuing factors which have created here a focal area of transport routes and economic activity. Mainz was a Roman town at the confluence of the Rhine and Main, but was overtaken by Frankfurt (Franks' ford) during the Frankish colonisation. Frankfurt developed faster due to its establishment as a 'Konigshof' and to its more central position on the plain for the routeways which developed during the medieval commercial period. From the tenth century onwards the Rhine–Main valley was centrally placed in the Holy Roman Empire and became a centre of exchange between the Netherlands and Italy. Frankfurt was also a 'Reichstad', a free city in the Empire with considerable industry and commerce. Mainz became an important archbishopric and was fortified, and both towns benefited from the great medieval fairs. Weisbaden lies on the north bank of the Rhine at the point where the Taunus mountains come close to the Rhine. It was a fortified town and seat of the Counts of Nassau, but became famous during the seventeenth century when its hot salt springs were popularised and it developed into a health resort and spa. The third apex of the triangle, Darmstadt, originated as the seat of the Elector of Hesse, and its planned origins are reflected in its rectilinear street plan.

The nineteenth and twentieth centuries have underlined the importance of the region in terms of access. Frankfurt is a focal point in the German railway network with the largest railway station in the Federal Republic, and it has developed industry on a large scale with engineering, electrical, chemical and consumer goods. The increase in Rhine traffic began during the nineteenth century, with the development of port facilities at Osthafen above the old city on the north bank of the Main. Today the West German Autobahn system has a major point of concentration in the Frankfurt Cross, and the outlines of the city region can be discerned in the triangular network of motorways which covers the whole area (fig. 12.3). In addition, the international airport is one of the busiest in Europe, with 11 million passengers per year, emphasising the city's role as a communications metropolis.

The most important present-day function of Frankfurt, however, is finance and commerce. It is the banking centre of West Germany, with the head offices of the German Federal Bank and no less than 148 German and 114 foreign banks. Its stock exchange is the largest on the continent, and 11 major trade fairs are held there each year.

Today the city has spread outwards and suburban growth has reached such proportions that to the north the formerly small spa towns which grew up at the foot of the Taunus massif—Bad Homburg, Konigstein, Bad Soden and Oberursel—have become dormitory suburbs. New townships such as Nordweststadt lie 4 miles to the north. Along the River Main, west towards Weisbaden, are the chemical complexes of Hoechst, the Opel car plant at Russelsheim and a number of other towns like Hofheim, so that the 17 kilometres between Frankfurt and Weisbaden are suburban in nature. To the south, Offenbach and Sachsenhausen now form part of the city. The residential town of Neu-Isenberg farther south is associated with the airport, motorway junction area and state forest, all of which occupy a broad belt of land just south of the Main. To the east along the Main is the jewellery-making town of Hanau. The zone thus described is closely linked in an economic sense, and rapid transport has ensured that all parts of the area are inside one hour's journey from Frankfurt. Commuting has developed on a large scale with complex movements of workers into the factories and offices of the city, which is ranked with Dusseldorf as a business centre. The whole city region has over one million people and is one of the most important growth areas in the EEC.

Mannheim—Ludwigshaven

There is an essential difference here in that these twin cities are, in their present form, the most important inland ports in the area, dependent upon the Rhine for imports of raw material and are major heavy chemical centres. They are perhaps more akin to the heavy industrial centres of the Ruhr than the other cities in the Middle Rhine. This is certainly true, but it must be remembered that there are very ancient settlements in the area. Landau and Neustadt are examples of settlement along the Weinstrasse, the foothill zone on the west bank corresponding to the Bergstrasse. Worms with its famous Leibfraumilch wines, Speyer and its textile industry, and Heidelberg, all lie within a dozen kilometres of the two main cities. Mannheim itself was founded, as a princely residence at the confluence of the Rhine and Neckar rivers, by the Elector of the Palatinate in 1720, and became a great theatrical and musical centre.

Mannheim's modern growth dates from the increase in Rhine traffic when it became the head of navigation for 5000-tonne barges in 1885. The advantages of river ports as input and processing points dependent upon low-cost waterborne raw materials are shown clearly here. Mannheim is a major distribution and transhipment point, a large railway junction, and one of the largest inland ports in Europe (fig. 12.2). Heavy chemicals, petrochemicals, dyestuffs, synthetic fibres and pharmaceuticals are most important, with grain milling also a feature. The twin inland port of Ludwigshaven developed on the west bank, the combined urban complex having over one million people.

Stuttgart and the Neckar Valley

Though not strictly part of the Middle Rhine region, the city of Stuttgart shows many of the features already mentioned. It is a city region based largely upon human resources and the convergence of routeways (fig. 12.4), and at least part of its prosperity derives from the river Rhine. Its site is an accident of history, and was chosen for a palace and fortified town from which the Dukes of Wurttemburg were to rule their principality from 960 AD onwards. The city was built in the ornate and baroque style and still has many elegant buildings. Its general situation must be one of the most beautiful in Europe for it stands in a saucer-shaped valley on the south side of the river Neckar with wooded and vine-clad hills around acting as natural boundaries. To the south-west lies the Black Forest, and to the south-east, the Swabian Jura.

This would appear to be hardly the situation for a major industrial city, but even in the Medieval period it became a focal point for Alpine routes from the south and routes from the Rhine via Heidelberg and the Neckar valley. In addition, the east–west routes from the Danube valley and Munich passed across the Neckar valley and Stuttgart. This pattern, like that of Frankfurt, was re-

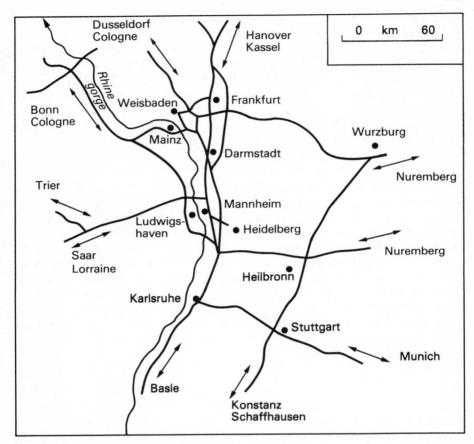

Figure 12.4 The autobahn network in the Middle Rhinelands.

emphasised during the nineteenth century when the railway system made the city into a focal point of South Germany, and also the Neckar became navigable for barges of up to 1350 tonnes.

The industrial wealth of the city was based traditionally on textiles from local wool, but the present-day industrial pattern is rather like that of Birmingham, with dependence upon the production and sale of high value goods, the assembly of semi-finished and component manufactures using skilled labour and the minimum of raw materials. Stuttgart is so far from raw materials that even with Rhine–Neckar transport, costs are relatively high, and skilled labour provides the one real resource. The city is favoured as it is the centre of a densely populated rural hinterland which provides a pool of labour, but in addition, there are many foreign immigrant workers. The machine-tool, automobile components, electrical engineering, and precision and optical instruments are supplemented by chemicals and pharmaceuticals, textiles, footwear and food-processing. Daimler–Benz, Mercedes, Audi and Porsche cars are built here, and Stuttgart is a major centre of the West German car industry. The IBM (Deutschland) computer company reflects the science-based and sophisticated nature of the manufacturing. Many industrial townships lie to the north-east of the city in the Neckar valley itself: Unterturkheim, Cannstadt, Feuerbach and Zuffenhausen. Some idea of the great significance of industry can be gauged from the fact that Stuttgart's industrial output is fourth among West German cities, and the Central Neckar valley produces one-third of the gross domestic product of the Land of Baden-Württemberg.

Stuttgart has considerable regional, industrial, political and cultural significance as the capital of Baden-Württemberg, and this is reflected in its position in the Central Place theory of Walter Christaller. Industrial satellite towns, based upon local supplies of labour, extend to a large distance up the valleys surrounding the city, north to Ludwigsburg and Heilbronn, south to Tubingen and Reutlingen, east to Goppingen and west to Pforzheim. Within this Stuttgart region there is a very dense movement of traffic, and the city is therefore a good example in southern Germany of a 'landeshaupstadt', or regional service centre. It is one of the large highly specialised cities of South Germany, with an extensive tributary rural area in the Neckar valley. Finally, it has a natural physical zone of influence, lying between the Odenwald to the north, the Black Forest to the south-west, and the Schwabian Jura to the south-east. Like Frankfurt, Stuttgart has developed and prospered because of its position at the hub of a communications network and a nodality in human terms. It is the perfect example of a city which has prospered because it was there.

Summary

There is thus a contrast between the Ruhr, with its heavy industry re-adjusting to twentieth century conditions, and these city regions of the Middle Rhinelands. Centres like Frankfurt and Stuttgart are much favoured because communications, markets and labour supply have replaced raw materials as the dominant factors in industrial location.

13

Belgium:
a study in regional contrasts

Local variations

Discussion of the European growth axis as a large-scale phenomenon tends to preclude examination of local variations within it. Belgium is such an example. Lying almost totally upon the central belt of economic activity, there are,

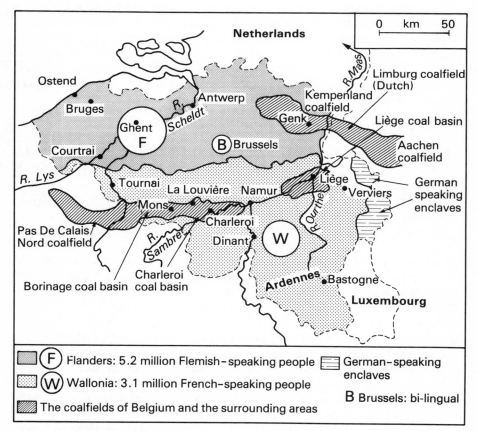

Figure 13.1 Belgium: Flanders and Wallonia.

nevertheless, four themes within the country (fig. 13.1) which present contrasting pictures:

1. The Brussels–Antwerp growth axis.
2. The coalfield belt from Mons to Liège which has similar problems to its western extension, the Nord coalfield of France and its eastern extension, the Dutch Limburg coalfield.
3. The highland area of the Ardennes which is an area of out-migration, although there is an interesting variation from the norm.
4. The language and cultural division between Fleming and Walloon complicates the economic differences within the country. Changes in recent years have swung the balance of ascendancy from Wallonia to Flanders, creating considerable intergroup tensions.

The Brussels–Antwerp growth axis

This is the most densely populated part of Belgium, and although the port and capital city are some 40 kilometres apart, they are beginning to show all the signs of conurban linkage as Antwerp rapidly becomes similar to Rotterdam as a major input point. Brussels has grown enormously since becoming the effective administrative centre of the EEC. They are connected by the Willebroek canal, railways and the E10 motorway, and show signs of creating a future conurbation on the southern side of the Rhine delta, of great similarity to the Randstad on the north. Indeed, if Ghent is included, a triangular growth area can be seen to be emerging (fig. 13.2).

Antwerp

The port and city is some 80 kilometres from the sea, but has a modern deepwater channel through the Wester Scheldt estuary, which is the southern arm of the Rhine delta, Rotterdam being on the northern arm. The Dutch delta plan will benefit Antwerp in terms of further waterway improvements and will also give better transport links with Rotterdam.

Antwerp is a very good example of a medieval city with the original sixteenth century walls and fortifications marked by boulevards which now enclose the present city-centre. The old city, about one square kilometre in extent, was the principal port and commercial zone in the whole Netherlands region up to the sixteenth century, but by the Treaty of Westphalia, 1648, the Scheldt was completely closed to sea-traffic, thus ensuring the rise and dominance of Amsterdam to the north. As a result, Antwerp and many other Belgian ports declined, and it was not until the early nineteenth century, with Belgian independence (1830) and increasing industrial traffic into the Rhine–Scheldt delta, that Antwerp began to prosper again. Growth was then rapid and in the late nineteenth century the earlier walls were replaced by the 'enceinte', an elaborate defensive complex with forts. This larger ring now constitutes the central area, and contains both the city centre, inner areas and railway termini.

Since the second World War, development has been particularly rapid. Residential districts on the east bank in particular fan out along the main roads

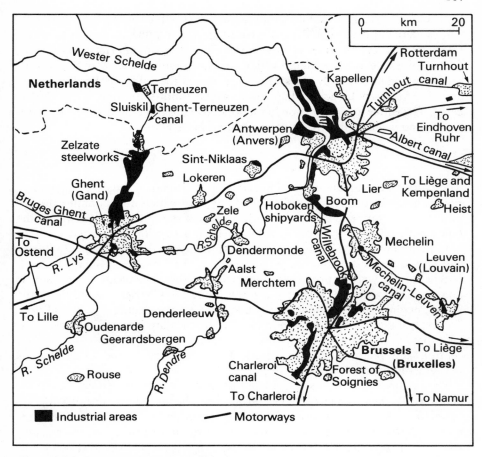

Figure 13.2 The Brussels–Antwerp–Ghent
growth area.

east towards Turnhout and south towards Lier and Mechelin. Road tunnels
under the Scheldt have led to modern developments on the west bank. Industrial
growth has followed the development of the port, and is well zoned to the north
and south of the city and along the river. To the north is a large and comprehensive dockland with oil refineries, car assembly plants, and the processing of
imported foodstuffs—mainly tropical products. To the south of the city along
the Scheldt, are shipyards at Hoboken and a variety of heavy industry continuing
along the river Rupel and Willebroek canal towards Boom. These include heavy
ceramics, cement, chemicals, textiles and brickmaking. There are also precision
industries, such as photographic processing, diamond-cutting, radio and electronics, which have grown with the increasing sophistication of the city's industrial capacity.

Antwerp has emerged as an international port, second in European rank after
Rotterdam, with a hinterland largely complementing that of Rotterdam. This
has a radius of up to 400 kilometres extending through Belgium into north-east

France and to Aachen, and including a small part of the southern Netherlands. The modern importance of the city is based upon communications. There are no raw materials here, but there is a low-cost input point with canal links to Brussels, Charleroi, Liège and the Meuse valley, and the Kempenland. Motorway links are becoming increasingly important, in particular the Antwerp–Brussels route, and the Antwerp–Liège–Aachen route, which follows the line of the Albert canal. The whole agglomeration has a population of three-quarters of a million people and is one of the fastest-growing areas in Belgium.

Brussels

The early extent of the city is indicated by the almost complete polygon of boulevards which marks the old walled city, and which now contains the administrative, commercial and shopping sectors of the central area as well as the oldest parts of the city, which are a considerable attraction for tourists.

Industrial locations are highly zoned, lying along the Senne valley to northeast and south-west. Along the Willebroek canal to the north, reaching towards Mechelin, are heavier processing industries, timber, chemicals, heavy metals and food processing, whilst to the south along the Charleroi canal lie textile works, engineering and cable works and the Clabecq steelworks. In addition, however, the city's light and specialised industries are immensely varied and widespread, including clothing, jewellery and cosmetics (Brussels is a fashion centre), and pharmaceuticals, electrical goods, printing and miscellaneous consumer industries.

The agglomeration now stretches for over 40 kilometres along the Senne valley and towards the south has extended around and beyond the Forest of Soignies, so this now forms an enclave of green belt surrounded by suburbs and commuter villages. Expansion eastwards to Louvain and south to Wavre has created an intensely suburbanised zone. Brussels is a bi-lingual island (French and Flemish) just within the Flemish-speaking part of Belgium. Near Wavre the city's expansion has crossed into the French-speaking (Walloon) section of the country with some resulting confusion. Brussels has gained its dynamism from being a regional and political centre at three levels. It has long been the provincial capital city for Brabant and the employment centre for much of East Flanders, and has exerted a strong centripetal attraction for the commuting workforce of these two provinces, although latterly there has been an increasing movement from all parts of Belgium, the attraction of the city contrasting with the declining areas of the south. Then there is its function as national capital of Belgium, now being rapidly superseded by its growth as administrative centre of the EEC. The Berlaymont Building, which houses the EEC Commission, is the nucleus around which so much activity occurs. The factor of Cumulative Causality is reflected in the frantic desire of industrial, professional and commercial companies to have their head offices at this most central point, and the building boom, often stimulated by British capital, is causing tremendous pressure upon land in the centre of Brussels as well as in the suburbs. Brussels has a population of over one million people and with Antwerp to the north constitutes a very definite growth axis.

Ghent

If Ghent is considered, with its 50 000 tonne capacity ship canal to Terneuzen on the Scheldt estuary, and other canal links to Bruges, plus the Ostend–Ghent–Brussels motorway, there is a third urban–industrial nucleus. Ghent has 250 000 people, and has cotton and synthetic fibres industries. Along the Terneuzen canal, in an industrial area reaching almost to the Scheldt estuary, are shipbuilding yards, chemicals, oil refineries, paper works and the integrated Zelzate Iron and Steel complex.

The Belgian coalfields with particular reference to the Borinage and Liège

Figure 13.1 illustrates the relationships of the smaller coalfields of north-west Europe, an almost continuous band stretching from Douai to Aachen. Whilst these are much less important than the major British coalfields and the German Ruhr, they were nevertheless a major factor in the nineteenth century as national sources of energy during the industrial revolution. The problems of each area today vary in intensity according to the extent of exploitation, the nature of the coal seams and the degree of exhaustion, but all have come under considerable pressure because of the alternative sources of energy and the need for low-cost fuel. Of all the Belgian coalfields the Kempenland, around Genk and Hasselt, has the longest term future (figs 13.1 and 13.3). It produces 7 million tonnes of

	1961		1969		1970		1972		1973	
	Production (million tonnes)	Number of pits	Production (million tonnes)	Number of pits	Production (million tonnes)	Number of pits	Production (million tonnes)	Number of pits	Production (million tonnes)	Number of pits
Kempenland	9·6	7	8·0	5	7·1	5	7·3	5	6·3	5
Sambre-Meuse	11·9	47	5·2	18	4·3	15	3·1	15	2·6	15

Figure 13.3 Coal production by the Kempenland and Sambre-Meuse coalfields.

coal per year from only five large collieries. In the Sambre–Meuse valley there are real problems. With early exploitation most of the best and thickest seams are exhausted and with difficult mining conditions and relatively small-scale old-fashion mines, these are high-cost coalfields. The Sambre–Meuse coalfield now produces only 2·6 million tonnes (1974) from fifteen remaining collieries. Its decline has been so rapid that there have been massive problems of readjustment in the industrial towns which stretch for nearly 140 km across Belgium. There are four regions: the Borinage, centred upon Mons (one productive colliery in 1972); the Central basin around La Louvière (one colliery); the Charleroi basin (seven collieries); the eastern or Liège coalfield (six collieries). The Borinage around Mons has been the worst affected of all.

Liège and the eastern basin

Although the basis of expansion here was coal, nevertheless the district of Liège has always been based upon more than extractive industry: this is the reason for its greater economic resilience during the last twenty years. The city was an ancient bishopric and city-state and as such has traditionally been a major service centre for the eastern regions of Belgium. It covers the Meuse valley in its confluence zone with the Ourthe, Amblève and Vesdre, the Verviers textile area and Ardennes foothills to the south, the fertile Hesbaye to the north-west and the Pays D'Herve to the east of the Meuse. By no means least, it is the cultural capital of Wallonia and third city of Belgium, with a conurbation population of 500 000.

In the Liège basin, the same problems of productivity arise as in the rest of the Sambre–Meuse valley, and there are only six productive collieries remaining. Perhaps the worst problem is the legacy of the 'old industrial landscape' with the masses of spoilheaps and tips on the Hesbaye plateaux above the deeply trenched Meuse valley, where most of the settlement lies. However, the industrial revolution has left Liège with much more than a mining economy. John Cockerill, an Englishman, was responsible for the first blast furnace in 1832, locomotive manufacture in 1835 and a large part of the metal-working tradition of the city. He was the first in Belgium to use the Bessemer process in 1863.[1] His company has now become Belgium's major steel-manufacturing concern and still maintains 60 per cent of its steel capability in Liège at Seraing. Cockerill has now merged with Ougree and Esperance at Jemeppe, to form a company of European standards in a major new industrial area up-river from the city, with a capacity of 7 million tonnes of steel per year. Other important metal manufacturing industries are zinc smelting, tubes, cables and small-arms, aircraft engineering and heavy electrical machinery; Liège has 75 000 workers in metals as compared to 18 000 in mining. 'Geographical Inertia' is characteristic of the whole area, with the heavy metal-based industries originally dependent upon local charcoal and water power from the streams running down to the incised Meuse valley, and subsequently, upon coking coal and local iron ores. Other important industries are chemicals, using the by-products of coking, glassware and tyre manufacture.

Verviers and Eupen, along the Vesdre valley to the east, form an associated industrial area manufacturing woollen textiles, originating on local wool from the Ardennes, and obtain water power from two reservoirs along the valley.

Despite the obsolescence of the industrial environment, unplanned piecemeal development crowded in the river valley, and unemployment of 6 per cent, nevertheless Liège has already adapted to a large extent to the decline in coal-mining and has bright prospects for the future. The reason is its location on the major link routes between the Rhine delta, West Germany, and France. Raw materials are now imported via the Albert Canal, particularly coking coal from the Kempenland and Ruhr, and iron-ore from Lorraine. The river Meuse provides a very useful means of transport for heavy goods. More important are the three motorway links (fig. 8.6). The motorways from Ostend, Brussels and

---

[1] *The Times*—Wednesday, May 31st 1972.

Antwerp lead to Aachen, Cologne and Frankfurt. The 'Autoroute De Wallonie' links Liège with the Sambre–Meuse towns and the Lille–Paris motorway. There are major development plans along two axes. Heavy industry is zoned along the river, with a nuclear power station at Tihange, up-river from Liège, an oil refinery on the Albert canal, and petrochemical works and fertiliser plants, which will join the predominantly steel and heavy engineering works of the river valley. Secondly, new light industry estates are zoned near the motorways on the plateaux on the outskirts of the city. Computers, electronic components, clothing, fibreglass and ceramics are produced at green field sites such as Hauts Sarts, north-east of Liège.

Charleroi

With its surrounding satellite towns, this is an agglomeration of some 400 000 people and its industrial structure has much in common with Liège. Although coal production has dropped markedly, there is a well established iron and steel industry, with chemical works and, more recently, plastics. This was also the centre of the Belgian glass industry, based upon local sands, which survives at Roux and Auvelais, although now suffering great competition from the Kempenland glass industry. Like Liège, Charleroi has a sufficiently broad and diversified manufacturing base to avoid the worst effects of the decline of coal.

Mons and the Borinage: La Louvière and the Central Basin

Although in strict terms the Borinage stretches only from the Belgian border to the city of Mons, provincial capital of Hainault, the area to the east including La Louvière is characterised by the same problems. These areas have experienced considerable economic decline and harsh adjustments have been necessary because of their over-dependence upon a single activity, coal-mining. Here there was little industrial development of any sort, and in 1953 coal-mining accounted for 56 per cent of employment. The seams of coal were almost exhausted, mines were very deep (over 1 kilometre) and in one particular colliery, Rieu De Coeur, galleries were specially refrigerated over one and a half kilometres below ground. As a small-scape producer (the Borinage produced 5·9 million tonnes in 1927, the peak year) it was a very high-cost coalfield. Not only was there heavy

	Miners	Number of Pits
1948–50	30000	28
1956	24000	9
1965	8000	5
1974	1500	1

The one remaining colliery in 1974 produces ½ million tonnes of anthracite yearly.

Figure 13.4 Changes in the Borinage coalfield.

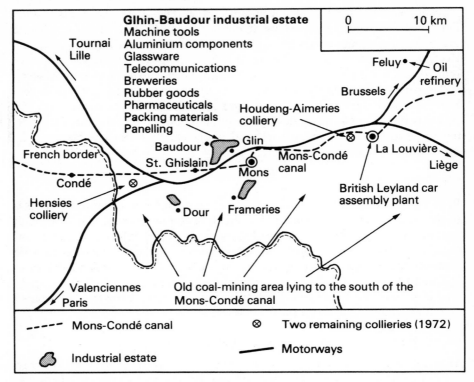

Figure 13.5 The Belgian Borinage: old and
new industry.

competition from oil and natural gas, but the increased cross-frontier competi-
tion and tariff-free conditions which arrived with the EEC meant that by 1958
Ruhr coal, even after being transported to Charleroi, was considerably cheaper.
With the reduction in Atlantic freight rates, American coal could be sold at
Charleroi for 841 B.f per tonne, whilst Borinage coal cost 971 B.f per tonne.
Productivity was lower, production was small-scale and inefficient from many
small pits, and Borinage coal could not be made competitive. The Conseil
National Des Charbonnages worked out a reorganisation and contraction plan
(fig. 13.4). Over the past 20 years the decline in coal-mining has been extremely
dramatic (fig. 13.5): with 28000 miners losing their jobs, unemployment stood
at 11 per cent in 1959, the worst year. The ECSC aided the region in two ways.
Loans were given, often in association with the Belgian Government, to lay out
new industrial estates and encourage investment in new plant. Since 1960 8000
jobs have been created in 48 new factories. The ECSC also shared with the
Belgian authorities the cost of retraining workers for new skilled jobs.

The changes in the region are threefold:

(a) Firstly, the Borinage became a region of out-migration, mainly to Antwerp
and Brussels and in 1949 and 1950 the employment force actually fell by 15
per cent from 67973 to 57400. Worse was to come, for in the period up to 1962

the employment force fell again from 57 400 to 38 344, a further decline of 33 per cent. This rate of decline is very unusual in advanced industrial countries.

(b) Secondly, however, considerable industrial diversification schemes began to take effect (fig. 13.5). There are three large industrial estates with consumer and light industries—pharmaceuticals, and electronic and telecommunications factories. Since 1960 48 factories with 8000 new jobs have been created. There is a British Leyland assembly plant at La Louvière and an oil refinery to the north. With increased employment in services, the industrial structure now approaches the Western European norm.

(c) Finally, with the introduction of fast electrified rail services between Mons and other parts of Belgium, many of the area's inhabitants now commute to work in Charleroi, Liège and Brussels. Over 3000 alone go daily to Valenciennes and other French towns.

The Borinage has adapted well, although the hardship was considerable during the 1960s. From being a mono-functional coal-mining area, it now has a solid industrial base. Many of the environmental problems still remain, as the landscape of the industrial revolution cannot be obliterated overnight. Its position and population are its main future resources: 5 million people, a large consumer market, live within 50 kilometres of the provincial capital, Mons. The area lies at the junction of two motorways—Brussels–Paris and the Wallonia motorway (Liège–Mons–Paris) (fig. 13.5). The raw materials may have vanished, but the Borinage lies square along a major growth axis.

The Ardennes massif

The Ardennes is a heavily forested upland (fig. 13.6), lying at about 350 metres OD but reaching 600 metres in the Haut Fagnes near the West German border. With rainfall reaching a maximum of 55 inches, it is a zone of marginal agriculture and experiences persistent out-migration. Most settlements are small and confined to the valleys of the Semois, Ourthe, Ambleve and Vesdre, tributaries of the Meuse. Farms are small and mainly in pasture, with some cereals (oats, rye or barley), and potatoes and fodder crops. In the sheltered areas such as the Semois valley, tobacco is grown and dried on local farms. Farms are abandoned yearly and the whole area is the least densely populated in Belgium with a population of under 200 000.

Forestry is an important occupation and timber is a major resource of the Ardennes, in areas such as Beauraing and Gedinne south of Dinant. There are isolated areas of economic activity such as limestone quarrying near Marche. The one major north–south routeway through the Ardennes is followed by the railway and E40 road which goes from Namur through Marche, Bastogne and Arlon to Luxembourg.

The drift of population is a continuing feature of the life of the area, but it is alleviated to a certain degree by two factors. One is the outstanding scenic beauty of the Ardennes which has led to a considerable tourist industry, and the second, inter-related, is the proximity of the region to the densely populated lowlands of Belgium, Holland, and West Germany. Its wealth potential increasingly lies in its landscape. With the attractions of woods and forests,

Figure 13.6 The Belgian Ardennes.

numerous chateaux, and the higher massifs and beautiful valleys like the Semois and Viroin, many towns have developed a tourist function. Dinant, La Roche, Bouillon, Houffalize and Spa (the original mineral springs have given their name to all towns of this type) all have a tourist function, and are supplemented by others with a market role such as Bastogne, Marche-en-Famenne and St. Vith.

Depopulation is also being partially reversed by the 'weekend cottage'. The second house is a popular idea in Europe, and the Ardennes are ringed with the dense urban populations of the Meuse valley, Brussels, northern France and Holland. Barvaux in the Ourthe valley particularly, and the Dinant and Marche areas of the Condroz have large areas of this sub-rural development which, if allowed to spread unchecked, will rapidly spoil the landscape it is designed to enjoy. In addition, the whole northern section of the Ardennes has fallen within commuting range of Liège and even Brussels, and towns such as Spa, Theux,

Aywaille and Remouchamps, in the Amblève and Lower Ourthe valleys, are becoming dormitories.

It is unfortunate that this development is taking place on the fringes of the Ardennes and is not really providing the stable natural rural focus for the centre of the forested plateau. There is a proposal for an entirely new town of 40 000 to be built between Marche and Libramont designed to use local resources such as timber for furniture and attract footloose industries for the under-used labour force. It would also act as a service centre with a full range of urban amenities. Its purpose, unlike most new towns, would be to check the depopulation of the region.

The regional and cultural dichotomy of Belgium: Flanders and Wallonia

Considerable economic differences between northern Belgium (the Brussels–Antwerp–Ghent region) and southern areas like the coalfields of the Meuse valley and the Ardennes uplands have been outlined above. Belgium is a bilingual and bi-cultural state, and the boundaries between the Flemings and Walloons approximately correspond to the economic lines of demarcation between growth areas in the north and areas of decline in the south (fig. 13.1). The recent history of the two groups adds another dimension to the dichotomy. Since Belgium has been a national entity (1830), the French speaking southern part, covering the provinces of Luxembourg, Liège, Namur, Hainault and south Brabant, has been known as Wallonia, and traditionally has been the dominant section of the population. French language and culture was dominant during the nineteenth century and Belgian administration, culture and teaching was in French. The French-speaking Walloons were an élite both culturally and in terms of prosperity, for this was the period of coal-based industrial growth of the Sambre–Meuse valley. Liège in particular was the nerve-centre of Walloon economic power.

The Flemish provinces lie to the north, covering West and East Flanders, Antwerp, Limbourg and North Brabant. During the nineteenth century the Flemings were really second-class citizens. They lived in an agricultural area with a stagnant peasant economy. Their language was a dialect of Dutch, and spoken (even if one adds Holland itself) by only about 15 million people in the world. Thus it was at a disadvantage in relation to French as a major language. From 1846 the 'Flemish Movement' set out to achieve parity for their language in their own country, and this, although a slow process, was achieved by the 1960s, when for all legal, educational and administrative purposes, Flemish and French became equal in national status. Belgium was divided in two parts by a language line, with Flemish spoken north of it and French to the south. Brussels is a bi-lingual island just north of the dividing line.

During the last twenty years a series of factors have added to this complete reversal of ascendancy of the two groups. Between 1947 and 1965 the population of Flanders rose by 618 000 (birth-rate 18·5 per thousand), whilst that of Wallonia increased by only 156 000 (birth-rate 13·5 per thousand). This has reinforced the Flemish majority position; they are now about 60 per cent of the total population, and the Walloons are very conscious of their diminishing relative importance within the state. Secondly, the economic shift of balance from Wallonia to Flanders which has been described in this chapter has reinforced the picture of 'two nations'. The sluggish growth, unemployment, dying coal industry, obsolescent plant, the 'Black Country' and 'satanic mills' image has depicted much of Wallonia. By contrast, Flanders now has a larger share of the country's wealth. The integrated steel mill at Zelzate, the development of Antwerp as port and large-scale industrial area, and the linking of Ghent to the sea are examples of the dynamism of port locations, and the Rhine delta in particular. The newer productive coalfield of the Kempenland lies in the provinces of Antwerp and Limbourg. The position of Brussels in the EEC structure is an additional factor in the growth of the Brussels–Antwerp–Ghent area. Some 81 per cent of American investment has gone into Flanders and the Greater Brussels area, only 19 per cent into Wallonia.

This picture of regional contrasts within Belgium attempts to show that not all regions within the European growth axis share in the increasing prosperity. Southern Belgium is one such region, but its process of adjustment is made much easier by its proximity to the European core.

14

Randstad Holland: the Ring City

The concentration of population

One of the most wealthy, urbanised and fastest growing regions within the EEC is the western part of the Netherlands, covering the provinces of North and South Holland and Utrecht. The concentration of population in these three provinces is shown by comparing the total population of the Netherlands, 13 million people in 1973, with the three provinces population of 6 million. Nearly half the country's total population is concentrated into 21 per cent of the country's area.

Specifically, the ring city is formed by two major urban regions, the cities of Amsterdam, Utrecht and Haarlem in the northern arc, and Rotterdam and The Hague in the south (fig. 14.1). Together with a number of smaller units interposed between, such as the famous old cities of Leiden and Delft, the new industrial centres of Zaandam and Ijmuiden, seaside resorts such as Scheveningen, Katwijk and Zandvoort, and other towns, the whole begins to take on the shape of a broken ring, or horseshoe.

The reasons for this major concentration of population lie mainly in the central position of these cities in relation to north-west Europe. The delta region of the Rhine and Maas, opening out to the North Sea, has traditionally been important for trade, commercial and industrial activity since the Medieval period and the days when Amsterdam was one of the foremost ports of the Hanseatic League. This was underlined during the colonial period when Dutch trade and wealth were second only to that of the British, and Amsterdam became the world centre of the diamond trade, quite apart from its food processing which originated from colonial raw materials. Even more relevant in the modern context is its position since the beginnings of economic integration in Europe. The delta now stands as the outlet for the Rhine basin, which is the major industrial, transport, and population axis of the community. The Randstad cities are literally at the centre of European integration (figs 10.1, 10.2).

This concentration of population, even in an extremely prosperous city region, causes problems and creates the need for very careful planning. The main geographical characteristics are convenient themes by which to look at the problems of planning this dynamic region.

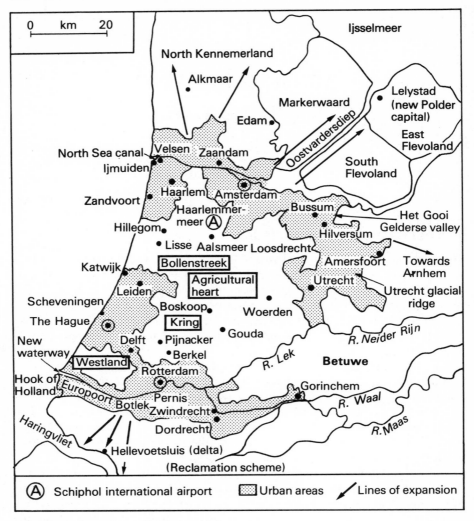

Figure 14.1 Randstad Holland: cities, greenheart and development plans (A = Schiphol International Airport)

1. The unusual pattern of urbanisation which has emerged in this polycentric city region.
2. The industrial scene and the concentration of resources at the Rhine mouth with the attendant dangers of pollution.
3. The needs of agriculture in this very fertile part of the Netherlands which produces 40 per cent of the country's total food.

These three characteristics will be examined in turn and placed in the context of two problems: severe competition for land and congestion.

The urban structure of the Randstad

The Randstad must be considered as a horseshoe of distinctive cities which are in danger of coalescing except perhaps on the south-east, where an open section

City	Population total of agglomeration (1000s)	Functions of principal city
Amsterdam	1036	Financial and commercial centre. The main service and retail centre entirely metropolitan in character.
Rotterdam	1066	Industrial, transhipment, storage terminals, import and export.
The Hague, including Delft	711	Administrative capital. Centre of Government and international agencies.
Utrecht	459	Historic university town, ecclesiastical centre, now provincial capital and regional service centre and communications centre.
Haarlem	239	Residential and regional centre. Engineering industry.
Leyden	165	Historic university town and regional centre for mid-western Randstad.
Dordrecht	172	Industrial town and a satellite for Rotterdam.
Hilversum	115	Residential and commuter town for Amsterdam.
Ijmuiden, including Velsen and Beverwijk	138	Outlet for North Sea canal with fishing port and steel works.
Zaandam	131	Industrial outlier to Amsterdam at the inner end of the North Sea canal.
Total large municipalities	4232	
Randstad (Total)	4353	(includes the 70 municipalities)
Total for North and South Holland and Utrecht	6146	
Total population for the Netherlands	13439	

Figure 14.2 The Randstad hierarchy: a summary (1973).

exists between Dordrecht and Utrecht. Its unique character derives from its 'rim' structure around the green centre, but also from its functional and hierarchical development. Unlike other European cities such as Paris or London, the multitude of functions normally carried out within the 'central business district' of a capital city is distributed here between several cities. There is a hierarchy of centres of vastly different sizes, some seventy municipalities in all (fig. 14.2), which can be conveniently grouped as follows:

Amsterdam

This historic city is the cultural, financial and commercial capital of the Netherlands and is the most highly metropolitan in character of all the Randstad cities with a population of 820000 (1973). The city is distinctive for its banking, finance and commerce, and luxury shopping facilities. As a tourist centre it has museums, art galleries and luxury hotels. The industries within the city are those of printing, fashion clothing and diamond-cutting. The distinctive city centre, with its semi-circular structure bounded by quiet tree-lined canals, is a major tourist attraction.

The expansion of the city has created several sub-zones on the periphery. To the south is the international airport at Schiphol and in an arc on the southern side of the city are the main industrial areas of Amstelveen and Sloetermeer, whilst its commuter zones lie farther east around Bussum and Hilversum, in the undulating wooded hills of the Het Gooi.

Herengracht, the historic centre of Amsterdam, with the old seventeenth century houses originally built for wealthy merchants.

Amsterdam North-West, one of the housing developments on the edge of the vastly expanded modern city.

On the north side of Amsterdam is the important industrial region around the North Sea canal. The canal was opened in 1876 to provide better communications from Amsterdam to the sea, but there are two industrial complexes associated with it, Ijmuiden–Velsen and Zaandam. At Velsen is the integrated Iron and Steelworks of Hoogovens, with blast furnaces, rolling mills and tin-plating mills. The complex is based upon the cheap importation of raw materials, coke from the USA, and ore from Sweden, Spain and North Africa. Nearer Amsterdam is Zaandam, where the North Sea canal reaches the city. Once important for shipping, it is now concerned mainly with processing of imported raw materials and foodstuffs of colonial origin and also local dairy and vegetable products.

Haarlem

An historic city which was associated with the Dutch war of independence against Spain in the sixteenth century, Haarlem is now mainly a residential and commuter area for Amsterdam and is the regional centre for South Kennemerland.

Utrecht

This is the one city of the Randstad which is a considerable distance from the sea, and has become an inland communications centre. It is a railway focus at the

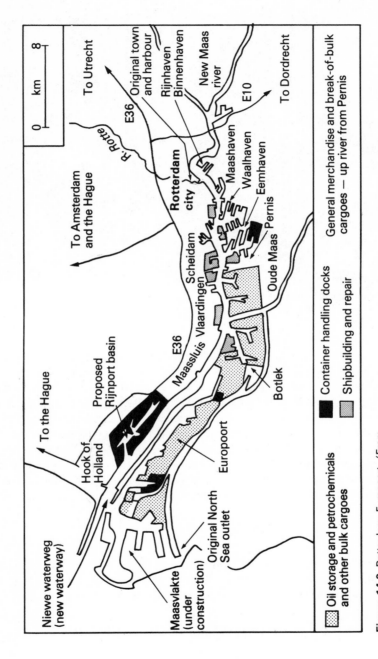

Figure 14.3 Rotterdam: Europoort. (From M. Vanderberg)

eastern end of the conurbation and has now become a motorway junction. It is, however, one of the oldest cities of Holland and also an ecclesiastical and university town and a provincial capital. It has room to expand to the east, with suburban development taking place on a low ridge of glacial origin, whilst beyond is Amersfoort and the Gelderse valley.

The Hague agglomeration

The two historic cities of Delft, famous for pottery, and Leyden, with its university, are very nearly joined by ribbon development to The Hague. This is a continuing pattern with Zoetermeer to the east and Wassenaar and Scheveningen to the north as residential outliers for the rapidly expanding Hague agglomeration. The Hague itself is the seat of government of the Netherlands and has most of the official administrative and public bodies, and many international agencies such as the International Court of Justice. Otherwise it is very much an attractive residential city, and has been called the largest village in Europe.

Rotterdam—Dordrecht

Of all the centres so far described, Rotterdam has experienced the most tremendous growth in size and international importance. As the raw materials input point and transhipment centre, it is a most dynamic industrial growth area, and the largest port in Europe. It will be dealt with in detail in the next section, but in the Randstad as a whole it is one of a number of cities which individually carry out very specialised and rather separate functions.

Rotterdam: Europe's leading port

Although the picture already given indicates the considerable number of industries associated with the other municipalities of the Randstad, there are two marked concentrations. One, already mentioned, is the belt along the North Sea canal from Ijmuiden and the Velsen Steelworks to Zaandam. By far the more important is the 30 kilometre stretch of water from the Hook of Holland to the city of Rotterdam itself along the New Waterway and thence along the distributaries of the Maas and Waal as far as Dordrecht (fig. 14.3). In 1962 Rotterdam moved ahead of New York in terms of cargo tonnage handled and in the decade since has become completely pre-eminent. Figure 14.4 illustrates the comparisons with other leading European ports. As late as the second World War it was a port of only moderate importance and in 1945 was in ruins as a result of bombing. It has a long history but its very sudden growth to prominence can be seen in three stages, in each case initiated by a major change in transport factors.

The early port, a dam on the River Rotta, itself a right-bank tributary of the tidal Maas, was a medieval fishing village with a very long and tortuous channel to the sea. Growth was slow and unspectacular, although by the end of the eighteenth century Rotterdam had grown to 50000, the second largest city of Holland. It was a prosperous pre-industrial port with the 'Oudehaven' tucked easily into the centre of the city, reflecting its small scale.

A

Port	Cargo tonnage (million tonnes)
Rotterdam	233
Marseilles	77
Antwerp	72
Le Havre	62
London	58
Genoa	57
Hamburg	47
Amsterdam	35

B

Year	Cargo tonnage (million tonnes)
1938	42
1946	8
1955	66
1966	130
1973	233

C

Commodity	Per cent trade (by volume)	
Oil	58	
Mineral ores	12	
Coal	4	bulk cargoes 84
Cereals	4	
Other bulk cargoes	6	
General cargo (break of bulk)	16	

Figure 14.4 Rotterdam: comparative trade figures. (A) comparative cargo tonnages, 1973; (B) growth of Rotterdam trade; (C) principal trading commodities, 1973.

The ultimate dominance of Rotterdam over both Amsterdam and Antwerp was ensured by the cutting of the New Waterway (Nieuwe Waterweg). This is wide, lock-free and cuts straight through the sandspit of the Hook of Holland to a point on the coastline where deeper water allows larger ships to enter the harbour. It became operational in 1872 and gave a new lease of life to the port at a critical time. The arrival of the steamship needing deeper channels coincided with the development of the vast hinterland of the port and the growing lines of waterway communication along the Rhine axis. At the same time as the Rhine and its tributaries became Europe's commercial artery, navigable as far as Switzerland, there was also rapid development of the Ruhr coalfield, Lorraine, the Saar, Limburg and the Sambre–Meuse valley. Rotterdam became the input and output point for industrial Europe, and to this major locational advantage was added the technical superiority of a modern deep-water channel. The docks of this period lie on the south bank opposite the old medieval harbour Rijn-haven, Binnenhaven, Spoorweghaven (Railway harbour), Waalhaven and

Rotterdam. The city centre and Euromast,
with the smaller inner city docks in the
background.

Maashaven. These are small by modern standards, and date from the nineteenth
century. They indicate the approximate extent of the port before 1945.

The really significant change came after 1946 when new opportunities presented themselves. Rotterdam's access to the Ruhr, and its position as outlet
for the Rhinelands, the most populous part of Europe, matched its adjacency to
the English Channel, the busiest stretch of water in the world. Even more important was the development of the EEC and its geographical axis along the
Rhinelands. The whole area of the Rhine delta assumed a new economic importance, and Rotterdam was one of the most central points on this axis. However, the single most significant change was the shipping revolution which developed from the great increase in size of ships during the 1960s and the increasing specialisation of cargo transport, with a distinction being made between bulk cargoes and break-bulk or transhipment cargoes.

The rapid decline of coal during the post-war period and its replacement
primarily by oil was the great opportunity for ports like Rotterdam to become
the reception, storage, and refining points for West European oil. Imports of
crude oil rocketed from 2·3 million tonnes in 1938 to 61 million tonnes in 1967,
indicating that Rotterdam's growth has been due in large part to her oil imports. The pipeline system to the Rhinelands (fig. 2.7) is an important supplement to the port facility which has helped to create a tremendous number of
processing industries, such as oil refineries, petrochemical works, chemical

Container dockyard at Pernis—Eemhaven.

plants and plastics fabricators. The port was well placed for the further boost to the bulk trade when the Suez Canal closed in 1967 and the era of the super-tanker began. Rotterdam's deep-dredged channels enabled it to become pre-eminent as a terminal port for raw materials, including crude oil, mineral ores, scrap-iron, timber and fertilisers, grain and coal, often requiring further processing. To accommodate the huge bulk-carriers, the deeper water areas from Pernis downstream have been developed since the 1950s, and by 1966 bulk carriers of over 200 000 tonnes d.w.t. could enter the port. The Pernis area is a complex of storage facilities, oil refineries and petrochemical works, followed by Botlek (1300 hectares) developed and in use since 1955 (fig. 14.3) and Europoort (4000 hectares) which has come into use during the 1960s with a capacity for 300 000-tonne oil tankers and 125 000-tonne grain carriers. The final phase is the reclamation of 2500 hectares of land at Maasvlakte, an ambitious scheme to provide even more land for industry and port facility. The post-war development of bulk shipping can be seen as a succession of newer, larger dock basins and industrial complexes, each one downriver from the original Rotterdam city docks and nearer to the sea, with over 30 kilometres of waterfront in all.

However, the upper harbour is just as important and adds the other element—the break of bulk, transhipment, or 'gateway' function (fig. 14.3). The development of containerised cargo-handling has revolutionised the loading and un-loading of the higher-value processed or manufactured goods which are pack-aged in smaller units. The 'gateway' port function is necessary principally to handle, transfer, and despatch to a variety of destinations. Traditionally this was a cumbersome inefficient operation, consuming time and labour. With the container, the high-value component or complete product is moved through the port as quickly as possible by efficient cargo-handling equipment. Larger ships have meant greater economies provided that 'turn-round time' has been cut. For example, on the Atlantic run 'dead time' in port has been cut from 70 to 20 per cent, with consequent saving on costs. On the dockside large areas of flat stacking space are needed for stacking and marshalling and also an efficient system of inland transportation. During the 1960s Rotterdam re-equipped itself for containerisation, so that it has become the foremost container port in Europe and even takes goods destined for the UK, formerly handled by London. It is the upper harbour which has largely been adapted. This is the small group of basins on the south bank of Rotterdam city, Rijnhaven, Binnenhaven, Spoorweghaven and Maashaven (fig. 14.3) where the clutter of merchandise is being replaced by huge cranes with 50 tonnes capacity and standardised boxes, and large storage zones. Waalhaven and Eemhaven are larger docks, the first one modernised, and the second built during the 1960s purely for container traffic. An extension downstream on the north bank is Rijnpoort. All the docks above Pernis are concerned with break-bulk cargoes. The successful operation of the 'gateway' function requires excellent communications to all parts of Europe, the river Rhine and its tributary systems of canals and navigable rivers being the main single advantage to Rotterdam in this context. In addition, however, the system of railways and Euroroutes allows fast transit to all parts of the EEC. The upper harbours are not only cargo-handling. Waalhaven and Schiedam are also the major shipbuilding sections of the port and its main Liner terminals. There are also many other industries: glass-making, car assembly, brewing and distilling, and food processing (chocolate and margarine) in the dock areas.

Without any doubt, Rotterdam's growth and prosperity is based firmly upon its bulk handling facilities and in particular, oil. One of the main problems is pollution. Water pollution is a menace and the Rhine is heavily polluted here by sewage, industrial and power station effluents from up-river and from West Germany (60 000 tonnes of chemicals per day are estimated). A more serious matter is air pollution at Botlek, Pernis and Europoort, where the oil refineries, chemical and petrochemical plants foul the air with hydrocarbons and sulphur dioxide. It is the downstream residential areas which suffer most—Vlaardingen, Maasluis, Rozenburg and the Hook of Holland. Finally, there are constant worries about housing and recreation, which relates to the ever-present problem in the whole Randstad: competition for land. In Rotterdam, industrial considerations have often completely outweighed any others. The symptom of this is the outward movement of Dutch people from the port and industrial area of the Rhinemouth since 1960. Although there is still an inflow of foreign migrant workers, the Dutch themselves are moving out.

In conclusion, it is relevant to consider the future of Rotterdam. Will the reduction in oil imports by the countries of the EEC have a lasting effect on the port and its further expansion? Will improvements in pipelines allow Marseilles and Genoa to reduce Rotterdam's oil hinterland? Rotterdam's bulk oil imports may not be a means of continual growth, as was assumed during the 1960s.

Europoort, Rotterdam, with the construction of dockside storage and industrial areas in progress.

The port and city will probably remain the major throughput point of the EEC because of its superb junction position between the North Sea and the Rhineland axis. Principal future growth will probably be based upon its break-bulk container cargo trade.

The Agricultural Heart

Western Holland is also a key agricultural area and formed the original core of the extensive schemes of land reclamation which began in the thirteenth century. The culmination of Dutch enterprise in this direction came in 1852 with the draining of the Haarlemmermeer of 18000 hectares. It is the future of the open centre of the Randstad (the greenheart), traditionally one of the most productive farming areas, which causes considerable concern. As the population grows, the cities within the system would no doubt ultimately coalesce, the valuable farmland now in the open centre would be developed, and the Netherlands would lose its most productive farmland. This is the essence of the continuing two-way planning problem; how to ensure continued urban development without giving up the agricultural land inside the Ring city.

Most of the Open Heart (fig. 14.1) is polder land below sea level. The principal characteristics of these polders are rich silts and clays, a reclaimed landscape of rectangular fields, and an intensive and varied agriculture. There are many lakes

Boskoop, in the greenheart of the Randstad, a horticultural region specialising in shrub cultivation, and exemplifying the intensive use of land.

which are commonly used for recreation, sailing and fishing, and have associated with them areas for picnics and camping, etc. Water drainage is essential through a system of ditches and dykes and the former importance of windmills is shown by their continued existence alongside the more modern pumps.

The intensive horticulture with which the Dutch have traditionally been concerned stems from the need to produce high value foods on a relatively restricted land area, and also from the demand which built up during the nineteenth century for large quantities of food by both the Randstad population, and the nearby industrial countries of Belgium, the United Kingdom and Germany. About 40 per cent of the Netherlands total crop of market garden products is grown here. There are considerable areas of specialisation, perhaps the best known of which is the small area between Leiden and Haarlem, the Bollenstreek (Lisse, Hillegem and Keukenhof), famous for flowers and bulb production. Aalsmeer near Schiphol airport is concerned with cut flowers (roses and indoor plants) and Boskoop to the south of Leiden is a specialist area of ornamental conifers and shrubs. Two major zones of vegetables occur: Westland and the northern and western fringes of Rotterdam. Westland lies between the triangle of the cities of The Hague, Rotterdam and The Hook, and contains the major concentration of glasshouses (1400 hectares in all). The predominance of glasshouses gives the area an urbanised appearance, but it grows a large proportion of Holland's tomatoes, cucumber, lettuce, leeks, carrots and spinach, etc. The Kring district north-west of Rotterdam (Berkel and Pijnacker) specialises in salad crops. In addition to vegetables, there are extensive areas under fruit, both soft and orchard, largely around Utrecht and to the south of the Neider Rijn. Melons and grapes are cultivated under glass.

Whilst horticulture has been traditionally the most significant form of farming, arable production, dairy farming and recreational use also make major demands upon the limited space of the Randstad. High yields are characteristic, potatoes, sugar beet and wheat being the principal crops. Much arable production is geared to the supply of food-grains for cattle, particularly the Haarlemmermeer near Amsterdam. This area has light sea-clay which is ideal for retention of nutrients, there is less wind-erosion, and with effective drainage it can be ploughed easily and the water table can be controlled. Dairy farming is of course most important throughout most of the inner Randstad. The southern region of the Betuwe between the Lek and Waal, the Gouda cheese region, and the Loosdrecht between Amsterdam and Utrecht are primarily grassland areas containing one-fifth of Holland's total cattle, and large numbers of pigs and poultry.

Competition for land

It must not be supposed that the Randstad open heart will inevitably remain agricultural, as there are tremendous pressures upon land. Recreation is one of these. The relatively short dune coastline extending through Scheveningen to Zandvoort has a great depth, often extending inland for five kilometres, but is in great demand from the Randstad cities for recreational purposes, and also from German cities in the Rhinelands, another result of the mobility engendered by the motor car. There is also the Utrecht ridge of glacial sands, stretching from Hilversum between Utrecht and Amersfoort. These low hills are wooded heathlands and provide parkland and scenic amenity areas. Some measure of land pressure can be gauged, however, from the fact that residential development from the city of Utrecht has spread on to the open land on the eastern side of the ridge.

Most critical of the pressures is the demand for land for housing and industry. The heavy industry and port installations of Rotterdam have been expanding at such a rate that, if continued, it is estimated that 6000 hectares of extra land will be needed by the year 2000. Although much of this will be built on reclaimed land at the mouth of the Niewe Waterweg to form Maasvlakte, this nevertheless illustrates the heavy demand for land. The expected growth of population up to 1980 may consume anything up to 40000 hectares of agricultural land, with over half a million extra dwellings. The ancient cities and their municipal areas are rigidly defined and are experiencing outwards population movement, and it is the outer suburban areas and the agricultural heart which are experiencing the growth pressures. Population projections estimate a rise from 5·5 million in 1961 to 6·6 million in 1981. The Randstad cities are already crowded and short of land for all purposes.

Regional planning

Some form of regional planning was a necessity from 1945 onwards. Dispersion of the population from the Randstad into the peripheral regions of east and north Holland, into towns such as Groningen, Nijmegen, Breda, Enschede and Tilburg, is encouraged, and these are growth poles with expansion plans of up to 200000 people. The historic cities are preserved as nucleii with buffer zones between them, and the agricultural heart in the centre is preserved absolutely. The only growth allowed in this central area is limited within existing historic towns such as Gouda or Woerden. The present morphology of the Randstad therefore is dominated by the horseshoe shape of urbanisation with an effective 'green belt' inside. The 1948 report *The Development of the Western Netherlands* contained the quite revolutionary proposal that in order to maintain the 'Greenheart' future growth be channelled outwards along the main transport routes in radial belts, themselves separated by wedges of open land. Four main avenues of development are expected (fig. 14.1). To the north of Ijmuiden and Haarlem is the peninsula of North Kennemerland, where growth could continue as far as Alkmaar, the old cheese-marketing town. On the east, the Utrecht ridge must be preserved as open land but beyond it are a number of very suitable nucleii from Amersfoort to Arnhem, Nijmegen and along the Rhine and Waal rivers almost to the German frontier. There is considerable potential for light industry here and this is a very important future area for development. These first two appear fairly straightforward, but two other avenues of development are less so. To the north-east of Amsterdam lies the polder of South Flevoland with its capital, Lelystad. This is a new area which, although retained mainly for agriculture, will nevertheless provide open space directly adjacent to Amsterdam, the present plan being that the Amsterdam–Lelystad strip will be urbanised. Along this strip will run the main highway from Amsterdam to Groningen, via Lelystad, and also the Oostvaardersdiep, the extension of the North Sea canal from Ijmuiden and Amsterdam. The second of these avenues lies to the south of Rotterdam and The Hague, into the delta of the Rhine and Maas. The whole area is being completely dyked against the sea and the formerly disastrous floods, and the Haringvliet has great potential as an alternative waterway and industrial site for Rotterdam's industries and port facilities. New towns are planned for Hellevoetsluis on the Haringvliet along with the extension of new roads south towards Middelburg to end the isolation of the delta. These various radial schemes are positioned to relieve the points of maximum congestion: Amsterdam–Haarlem north and north-east; Utrecht eastwards; Rotterdam and The Hague southwards.

The first and second Reports on Physical Planning in 1960 and 1966 emphasised the guided radial development of the congested Randstad cities. In the third report in 1974, however, the approach has become much more positive, with a 'spreading policy' designed to disperse the population to the underdeveloped regions of the Netherlands. There are now fiscal measures to slow down the growth of the Randstad, and twelve designated development and amenity centres, including Groningen, Leeuwarden, Emmen, Zwolle, and Doetinchem in the north and north-east, Venlo in Limburg, and Bergen-op-Zoom in the delta.

15

Denmark:
dairy specialist and
gateway to Northern Europe

Rural—urban change

Denmark is renowned for its dairy production based essentially upon the successful export of butter, bacon and eggs, and fresh, frozen and canned foods associated with her livestock—cattle, pigs and poultry. The total population of 4 million people has traditionally been rural, living in small market centres, coastal ports and agricultural villages. One of the remarkable characteristics of modern Denmark, however, is the enormous growth, industrialisation and increasing importance of Copenhagen, now a city of one-and-a-quarter million people, nearly a third of the country's total population. The purpose of this chapter will be to examine Denmark with this contrast in mind.

Land use

The extremely complicated glacial history of Denmark has produced two areas of landscape and land-use significance, one in West Jutland and the other in East Jutland and the islands (fig. 15.1).

West Jutland

The outwash plain and older morainic landscape of the Saale/Riss glaciation which covers the western part of Jutland form low sandy hills rising from the North Sea sand-dunes and coastal marshes. They were for long covered in heath interspersed with birch and oak—picturesque but wasteland and agriculturally unproductive. Soils are podsolised, known locally as 'blegsand' (bleached sterile ash-coloured sand) often with hard pan and accumulations of sour humus or peat. The reclamation of this area from the late nineteenth century onwards, is one of the success stories of Danish energy and of comparable importance to the similar Dutch areas in Groningen and Overijssel. The growth in population in Europe, coupled with the rising standards of nutrition, caused a rise in the demand for dairy produce: this led to an increasing need for more agricultural land which, in turn, began the systematic reclamation of the western heath-lands. The clearance of woodland and burning of the heath was followed by deep ploughing to break up the hard pan, regular draining and heavy applica-

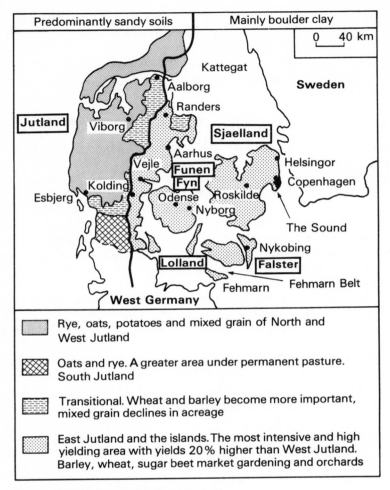

Predominantly sandy soils	Mainly boulder clay

0   40 km

Kattegat

Sweden

Aalborg

Randers

Jutland   Viborg

Sjaelland

Aarhus

Vejle   **Funen**

Helsingor

Fyn

Kolding

Copenhagen

Esbjerg

Odense   Roskilde

Nyborg

The Sound

Nykobing

Lolland   **Falster**

Fehmarn   Fehmarn Belt

West Germany

Rye, oats, potatoes and mixed grain of North and West Jutland

Oats and rye. A greater area under permanent pasture. South Jutland

Transitional. Wheat and barley become more important, mixed grain declines in acreage

East Jutland and the islands. The most intensive and high yielding area with yields 20% higher than West Jutland. Barley, wheat, sugar beet market gardening and orchards

Figure 15.1 Denmark: farming economy generalised. (From A. Mutton)

tion of fertilisers. The landscape of heather moor is now replaced to a very large extent by coniferous plantations, fields of pasture and crops, and some of the most modern farms in Denmark. These modern farms and the straight roads which lead to them are often dispersed throughout the countryside and are outside the old villages, a pattern indicative of late reclamation and secondary settlement. So successful has been the reclamation of the heathlands that today improved farmland covers three-quarters of the country. This 'inner colonisation' of West Jutland has made it possible for industrialisation and towns to spread with small loss to farmland.

East Jutland and the islands

A younger moraine landscape exists in East Jutland and the islands of the Danish Archipelago, that is the area east of the main stationary line marking the limit of the later Weichsel/Wurm glaciation. Here there is much more boulder clay, giving rise to a brown forest soil, which even here is a highly improved soil due to the rational application of manure over the centuries, continued soil ventilation by cultivation, and the practice of crop rotation. Thus there is now a man-made farmscape which bears little relationship to the original temperate forest, marsh and heath.

The development of intensive arable–livestock farming

Denmark's role as a high quality dairy-food producer is symptomised by its man-made farmscape, but has been principally created by the organisation and the vigour of the farmer, government, and indeed the whole population. The creation of this system is a result of the economic changes which were associated with the period post 1880. With large imports of low-cost wheat from USA and the new world grasslands, Danish farmers could not compete at all. The system of large manorial and crown farms and peasant subsistence farms existing side by side began to change dramatically. After a deliberate land policy to encourage the break-up of the large estates, and the establishment of family smallholdings, the typical Danish farm now has an area of between 10 and 30 hectares. There is, however, considerable variation across the country and in the sandy poorer soils of West Jutland, the individual farm tends to be much larger.

Alongside these changes in tenure to a tenant-farmer system, Denmark also turned to intensive dairy farming as the best way of utilising her small area, and utilising the only real advantage in her position, that of proximity to the two greatest industrial nations in Europe, Germany and Great Britain, who required large quantities of food. It is upon the cultivation of fodder crops that Denmark relies for her efficiency, since it must be stressed that nature has not really endowed her with excellent conditions for dairy farming. The climate is not particularly suitable for grass growing, with a rather inadequate precipitation of below 25 inches (63·5 cm), and spring comes later than in most dairy countries, giving a shorter growing season. Throughout the winter livestock must be stall-fed on fodder crops, some of which must be imported. The intensive use of land through arable farming and fodder crops is therefore essential in order to gain the maximum foodstuffs from a limited area (fig. 15.2). Grain crops, wheat, rye, barley and oats, usually occupy 45 per cent of total agricultural land; 20 per

Type of land use	Percentage of total land use	
Arable	66	total
Permanent pasture	9	cultivated
Woodland	10	land 75%
Heathland	7	
Urban	8	

Figure 15.2 Denmark: land use, 1973.

cent is under rotation grass; 18 per cent is under root crops including beet, mangolds, kohlrabi and potatoes; and only 13 per cent is under permanent grass. This is most unusual amongst dairy farming economies, which are usually predominantly pastureland. Denmark is probably the most intensive dairy farming country in the world. There are variations: West Jutland still has a greater acreage under rye; East Jutland and the islands have higher yields (fig. 15.1); around Copenhagen peas, beans, carrots and market garden and salad crops are important; the islands contain 75 per cent of the area of fruit and market garden crops. The main theme is animal husbandry, with 85 per cent of crops used as stock feed. The highest yields (67 units per hectare) come from root crops, which are at home in the Danish soils and climate with its long autumns, and roots and grass provide rough coarse feed. Cereals yield only an average of 39 units per hectare, but are invaluable because they supply the carbohydrate for concentrated feedstuffs. Proteins are supplied mainly by oil seeds which have to be imported.

Danish cattle are principally of two national breeds. Black and white milch cows are found mostly in West Jutland because of their hardiness and ability to thrive in areas of poor grass and fertility. The Danish Red breed is widespread throughout the country. Jerseys and Shorthorns are increasing in popularity. Yields of milk are very high (3600 kg per milch cow per annum), and the vast bulk (61 per cent) goes for butter-making. Cheese-making consumes 13 per cent, and the rest goes for cream, condensed milk and milk-powder, with the intensive nature of the operation apparent as the skimmed milk is returned to the farms for pig-feed. The number of pigs has increased considerably to 6·5 million, the main variety being the Landrace. Skimmed milk from the dairies is added to grain, potatoes and sugar beet toppings to feed these animals which produce the high quality ham and bacon for which Denmark is famous. The third element in the economy is becoming increasingly a battery-rearing operation associated with smaller farms of less than 10 hectares: eggs and poultry meat account for 12 per cent of the total value of farm produce.

The most important single characteristic of Danish farming is its dynamic efficiency. The cooperative movement is carried to its ultimate limits in the loan of machinery, the dissemination of research, and the organised processing and marketing of produce in creameries and factories. Government aid, the

Export	Percentage of total exports
Food and beverages	35·3
Minerals and fuel	2·2
Crude materials	7·2
Machinery and transport	27·0
Other manufactures	28·0

Figure 15.3 Denmark: principal exports, 1973.

systematic construction of Esbjerg as a port for trade with the UK, agricultural schools, and price guarantees are matched by unparalleled inspection standards. The significance of dairy products is shown by the fact that farm produce provides just under half of Denmark's exports by value. Agriculture is very dependent upon export markets for its continued prosperity, and Denmark's dilemma in the 1960s was that her two greatest markets, the UK and West Germany, were within different tariff groupings, EFTA and EEC. The accession of the UK with Denmark to the EEC meant that these two major markets were assured. Denmark's principal contribution to the community is as a very significant supplier of dairy foods (fig. 15.3).

Industrial and urban changes

The traditional picture of rural Denmark has now changed considerably into one of rapid industrialisation and urbanisation. There has been a marked change in the employment structure of the country. The number of workers in industry and the services has risen whilst those in agriculture have fallen dramatically (fig. 15.4).

Employment sector	Percentage of employed population		
	1950	1970	1973
Agriculture	25	11·5	9·5
Manufacturing	29	32·5	33·8
Services	47	56·0	56·7

Figure 15.4 Denmark: employment.

Denmark is unique in the EEC for the proportions of its total population which is concentrated within the capital city. In 1973 the Greater Copenhagen district had a population of 1·6 million out of 5 million, approximately 30 per per cent. The development of the city may be considered under four headings: the site and origins; the establishment of the 'Freeport' in 1894; modern residential expansion and the city as a tourist attraction; development as a communications centre linking northern and western Europe.

Copenhagen and the Baltic Sea

The old city of Copenhagen (fig. 15.5) was built as a safe anchorage and deep water port on the narrow strait between Zeeland (Sjaelland) and the small island of Amager, and it developed an early commercial importance as one of the major trading ports of the Hanseatic League in the thirteenth century. Its traditional role was as entry port into the Baltic Sea via the Ore Sund, the sound between Denmark and Sweden. The part of Sweden directly opposite Copenhagen was Danish territory (the province of Scania) until 1660, and thus the city was originally in a much more central position to Denmark as a whole.

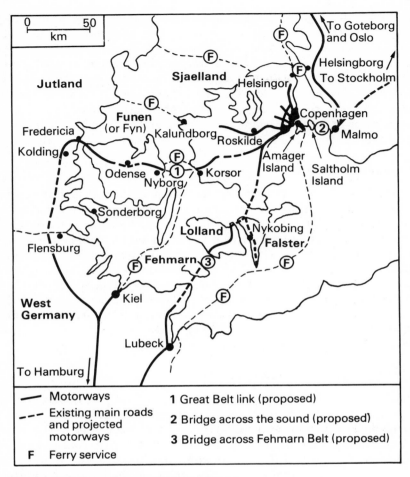

Figure 15.5 Copenhagen and the Danish
Islands: developing transport links.

The Kiel canal and the 'Freeport'

A change of critical importance came with the opening of the Kiel canal in 1894, which provided the city with serious competition by giving a more direct entry into the Baltic, and therefore threatened its role and prosperity as entry point to the Baltic. One answer to this problem was the development of the 'Frijhaven', Copenhagen Freeport, which was built at the northern end of the existing city harbour where it joins the Ore Sund. This has now become one of the largest entrepot ports of Europe, and of the 22 million tonnes of imports entering Denmark by sea in 1970, over 50 per cent came through Copenhagen, and included petroleum, coal, metal ores, timber, fertilisers, oil seeds (agricultural and industrial raw materials). Perhaps more significant was the resulting industrial expansion—over 45 per cent of Denmark's industrial workers are now employed in Copenhagen. Shipbuilding and repairing, marine engineering, oil storage for bunkering, and the generation of electricity are large-scale activities. There are also grain mills, milk and meat processing factories, and cattle-cake as a by-product, vegetable canning, tobacco processing, and brewing (particularly the Tuborg and Carlsberg lagers) and fertiliser (phosphates), all of which have a clear association with agriculture. The industrial base, however, is very varied, with engineering, electrical, radio, automobile assembly, printing, textiles and shoes, rubber, soap, paint and pharmaceuticals. Special mention must be made of furniture, stainless steel and glassware, high quality Danish consumer goods specialities.

The expansion of the city

The expansion of the city since the eighteenth century has dramatically changed the balance of its structure and morphology. Amager Island was the initial area of expansion with Christianshavn and Sundbyern to the south of the old city. In the present century, however, the west and north have figured largely in an exceptional rate of growth, with the main area of suburban expansion in the districts of Fredericksberg and Gentofte. These are added to Copenhagen itself to give a total population of 1·6 millions. The inner city is surrounded by the old canal and a ring of gardens of which the Tivoli is the most famous. A thriving tourist industry is based upon the attraction of the old city, the Christiansborg and Rosenberg palaces and the specialised traditional industries such as the Royal Danish porcelain factory, and silverware and other fine craftwork.

Copenhagen as a communications centre

A large part of the increased importance of the city since 1960 is its developing function as a communications centre. Ferry services across the Sound via Helsingor to Halsingborg, Malmo and Halmstad in Sweden, and to Travemunde (Lubeck) illustrate the position of the city as a bridge between continental Europe and Scandinavia. The international airport at Kastrup on Amager island is just six miles south of the city centre and in addition to European flights, there is the Polar route to Canada and Tokyo. Three major projects are now under discussion which will increase the nodality of the city as a European–Scandinavian land-bridge (fig. 15.5): (1) A fixed link over the Great belt (railway or six-lane motorway) to link Zeeland with Funen and Jutland and thence to West Germany; (2) a bridge across the Sound to Malmo via the Danish island of Saltholm (where the new international airport is planned); (3) a third bridge over the Fehmarn belt via Falster and Lolland across to Puttgarde on the German island of Fehmarn and thence to Kiel and Lubeck. These fixed links would be a critical step forward for the city, and would help continue its present growth. The single most significant of the three is the link across the Sound which could eventually result in the fusion of Malmo with Copenhagen to create a conurbation, the first in Scandinavia, which would spread along both the Danish and Swedish coasts of the Sound.

16

Piedmont, Lombardy and Liguria: the economic core of Italy

The wealthy north

The administrative regions of Piedmont, Lombardy and Liguria today form the extreme north-western corner of Italy, and represent a small proportion (some 20 per cent) of the total area of the country, yet they occupy a dominant place in the Italian economy. Piedmont originated as the Duchy of Savoy and from the

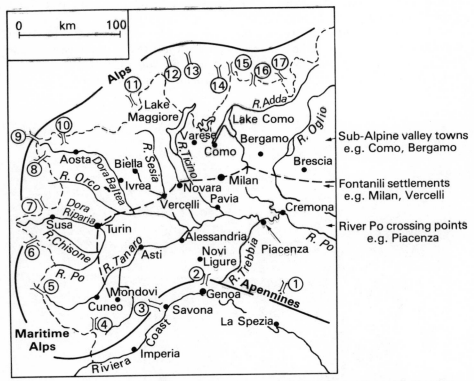

Figure 16.1 Lombardy, Piedmont and Liguria. *Appennine coastal passes:* 1. Cisa pass; 2. Giovi pass; 3. Altare pass; 4. Tenda pass. *Alpine passes:* 5. Maddalena; 6. Mt. Genevre; 7. Mont Cenis; 8. Little St. Bernard; 9. Mt. Blanc tunnel; 10. Grand St. Bernard; 11. Simplon; 12. St. Gotthard; 13. Luckmanier; 14. San Bernadino; 15. Splugen; 16. Maloja; 17. Bernina.

sixteenth century its main city, Turin, has exercised an important influence over the formation and subsequent industrialisation of Italy. Lombardy is centred around the ancient Duchy and city of Milan, although it covers much of the central part of the Po basin. Liguria is a narrow coastal strip with the port of Genoa as its major focal point. Structurally the three regions are dissimilar. The Ligurian coast forms part of the Maritime Alps and is composed largely of sandstones and limestones with fast flowing streams and steep valleys making communications very difficult. The apparent uniformity of the Po basin masks a landscape which is rich in contrasts (fig. 16.1). It varies from the sub-alpine hilly margins, with long tributary valleys such as the Dora Baltea and Dora Riparia, to the upper and lower plains divided by the line of fontanili springs and broken by the occasional low hills of moraine, such as the Serra Ivrea north of Turin, and the deeply incised hill country of Monferrato and Le Langhe, south of Turin. Climatically there are also considerable contrasts. Liguria is sheltered from the north by the Apennines and enjoys a dry summer and a mildness of climate more truly mediterranean and reminiscent of southern Italy. On the other hand, the plain of Lombardy has cold winters of continental origin, hot summers (24°C) with a tendency to thunderstorms and a well distributed rainfall. This stimulating climate can be related to the traditional energy of the peoples of northern Italy.

Overriding all these differences, however, is a common feature. This is the continuing dominance of the Italian economy by the three cities of Genoa, Milan and Turin, and their respective hinterlands. During the Middle Ages the significant factors were the natural endowment of a well-watered plain and

The autostrada via the Grand St. Bernard Pass linking Aosta, Italy, with the Rhône valley in Switzerland.

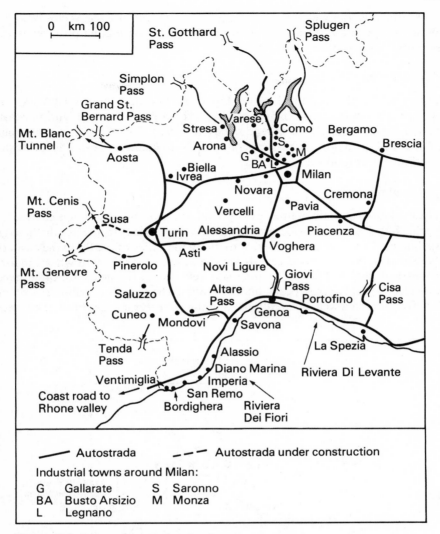

Figure 16.2 Autostrada network and major routes through the western Alps.

climate beneficial to large-scale agriculture. The control of water supplies both for irrigation and power has been an essential feature throughout. Equally as important a factor has been the proximity to the passes into France, Switzerland and northern Europe, and the maritime access via Genoa. This has encouraged enterprise, new ideas, commerce and industry, best illustrated by the extraordinary vitality of city life throughout the region's history. In the post-1945 period this proximity to north-western Europe has been physically reinforced by road tunnels, such as the Mont Blanc, and by the growing network of autostrada (fig. 16.2). The EEC has brought a fundamental change in attitudes and in economic integration, which has benefited Italy as a whole enormously.

This populous triangle, rich in farmland, industry, and city life, is closest to the West European growth axis, and has developed a dominating position as the economic core of Italy.

Agriculture

The extensive plain, drained by the Upper Po and its tributary network, the encircling mountains and their foothills, and the south-facing Ligurian coast, exhibit a wide variety of farm landscapes (fig. 16.3). The whole area is also one of the EEC's major warm-temperate food-producing zones. The principal divisions are as follows:

The Piedmont plain

The Piedmontese plain of fine fluvio-glacial deposits and alluvium is centred on Turin, but describes a wide arc from the Cuneo basin in the south through Savigliano, and is continued eastwards along the valley of the Po to the basin of Alessandria. Non-irrigated cereals are the dominant type, with wheat, maize, potatoes, beans and fodder as the main field crops; the fields are often lined with tree crops of apples, pears, plums or vines. The numerous tributaries of the Po give the area a well-watered look, and the river terraces are broken by steep

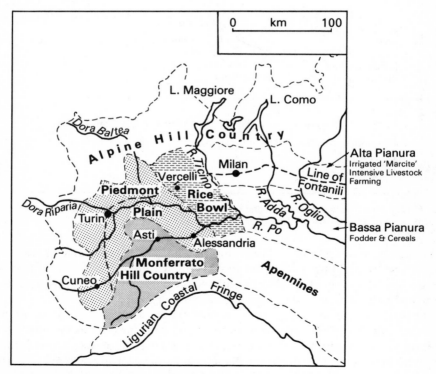

Figure 16.3 Agricultural regions. (From D. S. Walker)

bluffs commonly in woodland, whilst the flood plains are often irrigated. The plain of Alessandria, in particular, specialises in market gardening, with sugar beet at Marengo, and is the chief granary of Piedmont. The farms are substantial holdings, often over fifty hectares, with large, prosperous looking farmhouses, grain silos and outbuildings.

Monferrato hill country

To the south of Turin lie the foothills of the Apennines, the Monferrato and Le Langhe hill country. The northward-flowing river Tanaro follows an attractively varied landscape of cuestas, vales and rolling hills, with many hill-top villages and market towns such as Mondovi and Ceva, which lie on the route to the coast at Savona. The speciality of the area is viticulture, particularly around Asti and Alba. Here there are nearly 150000 hectares of specialised vineyards which produce the famous sparkling Moscato D'Asti, and Torinese Vermouth. There is also a large production of red wines notably Barbera, Dolcetto and Barbaresco. In other parts there is a patchwork of cereals, pasture and cattle raising, with some fruit and market gardening, but farms are small, generally 2 to 3 hectares, and this part of Piedmont suffers from the drift of population to the cities. As the higher slopes of the Apennines are reached, there are hazel nuts, truffles and chestnuts in valleys such as the upper Tanaro.

The Alpine hill country

To the north and west of Turin the plain merges into the Alpine hill country. At the exits to the Val Di Susa and the Val D'Aosta there are extensive moraines which form irregular hills. The Serra D'Ivrea is one example, its surface covered with heathland and chestnut woods. The Val D'Aosta, which carries the beautiful Dora Baltea river has the classic Alpine succession of pasture and tiny fields of hay, rye and potatoes on the flats and orchards on the lower slopes, followed by terraced vineyards supported on trestles to counteract the effects of damp from the high rainfall (100 cm). Above this are bare slopes and the high pastures used for the spring migrations of farm animals. There are also abandoned terraces and farmhouses, indicative of the retreat to lower slopes and more beneficial soil. In the western Italian Alps as a whole only 6 per cent of the land is classed as cultivated. In the upper Po valley to the south-west of Turin are the sheltered valleys of the Saluzzese with orchards, vines, palms and magnolias, and a four-year rotation of cereals with hay and root crops.

The 'Rice Bowl'

Probably the most distinctive farming type is the Rice Bowl of Vercelli and Novara. Half a million hectares of heavy clay soils are irrigated in vast monotonous fields which are carefully terraced and bordered with screens of Lombardy poplar and willow. The farms are large, usually over 50 hectares, and isolated, mostly built around a courtyard and containing grain stores, machinery sheds and accommodation for seasonal workers. Up to 80 per cent of the land is under rice. The ploughing, cultivation and harvesting of the rice is done by machine, but the planting is done by hand, with seasonal female labour. Yields are high, averaging twelve tonnes per hectare. There is heavy use of fertilisers, and although monoculture has traditionally been the pattern, there is now a growing diversification towards rotation fodder and milk production. The Vercellese is an example of the early use of irrigation for intensive production. Fontanili springs were used as early as the thirteenth century, but the real intensification of farming came with the construction of the Cavour canal in 1863. The Vercellese is an excellent example of large-scale, heavily capitalised farming, with irrigation as the basis for intensive rice production.

The Alta and Bassa Pianura around Milan

The part of Lombardy which is centred upon Milan lies mainly between the Ticino and the Adda, and exhibits a more straightforward division than Piedmont, with the water-rich Fontanili zone dividing the Alta Pianura, north of Milan, from the Bassa Pianura which stretches south to Piacenza on the river Po. The excellent supplies of water and their control and exploitation are the key to Lombardy's historic agricultural productivity. About 60 per cent of the farmland is irrigated, and of this 40 per cent comes from the Fontanili which has been used since the eleventh century. The rest comes from the extensive canal system which utilises the waters of the Ticino, Adda, Lambro, Sesia and Oglio rivers, by crossing the interfluves in an east–west network stretching from Turin to Brescia. The most important of these are the Cavour and Villoresi canals.

Along the line of Fontanili, the high water table encourages dairy farming. The cattle are reared on water meadows (Marcite) which are irrigated continuously ensuring a large number of fodder cuttings (10 are usual). The cattle are stall-fed in the 'cassini', which is a special variety of the 'Corte', the large Italian courtyard farm. The production of milk is geared to cheese-making, in particular Parmesan and Gorgonzola, and butter.

South of the Fontanili, on the lower plain, irrigation, though still important, is more intermittent, and fodder crops are grown in conjunction with wheat and maize. There is often a seven-year rotation, with four years of cereals, followed by three years of meadow, indicating the continuing importance of dairy farming. The main hazard on the low plains is of flooding, creating the necessity for high levees.

The intensive livestock economy thus described is not typical of Italy, nor is the capitalised farm operated with wage labourers generally typical of the Mediterranean area. The medium-sized and large farm holdings with their prosperous 'Corte' are a particular feature of the Lombardy and Piedmont plains. The urban life of the cities of Milan and Turin has been sustained since the Middle Ages and has been a major impetus to the efficient production of food, the utilisation of new techniques and the specialisation associated with commercial agriculture. The administration of these provinces was more enlightened than most, and the break-up of the large medieval estates into viable farm holdings was carried out in the nineteenth century.

The Ligurian coastal fringe

Liguria forms the maritime facade for the interior plains of Lombardy and Piedmont. It also forms a considerable barrier, with over 65 per cent of its land area classed as mountainous and the rest hilly, with only limited alluvial flats. Agriculturally, Liguria is therefore a difficult region, with only 11 per cent of the land cultivated. Tree crops dominate, with olives covering 50000 hectares and vines 40000 hectares.

There are three sections to the province, the Riviera Centrale, containing the port of Genoa; the Riviera di Levante, stretching eastwards to La Spezia; the Riviera di Ponente, which stretches from Genoa westwards to the French frontier, and it is this last section which has the most interesting and specialised agriculture. The Riviera Di Ponente is often called the 'Riviera of Flowers' or Riviera Dei Fiori. It faces south-east, and is sheltered from the north by the Apennines. It has drier, milder conditions than the rest of Liguria, and its sheltered bays have many sub-tropical plants, exotic palms, cypresses and bougainvilleas. There is a string of popular holiday resorts from Ventimiglia on the French frontier to Alassio, and the hillsides are heavily terraced with stone walls and covered with glasshouses for the cultivation of garden flowers. Floriculture covers 27000 hectares along this coast, and Ventimiglia has a famous traditional flower market. San Remo in particular is well-known for the cultivation of roses and carnations. Citrus fruits, early vegetables, and orchards of apples and plums are found on flatter alluvial fans of irrigable land, as at Albenga and Diano Marina. Vines, figs and olives alternate on the lower slopes with chestnut woods, and there is considerable woodland on the upper slopes, petering out into poor pasture.

The Italian industrial triangle

Although there are other heavily industrialised zones in northern Italy, notably at Marghera near Venice, and Bolzano in South Tirol, nevertheless the major industrial concentration in Italy lies within Lombardy, Piedmont and Liguria. Here lies the core of Italy's wealth production. Lombardy has little more than one-seventh of Italy's population, but provides one-fifth of the national product, and 40 per cent of industrial exports. It has a quarter of the industrial workers, and provides over 35 per cent of the taxes paid by industrial companies. Its industry is broadly based upon a vast number of small and medium-sized concerns. Around Milan there are over 100000 industrial concerns, and the largest factory in the city employs 18000 workers, a small figure when compared with the 70000 workers of the main Fiat factory in Turin. Piedmont provides one-tenth of the country's national product, and one-seventh of the industrial output, but, unlike Lombardy, its wealth is built around a few large enterprises. Fiat of Turin employs 186000 workers, and thousands more are directly dependent upon it for a livelihood. Turin is an excellent example of a company city, and certainly its life revolves around the car industry. Liguria's wealth is based first upon the port of Genoa and its subsidiary port, Savona, and the modern steel mills, shipbuilding yards and engineering industries which lie on the coast between the two ports. The other source of wealth lies in the old established tourist trade along the Riviera Dei Fiori. Many well-known resorts line the coast for 150 kilometres eastwards from the French Riviera around the Gulf of Genoa.

Milan

Milan originated as Roman Mediolanum, and became a famous ecclesiastical centre during the latter part of the Roman Empire. During the revival of city life in the eleventh century it again prospered and was a medieval industrial, commercial and banking centre of great importance. The city typifies the extra-ordinary tenacity of the cities of the northern Italian plains, as it survived the centuries of stagnation of Spanish rule, and from the nineteenth century on-wards industrial development came steadily, with the concentrated economic advantages which Lombardy could now exploit. These were the accrued agri-cultural commercial wealth, the enterprising spirit of the population, and hydro-electric power from the Alps. Perhaps most important was the development of modern communications so that the city could assume its natural position as the chief focus of road and rail routes within the plain and across the Alps, and to the Ligurian and Venetian coasts.

Food processing (pasta, confectionery, etc.) is concentrated in the Greater Milan area. In particular, cheese making, with the famous Gorgonzola, Parmesan, Bel-Paese and Stracchino cheeses, is found in Milan and the cities to the south—Lodi, Pavia and Piacenza.

The industries which are basic to the prosperity of the area are, however, engineering of all kinds, textiles, and chemicals. The textile industry is located mainly in the upper plain to the north of Milan, and is associated with the growth of a major agglomeration of industrial towns (fig. 16.2) stretching north to the Alpine valleys, which were the original source of power. The cotton industry is represented strongly to the north-west at Busto Arsizio, Legnano, Varese and Gallarate, and to the north-east at Monza and Bergamo. Silk is manufactured in Como, and woollens in Bergamo province, whilst the newer synthetic fibres are present in Milan itself.

The chemical industry is concentrated in Milan and Novara, with many factories of the Montecatini group. There are several petrochemical plants, and an important feature is the existence of substantial natural gas deposits in the lower plain. The headquarters of ENI, the state oil and gas agency, is at Milan. Fertilisers, artificial rubber and Pirelli tyres are all important, whilst there is a major pharmaceuticals industry in Milan, based largely upon the high level of demand in the northern cities.

It is in the engineering field, with all its varied aspects, however, that the real industrial vitality of Milan is based. Prior to the post-1945 movement to the integrated coastal steelworks, Italy's steel industry was dominated by Lom-bardy, and there were steelworks based on scrap at Sesto San Giovanni, Bergamo and Brescia. Their output is small, under one million tonnes per year, and insufficient for the metal working. Foundry and steel-making equipment, presses, lathes and engines, and heavy electrical generating equipment are located at Milan. The vehicle industry is represented by Innocenti and Alfa

Romeo. The light engineering section includes machine tools, calculators, precision instruments, textile machinery, motor scooters, motor cycles and sewing machines. In this last area, Singer at Milan and Necchi at Pavia are especially significant.

The footwear industry is centred at Vigevano to the south-west of Milan, but Milan itself and Varese are other centres. Paper and furniture manufacture is also represented strongly in the satellite towns of the upper plain from Vercelli to Como.

The great variety of industry in Lombardy, particularly Greater Milan, is a reflection of its mature industrial structure. Milan itself is a city of almost capital rank. It is certainly the financial capital of Italy with major commercial, insurance and banking operations of greater significance than those of Rome. It has the country's most significant trade fair, is a great publishing centre, and its cultural activities are metropolitan in character.

Turin

This is the chief city of Piedmont, and stands at the confluence of the Dora Riparia and Po rivers, but the modern significance of its position is the control of the passes emerging from the western end of the Alps. It rose to importance only in the sixteenth century when chosen as the capital city of the House of Savoy, under whose guidance it became the chief force in the unification of Italy in the mid-nineteenth century. During the twentieth century, with the development of roads, railways and modern autostrada, the importance of its position has again been underlined (fig. 16.2). It controls the important routes south to the Ligurian coast and Riviera, westwards via the Mont Genevre and Mont Cenis passes, and northwards through the Dora Baltea river valley to the Grand St. Bernard pass into Switzerland and the Mont Blanc road tunnel into France.

Turin is, however, the second industrial centre of Italy. The rulers of Savoy were instrumental in giving Piedmont a measure of industrialisation which was exceptional for Italy. The Turin arsenal was followed in 1900 by the car companies of Fiat and Lancia, and by Olivetti. It was the utilisation of the hydro-electric power of the Alpine valleys and the development of the strategic industries under Mussolini in the 1930s which firmly established Turin as a leading industrial city. The engineering industry, particularly car manufacturing, has boomed since 1950, and the population of Turin has passed one million, with the absorption into the city of nearly half a million Italians from the south. Car production is dominated by the large integrated Fiat factory at Mirafiori; Fiat in Turin employs 186000 workers and produces over a million cars per year. They also produce a vast range of electrical and engineering products such as marine and aero engines, electric motors, railway stock, tractors and domestic appliances. They are even concerned with the construction of Alpine tunnels and nuclear engineering. Turin (and Ivrea to the north which now has the main Olivetti typewriter factory) are examples of 'company towns'. Ancillary industries such as sheet steel, machine tools, rubber and ball-bearings, complete the picture of car assembly.

Although Turin does not have a constellation of subsidiary industrial towns like Milan, nevertheless there are a number of important rank. To the south are Alessandria and Cuneo, both route centres, Novi Ligure (steel), and Asti, a famous wine processing town. To the west is the Dora Riparia valley to the Mont Cenis pass, which leads to Chambery, and some evidence of industrial overspill from Turin is present, with many light industries at Susa and Busso-leno. To the north-east lies the woollen textile town of Biella.

Perhaps the most interesting area of development is the Dora Baltea valley. Along it runs the autostrada to the Mont Blanc tunnel and Grand St. Bernard pass, rapidly becoming the most important routes through the western Alps (fig. 16.2). Hydro-electric power is well developed and aluminium works at Borgofranco and Rayon at Chatillon are based upon this. At Aosta itself is a small steelworks, based upon local supplies of magnetite. Another source of wealth is the rapidly developing tourist industry, of both winter and summer resorts. Courmayeur and St. Vincent in the Val D'Aosta now have a greatly in-creased accessibility. Before the construction of the modern roads and tunnels in the 1960s, the Val D'Aosta was isolated from France and Switzerland for seven months of the year. This change typifies northern Italy's new close relationship with north-west Europe.

Genoa

Genoa was a flourishing port in the Middle Ages, when it rivalled Venice in the Levantine trade, but its importance shrank from the sixteenth century onwards with the growth of Atlantic shipping. It was Cavour, the Piedmontese states-man, who saw its potentialities as an outlet for the whole of northern Italy and the Alpine regions. Under his guidance the port facilities were considerably improved and a railway link from Turin established. At the same time the Suez canal had a major regenerative effect upon Mediterranean shipping.

Although the port has a major disadvantage stemming from its mountainous coastline and consequent lack of space for development, nevertheless, there is a transport factor of the greatest significance. The mountains are at their lowest and narrowest point behind Genoa, and this funnels traffic from the interior into the Giovi pass (fig. 16.2), which is traversed by two railways and the auto-strada. There is also the higher Bochetta road pass close by, and the Turchino railway route. These are important not only in allowing Genoa easy access to Piedmont and Lombardy, but in addition the trans-Alpine passes have facili-tated the extension of its hinterland to Switzerland and beyond. It is thus the natural outlet for Turin and Milan, and is an important corner of the Italian industrial triangle.

Genoa is now second in importance only to Marseilles on the EEC southern flank (chapter 8, fig. 8.8). There are 17 miles of quays extending along the coast and its industrial suburbs, Sampierdarena, Cornigliano, Sestri, Pegli and Voltri, extend to the west of the city. Genoa deals mainly with imports, 90 per cent by tonnage of its total trade. Oil accounts for half the total tonnage, coal, mineral ores, grain, tropical foods, chemicals and textile fibres also being important. It is thus a major input point for raw materials, and associated with the oil terminals are the pipelines which carry oil from Genoa to Milan, Aigle in Switzerland and Ingolstadt in southern Germany.

Heavy industry has developed along the coast, particularly shipyards at Sestri and Voltri. At Cornigliano is one of the coastal integrated steelworks developed since 1945, entirely dependent upon imports of scrap iron, West African iron-ore and coal. There is also oil refining, metal smelting, machine tools, marine, electrical and railway equipment. Food processing based upon imports is also an important activity, with vegetable canning, grain-milling, soap manufacture, sugar refining, paper and pottery.

The other two Ligurian ports illustrate the importance of hinterlands. La Spezia to the east has an excellent harbour, but is handicapped by difficult passes through the Apennines. Savona by contrast, on the western side, has developed a special relationship with Turin, to which it has easy access via the Altare pass. These links have increased rapidly since 1972 with the development of the auto-strada from Turin, a spectacular example of modern engineering which joins the coastal autostrada at Savona.

Tourism along the Italian Riviera

The Riviera Di Levante, eastwards of Genoa, has a rugged coast of great beauty, with famous resorts like Portofino, Rapallo and Santa Margarita. The section of the coast west of Genoa has already been described as the Riviera Dei Fiori for its associations with fruit and flowers. It too, has a beautiful rugged coast-line and many seaside resorts including Ventimiglia, San Remo, Diano Marina and Alassio, which nestle in sheltered bays backed by wooded hills. The whole riviera coast has begun to feel considerable competition from newer tourist areas around the Mediterranean sea. It suffers from overcrowding due partially to its longstanding popularity, and partially to the difficulty of access by the inadequate roads. The recent completion of the autostrada running along the entire coast from Avignon to Genoa and La Spezia, with interior links to Milan and Turin may well have largely removed this disadvantage (fig. 16.2). The re-vitalising effects of fast road transport are important to the whole region, but perhaps most of all to this beautiful Ligurian coast.

17

The Mezzogiorno: Italy's problem region

The poor south

The contrasts between northern and southern Italy are dramatic. The well-watered environment of the Plain of Lombardy, with its great traditions of urban life, commercial agriculture, bustling industry and busy transport networks, has no counterpart in the south. More than any other member of the Community, Italy is a land of two nations. South of Rome there is a clearly identifiable atmosphere of impoverishment, lack of activity, and a quite distinct feeling that this part of Europe is sub-tropical in climate and culture. To be more

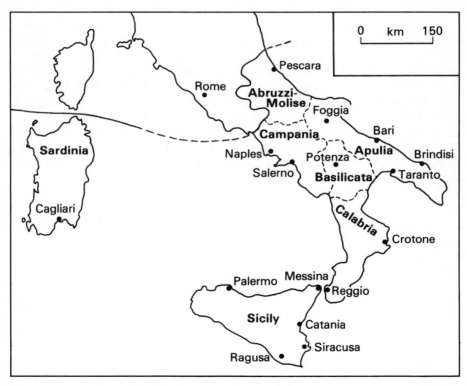

Figure 17.1 The seven Provinces of the Mezzogiorno.

Region	Gross Domestic Product Lire ($\times 19^9$)	
	1960	1970
Italy	19286	51849
Lombardy	4147	10982
Apulia	823	2430
Basilicata	111	355
Calabria	374	1021
Abruzzi Molise	370	998
Campania	1225	3330

Figure 17.2 A comparison of Gross Domestic Product. (From EEC Regional Statistics)

specific, Italians refer to the area as 'Il Mezzogiorno', the land of the noon-day sun. The Mezzogiorno comprises seven of Italy's nineteen administrative regions (fig. 17.1) and contains over 20 million people. During the period from 1950 to 1960 it contained 40 per cent of Italy's population, and yet produced only 20 per cent of the country's gross domestic product (fig. 17.2). Its average income per head was less than half that of northern Italy, and one-fifth that of France. Its population of nearly 20 million people was twice that of Greece, which has much the same total area. Emigration from the Mezzogiorno has been persistently high. During the period from 1900 to 1920 over 8 million Italians emigrated from the south, often to the northern cities, but in very large numbers to North America and other parts of the New World. In the 1950s more than half the houses in the south were without drinking water, and 40 per cent without sanitary facilities. Most significant of all, because it underlines the basic problem, was the picture of agricultural unemployment. In 1950 the south had 57 per cent of its population employed in agriculture and only 20 per cent in industry, demonstrating its basically under-developed structure. The problems could be summarised as: a low level of economic activity; income levels well below other parts of the EEC; poor living conditions; an overwhelming dependence upon agriculture with resulting rural overpopulation. Persistent out-migration has been one traditional answer to the situation, but it has not been enough. The population has continued to increase steadily and has remained stubbornly too high for the resources of the land to sustain. In the immediate post-1945 period the imbalance between Italy's south and north remained. The Mezzogiorno was one of Europe's most intractable problems.

The disadvantages of the Mezzogiorno: physical, historical and economic

Water shortage

The small amount of rainfall and its seasonal occurrence are a major problem. Many parts of the south have only 500 mm of rainfall per annum, and in addition the summer drought, high rate of evaporation and considerable unreliability of rainfall create desiccated conditions for up to five months during the summer. Yet it is precisely during the summer period that the high sub-tropical temperatures would permit the growth of crops not easily cultivable anywhere else in the Community. Unless irrigation water is available, and this is not easy because most rivers dry up in summer, intensive summer cropping is impossible, and the common answer to the drought is a wasteful fallow. There is generally under-utilisation of the land with extensive farming and heavy reliance upon wheat, olives and livestock grazing. Even grazing is limited owing to the absence of good year-round pasture, and the numbers of sheep and cattle are low compared to those in the north. The whole agricultural environment of the south is harsh, inferior, and marked by low productivity.

A mountainous landscape

Southern Italy is dominated by the Apennine mountains, and it has been estimated that over 40 per cent of the land area is mountainous and too steep for any form of cultivation. Another 45 per cent is classified as hill country which is prone to considerable soil exhaustion. Most of the southern Apennines are formed of limestone, much of which is dolomitic. This hard dolomitic limestone gives a landscape of sharp peaks and bare slopes with the smallest vestiges of maquis or scrub vegetation. In the Abruzzi is the highest peak, Corno Grande (2915 metres). In other areas such as Apulia the limestone gives bare karstic conditions. By contrast much of Calabria is granitic with the Pollino massif reaching 2275 metres. Extensive plains are limited, and lowlands are confined to Foggia, the Naples–Salerno plain, and the 'heel' around Taranto. There is a basic poverty in the Mezzogiorno with its high proportion of uncultivable land, rugged and eroded slopes, dried-up river beds and desiccated landscape.

The legacy of the past

The history of the area has had a dramatic effect upon this landscape. From the period of the early Greek and Roman civilisations, the south was a major granary with widespread cultivation of vines and the olive. With the collapse of Roman power from the fifth century onwards, there was a prolonged period of political chaos and insecurity, with a succession of invasions from the north and piracy from the sea (Barbary pirates). Settlement moved inland and tended to concentrate in closely-knit villages, often of great size, clustered around a castle or on hilltops, where they could be more easily defended. The plains were abandoned and the foothills and mountain slopes became over-grazed and de-forested, with ensuing soil erosion, extensive gullying on the hillsides, and low-land flooding leading to swamps and malarial infestation. From the eleventh century onwards the whole area, as the Kingdom of Naples, came under the corrupt rule of the Spanish House of Bourbon. Feudal serfdom with large absentee landlord estates called 'Latifundi' persisted into the middle of the twentieth century. These Latifundi are generally large estates covering over 200 hectares which exist on the plains and which practise monoculture based upon wheat alternated with fallow. This is extensive farming and under-utilises the

Calascibetta, Enna. A typical hilltop town
surrounded by rugged hill country in the
centre of Sicily.

resources of both the land and the people. Most of the south's sheep and cattle
are grazed on the Latifundi, and transhumance is practised with livestock being
taken to the nearby mountain slopes. The blight which the Latifundi have
brought to the south is seen in the under-employment of the farm labourers.
Many peasants would have five or six weeks working time on their own plots of
land, and then would look for work on the Latifundia, some distance away. The
peasants wait, early in the mornings, in the piazzas of the towns and villages for
the farm overseer to hire them for the day. Generally they would average only
100 days work per year, illustrating the low economic level at which the south
existed well into the mid-twentieth century.

Too many people on the land

Pressure of population led to the increasing subdivision and fragmentation of
land holdings. In 1950 over 70 per cent of holdings in the south were of less than
three hectares. These are the other side of the picture, known as 'Minifundia'.
They usually existed on the poorer hilly and mountainous land which experienced considerable sub-division amongst tenants and share-croppers. In
1950, 45 per cent of all agricultural workers in the south owned no land at all;
28 per cent were share-croppers who surrendered up to 60 per cent of their crop
to the landowner as rent; only 27 per cent owned their own land. Fragmentation
of farm holdings was the norm, with peasant farmers cultivating anything up to
ten widely scattered plots of land. Such a system of tiny holdings, particularly
with a proportion being share-cropped, is often inadequate to support a family.
Crop specialisation is almost impossible because of the need to maintain the

family's food supply, and the pattern of farming is subsistence, with very little entering commercial channels. Methods of cultivation were antiquated and labour intensive; insecurity of tenure was damaging to morale, and not conducive to mechanisation and capitalisation. Economic feudalism was the most distinguishing feature of the Mezzogiorno.

Isolation and a lack of raw materials

The essential bases for industrial development were lacking, as there was no coal, or other raw materials of any significance, and the development of hydroelectric power, so important in the north, was retarded in the south by the intermittent river regimes. Only Naples had any significant industrial capacity, and throughout the south industry was limited, inefficient, and mainly small-scale artisan in character. Perhaps most important of all was the isolation of the south from the mainstream of European development during the nineteenth century, whilst the rest of Europe was industrialising rapidly. The great length of peninsular Italy (1000 km) and its physical nature was an inhibiting factor in communications. The backwardness associated with the corrupt rule of the Bourbon kings of Naples until 1861 had meant that there was hardly any infrastructure of roads and railways. In 1861, the Mezzogiorno had only 99 km of railway, whilst in Italy as a whole there were 1798 km. All this contrasted markedly with the north of Italy (chapter 16) whose most important foundation for industrial wealth lay in its relatively easy access across the Alpine mountain passes into the core area of Europe. Furthermore, after the unification of Italy in 1861, the contrasts between north and south increased. The economic disadvantages of the south, remoteness from markets, higher fuel costs, and a feudal system of agriculture, were compounded by the illiteracy and unskilled nature of the population. In the newly unified Italy, the north held all the basic advantages, and as it rapidly became industrialised from the 1870s onwards, the gap between the two Italys steadily widened.

The Cassa per il Mezzogiorno

There have been piecemeal attempts to reform and reconstruct the economy and environment of the south. Various projects to reclaim marshland and eradicate malaria, and to improve river channels and combat soil erosion were made during the nineteenth century. During the inter-war period, the Fascist government introduced a programme to drain and irrigate the land and improve agriculture. It was in the immediate period after 1945, with land hunger and large-scale unemployment causing considerable unrest, that the problems of the south became really acute, and were brought to the attention of the government and public opinion. Furthermore, statistics were more readily available, which allowed assessments to be made and remedies to be suggested. A long-term strategy was favoured and a supra-regional body was proposed with direct powers and massive investment backing which could see the south as a whole and which would be able to plan a coordinated and vigorous policy of rehabilitation.

In March 1950 the Cassa per il Mezzogiorno was established by the Italian

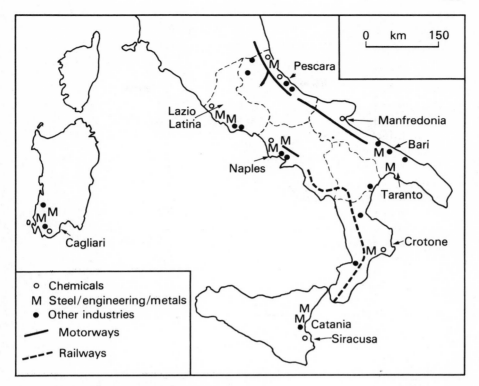

Figure 17.3 EIB loans for industrial and transport projects up to 1972. (Source: EEC statistics)

Parliament as an executive body with powers to carry out a ten-year basic development plan. It was to operate in the seven regions of the south and also a small part of Latium near Rome. There was a considerable battery of aids for the Cassa. In addition to the power to initiate development projects, it also had coordinating power over development in every sector of the south's economy. The investment of government money was supplemented by private investment, both Italian and external, and by loans from the World Bank. Since the development of the EEC, the European Investment Bank (EIB) has made substantial loans (fig. 17.3), over 300000 million Lire (58 per cent of total EIB loans) during the 1960s, and the Agricultural and Social Funds have also helped considerably.

Agricultural improvement

Agriculture initially accounted for the major efforts of the Cassa, and the original planned pattern of investment earmarked 77 per cent of investment for agriculture (fig. 17.4). (Industry was not included at all in the original plan.) There were two principal methods of agricultural change: land reform, and the modernisation of farming techniques. Special agencies 'Ente Di Riforma' were set up to

	Expenditure (%)		
	1950 (proposals)	1950–65	1966–69
Agriculture	77·0	56·1	24·7
Infrastructure (aqueducts, drainage, highways, etc.)	20·5	22·4	19·6
Tourism	2·5	4·2	8·1
Industry	–	6·9	36·0
Technical assistance and training of workers	–	10·4	11·6

Figure 17.4 The Cassa Per Il Mezzogiorno.
(From Allen and McLennan)

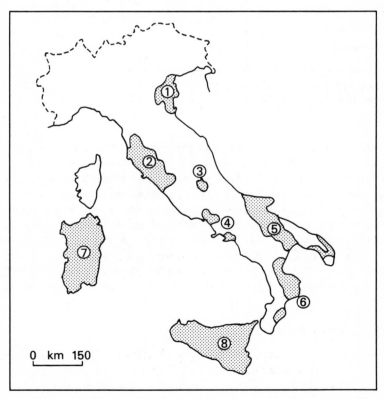

0 km 150

Figure 17.5 Land reform agencies. 1. Delta Padano; 2. Tuscany–Lazio; 3. Fucino; 4. Volturno; 5. Apulia–Basilicata; 6. Sila; 7. Sardinia; 8. Sicily. (From Mountjoy)

administer nine areas of land reform (fig. 17.5). These areas were set up by government decree and were not directly under the jurisdiction of the Cassa, and not all of them were in the Mezzogiorno as previously defined. Nevertheless they performed a valuable function, thereby providing landless peasants with holdings by expropriating large and inefficiently run Latifundia. The large estates which were expropriated were those which generally were extensively cultivated, and which had received virtually no investment. Particularly well run farms were termed 'model farms' and exempted from expropriation. The whole object was to carry out close settlement, to provide new villages and to increase productivity with irrigation and land improvement schemes, so that intensive cash-crop farming on small holdings would replace extensive wheat cultivation. Viable family holdings (poderi) were created; in irrigated areas the minimum size was 5 hectares, whilst on hillsides it could be up to 50 hectares. Over 114000 families received land in all, and the typical pattern of change may be seen in the work of the Ente de Riforma Apulia-Basilicata, covering the 'heel' of Italy. A total area of 201000 hectares was expropriated from 1500 landowners, and assigned to 31000 families. The change to this much closer pattern of settlement has involved the construction of roads, power and water supply,

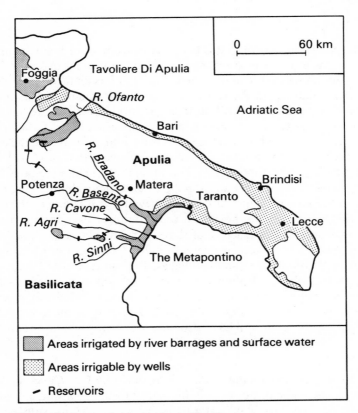

Figure 17.6 Irrigation in Apulia and Basilicata. (From Mountjoy)

land reclamation, new farmhouses and villages. A complete new infrastructure has been developed, with 15000 farmhouses, 50 service centres and villages, 1700 kilometres of roads, and 7500 wells. A large programme of irrigation has transformed the lowland areas of the Metapontino, the Bari–Brindisi coastal strip (Salentine peninsula) and the Tavoliere Di Apulia (fig. 17.6). The 'wheat and olive' landscape has changed to one of citrus fruits, vegetable and industrial crops, and livestock numbers have increased dramatically. The Metapontino (fig. 17.6) illustrates the transformation of the landscape. It was formerly a malarial coastal plain, reclaimed after 1945, the marshy areas drained and the mosquito eradicated. The five rivers irrigate the entire coastal strip and are responsible for the cultivation of 8 million vines, 350000 citrus and other fruit trees. Some 750000 pine trees act as windbreaks. Oranges, peaches, apricots, pears, salad vegetables, sugar-beet, tobacco and tomatoes are the principal high-yielding crops.

The transformation of large areas has been impressive. The largest and least efficient Latifundi have disappeared, and much of the day labour system with them. There has been a notable increase in intensive farming in fruit and vegetable crops. It must be remembered, however, that land reform has only affected 10 per cent of the cultivated land in the south.

Infrastructure

The Cassa per il Mezzogiorno has been the instrument of financial assistance for many of the improvement schemes initiated in the areas of land reform. As well as irrigation schemes and new farm houses, it has financed crop and stock improvements and begun the task of consolidating fragmented holdings into viable units. A significant contribution to the rural infrastructure has been the establishment of packing, processing, and refrigeration units. Finally, because the most permanent weakness of the south is its need to overcome the relatively long distances from the markets of western Europe, the Cassa has been very active in developing transport, distribution, and marketing facilities for agricultural products. Aqueducts and reservoirs and the draining of marshes are primarily associated with agriculture, but they also contribute to the improvement of village life. Schools, hospitals, and training centres are directly associated with the social infrastructure of the south. The Cassa has installed main water supplies for 8 million people, and aided local authorities to build the systems for distributing the water to villages. The construction of hydro-electric power stations, whole telephone systems, 29000km of new roads and the improvement and reconstruction of as many more, and the railway system from Campania into the toe of Italy at Reggio Calabria, have made large areas of the south more accessible and have also improved living conditions immensely.

Industry

During the early period, up until 1957, the main work of the Cassa was to inject new vitality into agriculture, village life, and into the environment generally, whilst hoping that this would stimulate demand, and provide conditions favourable to the growth of industry. However, by 1957 it was realised that there would have to be more definite intervention in the industrial sector to provide new employment and to ease the burden on the agricultural sector. The passing of the Industrial Areas Law in 1957 empowered the Cassa to support the establishment of industrial zones in the south, and figure 17.4 illustrates the shift of resources into the industrial sector after 1965. There were various encouragements to industrialists. The Cassa itself provided capital for new projects and for modernisation of existing concerns, up to as much as 85 per cent of the cost. There was also exemption from local taxes, rail-freight concessions and exemption from customs duties on imported raw materials. The European Investment Bank (EIB) has been of great importance here and has helped to establish a large number of factories of various kinds (fig. 17.3). The largest single contribution has come from the government-controlled companies such as ENI and IRI; by 1964 they were required by law to place 40 per cent of their investment in the south. Much of the growth has been in heavy industry, mainly in iron and steel, shipbuilding, heavy engineering, cement, oil-refining, and petrochemicals, because of the nature of the state controlled companies. Major projects of international significance include the Taranto and Bagnoli steelworks, and the large Montedison petrochemical complexes at Brindisi and Siracusa–Augusta in Sicily. The continuing problem has been that these are mainly capital-intensive heavy industries and they do not provide very large employment possibilities, nor do they necessarily stimulate the development of lighter consumer goods industries, which are essential to balanced growth. Another problem was that although an enormous amount of investment had been poured into the south (2500 million Lire by 1975) it tended to be dissipated over the whole area.

Growth poles

The development of a limited number of centres which were individually capable of faster growth was adopted during the latter half of the 1960s. The idea is based upon the economies of scale which accrue when the infrastructure, industrial linkages, and trained labour supply are concentrated into a smaller cohesive area. Altogether, 42 nuclei of industrial development were designated, and subsequent experience has shown that five major areas were of greatest significance, and these have become 'growth poles' (fig. 17.7) into which most investment has been channelled. Three of the most important of these are the Naples–Salerno pole, the Bari–Brindisi–Taranto triangle, and the Siracusa–Augusta pole.

1. **The port of Naples** has declined considerably in relation to Italy's other ports and now occupies fifth position after Genoa, Trieste, Augusta, and Venice. Nevertheless its shipbuilding and repairing industry continues. This has been supplemented by the Bagnoli Steel plant, cotton textiles, Alfa-Romeo cars, Pirelli cables, Olivetti office machinery, and Montedison Petrochemical and Plastic works. There is also the development of the nucleus of an Italian aircraft industry based upon a joint Fiat/IRI venture, 'Aeritalia'. There appears to be the basis of a fairly diversified industrial structure in the Naples area.

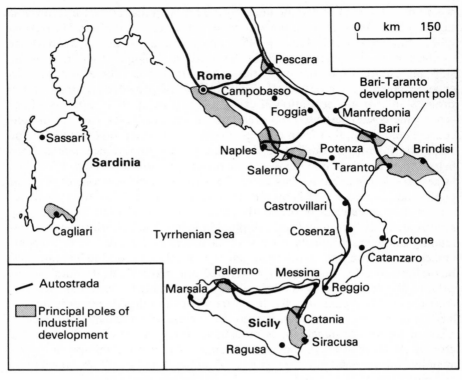

Figure 17.7 The Mezzogiorno: motorways and industrial development poles.

2. **Siracusa–Augusta.** The development here is based largely upon petrochemicals, for two reasons. There is a small oilfield at Ragusa, and considerable sulphur and potash deposits in eastern Sicily. More important are the deep water facilities between Augusta and Siracusa which have led to the development of major port installations, with Augusta being able to accommodate 250000-tonne tankers. Rapid development of one of the largest oil refinery, chemical and petrochemical complexes in Western Europe is taking place. Cement and the refining of non-ferrous metals are other activities.

3. **Bari–Brindisi–Taranto.** The integrated iron and steel works at Taranto, built in 1960, dominates this area. It is one of the largest steelworks in Europe with a capacity of 10 million tonnes per annum. Its coastal site and the facility for low cost imports have been instrumental in its success, and it has been accompanied by a large industrial estate with an agglomeration of engineering and machine-tool factories, agricultural machinery and consumer goods industries. At Brindisi is the Montedison petrochemical factory, producing plastics and ethylene. The EEC Commission has drawn up a detailed development plan for this growth pole and has invested over 150000 million Lire in industrial plant.

Tourism

The recognition by the Cassa that tourism can play a major part in economic development has meant the increasing allocation of funds for hotel building and modernisation and other tourist amenities. The south has much to offer the tourist: beautiful empty beaches; dramatic mountainous scenery; architecture of every type and period. It is the more attractive by comparison with the over-crowded northern Italian resorts. Hitherto there was one major drawback—inaccessibility.

Autostrada

The construction of autostrada has now shrunk the distances quite dramatically. The Autostrada Del Sole, running from Bologna through Rome and Naples to Reggio Calabria is the most well-known, but there are autostrada running down both west and east coasts, with two cross-Apennine links from Naples to Bari and from Rome to Pescara (fig. 17.7). The remoteness of the south is now disappearing both for the tourist and the industrialist, and the autostrada may well prove in the long run to be the most important single factor in its development.

The Mezzogiorno in 1975

The problem has proved deep rooted and complex: the Cassa has been in existence now for 25 years, during which 7500 billion Lire has been invested in the south, but it is still difficult to see whether the economy has reached the 'take-off point' or whether the 'multiplier effect' is operating, and capable of sustaining long-term growth.

Yet there is no doubt that there are the beginnings of substantial industrialisation, and the employment structure has shown quite dramatic change as seen in the percentage figures in fig. 17.8.

	Agriculture	Industry	Services
1950	57	20	23
1970	33	32	35
1973	28	32	39 (estimated)

Figure 17.8 The employment structure in the Mezzogiorno, 1950–1973.

The industrial and service infrastructure is much sounder, and agriculture has lost 2 million workers.

Agricultural productivity has improved considerably in the land reform areas (fig. 17.9) with a much greater emphasis on intensive crops and dramatically increased numbers of livestock. But this has to be taken in context, noting that land reform has so far affected only 10 per cent of the cultivated land in the

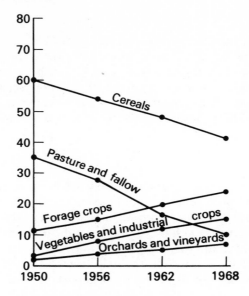

Figure 17.9 Changes in land use in the Mezzogiorno. (From Mountjoy)

south. The largest remaining problem is that of rehabilitating the eroded mountain slopes and bringing the hill farmers into a modern farming system.

The gap between the south and north of Italy remains, because, in spite of considerable advances in per capita income in the south (67 per cent 1951–65), the north has experienced such boom conditions in the decade up to 1970 that the gap has closed only partially as fig. 17.10 shows.

	Income per capita (Lire)	
	1950	1970
Italy (average)	188 000	605 500
Lombardy	276 000	758 400
Liguria	284 000	787 800
Apulia	110 000	481 700
Basilicata	97 000	376 800
Campania	106 000	483 700
Calabria	80 000	371 300

Figure 17.10 Changes in per capita income (Lire), 1950–1970.

The per capita income in Calabria is still only half that of Lombardy and Liguria, although in Apulia and Campania the figure is drawing closer to the national average. Clearly the improvement has been very uneven and an immense amount remains to be done.

As part of the economic rehabilitation of the south, emigration will still be necessary for a long time to come. During the 1960s it was running at an annual rate of 140 000 per year, and in 1970 it was 150 000 (fig. 17.11). It is still therefore

	Net emigration (in thousands per annum)	
	1966	1970
Campania	26·4	34·9
Abruzzi/Molise	15·0	6·5
Apulia	27·5	26·4
Basilicata	8·6	10·7
Calabria	23·3	26·1
Sicily	33·5	36·8
Sardinia	6·5	8·9
Total Mezzogiorno	140·8	150·3

Figure 17.11 Net emigration from the Mezzogiorno. (From EEC Regional Statistics)

of major significance in siphoning off the excess rural population. Most of the emigration is inter-regional, to the northern cities, but emigration to other EEC countries, notably West Germany, also occurs. The movement from the south should be seen as part of the process of making agriculture more efficient, of raising the per capita income of the remaining population, thus increasing demand for goods and services and giving greater incentive to industrialisation. It would seem that the Cassa per il Mezzogiorno has achieved much in 25 years, and that in the decade up to 1980 the infrastructure which it has created may reach the self-sustaining 'take-off' point.

18

Eire:
the EEC's Atlantic Fringe

On the regional maps of the European Community, Eire is typecast as a peripheral, underdeveloped region (chapter 10). Its environmental problems are very different from those of the Mezzogiorno, but they have produced many of the same effects. These include endemic poverty in many areas, a rural subsistence economy with very low productivity, a great excess of population employed in agriculture, few industries and a low level of urbanisation, and a high and sustained rate of emigration since the early nineteenth century.

Emigration

The problem of emigration has been central to the economic geography of Eire. Up to 1840 the population of the island as a whole (including Northern Ireland) had expanded to approximately eight million. The countryside was relatively prosperous and had sustained the large-scale cultivation of the potato, which was the staple food of the rural population. It was the failure of successive harvests due to potato blight during the 1840s, and the resulting famine and starvation which led to the initial waves of emigration, many of the emigrants going to the New World. The country never recovered, and the whole basis of rural life was undermined, resulting in a halving of the population in the century up to 1940. Eire's population in 1973 was 3051000, the lowest density in the EEC. It has been estimated that people of Irish descent living in America, Great Britain and elsewhere total something like 16 million, over five times the number remaining in Eire itself.

The question of the great emigration needs a little more analysis in depth. The potato famines lasted for a very short period, but they triggered off a century of decline at the same period when most of Western Europe was growing substantially in population. The answer is probably to be found in the harsh and difficult nature of the rural environment, the essentially subsistence character of farming, and the low income levels and depressed spending capacity of the population. This picture must then be placed in the comparative context of the rest of Europe and the New World. The decline of population began before the start of the nineteenth century, with the commencement of the industrial revolution in Europe. In Ireland there was no industrial base to absorb the movement off the land because there were almost none of the resources to sustain the initial industrial growth which in countries like Britain were supplied by the huge reserves of coal and iron-ore. The attraction of employment, high wages and rising standards of living lay abroad, and there was little alternative for the Irish but to emigrate. The potato famines gave a large impetus to this movement, but the underlying cause of Ireland's depopulation lay in its lack of industrial resources at the critical period of the industrial revolution. The fact that Ireland was politically part of Great Britain at this time was also a contributing factor in terms of the close links and ease of access by which there was almost a positive inducement to emigrate to the more advantageous environments outside Ireland.

Eire today

Dublin, the capital city, is in a class by itself, and with its port, Dun Laoghaire, has 710 000 people. Cork (125 000), Limerick (60 000), Waterford (30 000), and Galway (27 000) are the only other regional centres of any size and importance. Agriculture is by far the most important single activity in Eire, accounting for 25 per cent of the labour force (fig. 18.1). Eire is thus characterised by an under-developed urban hierarchy and a greatly enlarged agricultural sector.

	Agriculture	Industry	Services	Work force total
Eire	25	31	44	1 139 000
East	6	39	55	415 000
South-East	34	27	39	121 000
North-West	51	18	31	30 000
Donegal	44	24	32	43 000
Mid-West	34	28	38	102 000

Figure 18.1 Eire: percentage employment in each region (1973). (*Economist*)

In western Eire these characteristics are even more extreme—here the rural population accounts for over 80 per cent of the total. Substantial amounts of land are uninhabited mountains or ill-drained boglands. Settlement is dispersed and villages are rare, the main unit of rural settlement being the single farm. Towns are generally very small, often having only 1500 people, but have the range of social and economic functions normally associated with a town.

In many western counties the proportion of the population engaged in agriculture rises to 50 per cent (fig. 18.1). Poor soils, small and fragmented farms, lack of capitalisation and cooperative organisation, characterise a subsistence-oriented rural economy. Although total population decline has now been arrested in Eire generally, many parts of the west are still threatened with decline. This is because of selective migration by young people, which adversely affects the birth rate and causes stagnation in many rural communities. The farm population is relatively old, and in the western region nearly 60 per cent of the farmers are over 50 years of age, representing a major obstacle to change.

The north-western regions

The north-west of Eire typifies the picture which has been presented. It is agriculturally poor, and very sparsely populated. Donegal has granite and metamorphic mountains rising to 650 metres, glaciated and often bare of soil. The lower lands are erosion platforms containing waterlogged areas with shallow lakes and extensive blanket peat-bogs. Only about 40 per cent of the total area is improved farmland and even good pasture-land is scarce. On the coast are rocky headlands and deep inlets. Rainfall is heavy (up to 1500 mm per year) and the land is bleak and windswept with severe exposure to Atlantic gales. Tree growth is impossible in many areas. Population is sparse and is based upon subsistence farming with the cottages usually situated in the sheltered lee of the mountains. Potatoes, hay and occasionally oats, are the only crops possible. Sheep are more numerous than cattle and their wool serves as the basis for the manufacture of homespun cloth, knitwear and the Donegal Tweeds. The only town of any size is Donegal (1500 people) which acts as county town and market centre, and typifies the restricted development of most Irish towns.

The mountains of Mayo and Connemara are scenically beautiful, but are also similar regions of difficulty. They form dissected masses of metamorphic rocks rising to 800 metres. There is a combination of bare ice-scoured rocks and peat-bogs, and the mountains are practically uninhabited. Where there is settlement, it is characterised by isolated and tiny farms and cottages, with low standards of living. These north-western coastlands lie on the remotest fringes of Europe and illustrate both the worst extremes of the Atlantic mountain environment and some of the most marginal economic conditions in the whole of the Common Market.

The South and East

The southern and eastern parts of Eire, including particularly the Limerick–Shannon lowland, the south coast from Cork to Wexford, and the East Central Plain centred upon Dublin, have a kinder physical environment and a greater accessibility to the United Kingdom and the rest of Europe. About 90 per cent of the East Central Plain is improved farmland. The generally humid atmosphere encourages a thick growth of grass on limy glacial drift soils. Dairy farming and market gardening exist around Dublin to supply the large urban market, but beef cattle are of the greatest importance. Live cattle, both store and fatstock, are exported. To the south-west the region merges into the dairy farming zone of Limerick and the Golden Vale. The southern coastlands around Waterford and Wexford have the sunniest climate in Ireland and the proportions of arable land are relatively high, rising to one-third of the total farmland on the Wexford plain. The Wexford plain is known as 'The Garden of Ireland' with fertile soils based on weathered sands, clays and marls supporting crops of oats, barley, potatoes, wheat and sugar beet. Cork, with its outport Cobh, is a port of call for transatlantic liners. It has good rail links with Dublin, has an excellent ria harbour, and is the second largest town in Eire. It has a considerable manufacturing base with a small steelworks, vehicle assembly, agricultural machinery, rubber, clothing and footwear, and food processing of various types.

The growth of Dublin in particular has been a feature of the last 40 years. Although a small city by British standards, Dublin and its outport Dun Laoghaire have increased their share of the country's total population to 25 per cent. The city is six times as populous as the next largest town, Cork; it accounts for half the total industrial output, and employs over two-fifths of the total industrial labour force of Eire. Its industries include engineering, clothing, footwear, meat canning and bacon processing, brewing, distilling, biscuits and jam, tobacco, and fertilisers. Dun Laoghaire is the principal passenger port of Eire. Dublin port and city dominates the external trade and economy of Eire to an increasing extent. Consideration must therefore be given to the steadily increasing imbalance between the western underdeveloped region on the one hand, and the richer south and east on the other.

The western underdeveloped region

Although the whole of Eire qualifies for aid under the EEC Regional Policy, the western part of the country is markedly poorer, economically marginal and more isolated than the east. Its dependence upon subsistence agriculture is such that purchasing power is often minimal. Average income per head is a useful indication of the differences. In 1970 in Dublin it was £517, in the west generally £324, and in Donegal only £305 (in the UK it was over £900). These are highly significant figures when placed into the context of the EEC, and are underlined by the pattern of emigration. The marked reduction in emigration from the country as a whole masks the inter-state differences. From 1966 to 1971 the average yearly net loss of people from Dublin and the east was less than 1 per 1000, whilst the west and northwest lost 10 per 1000. The single most pressing regional problem is the maintenance of a viable population in western Eire.

In 1949 the Irish Development Authority (IDA) was established with two important principles: (1) the encouragement of industrial investment (particularly for export-oriented industries) by means of incentives; (2) the ending of restrictions on foreign ownership of Irish companies. From 1960 to 1973 foreign capital investment rose dramatically to total £257 millions, with the creation of 53000 new jobs. The problem was that much of this investment continued to go into the south-east and Dublin area.

The Underdeveloped Areas Act 1952 designated the 'Western Underdeveloped Region' (fig. 18.2). It comprises 12 out of the 26 counties of the Republic, and includes one-third of the total population. Industries established within the region are eligible for a higher rate of aid than in the rest of the country. Aid falls into four groups: capital grants of up to two-thirds; long-term loans at favourable interest rates; tax relief of 20 per cent on buildings; and grants towards the training of workers. There is also the Shannon Free Airport scheme within the region, which operates under much the same advantages and in which companies producing for export markets can import and export without customs duties. The launching of the 'Small Industries Act' of 1969 is another attempt to assist the modernisation and enlargement of many existing

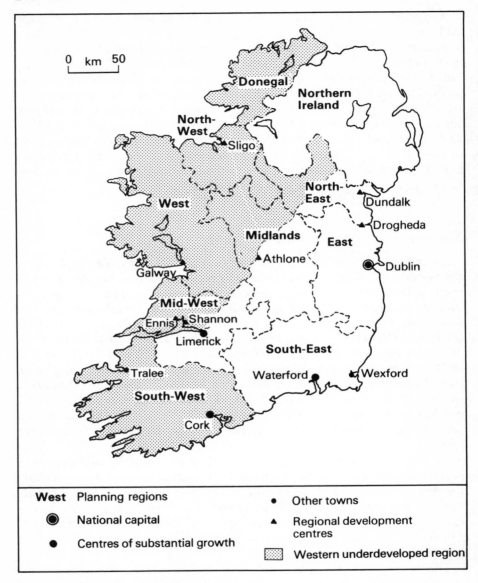

Figure 18.2 Eire: planning regions and regional development areas. (From Buchanan, 1968)

local craft industries scattered throughout the small towns in the west: the Irish linen industry is an example.

In 1968 Professor Colin Buchanan recommended to the Irish Government the strengthening of the urban hierarchy by means of the designation of regional development centres (fig. 18.2). The IDA has taken up its basic theme, and progress is being made to attract investment initially into the three large regional centres of Cork, Waterford and Wexford, which have an existing industrial base. Perhaps more significant are the' projects established in areas which are still losing population. Two examples of textile factories are Snia Viscosa (Italian) in Sligo and Courtaulds in Donegal. The lower wage levels and the reserve of under-employed female labour are two significant factors. Most industry is associated either with the agricultural processing section (such as milk-processing and fertilisers) or else is classed as 'footloose', covering a wide range of light industries and consumer products which range from bathroom scales at Sligo to ball-bearings at Tralee.

The Mid-west regional plan

The Mid-west comprises the counties of Clare, Limerick and part of Tipperary, 265000 people in all. The regional plan focuses upon the proposed growth zone of Limerick–Ennis–Shannon. It is the development of the Shannon Industrial Estate since the 1960s which has provided the basis for the country's third largest industrial concentration after Dublin and Cork. The Airport Act of 1947 established Shannon as the first customs-free airport in the world. The Airport Development Authority promotes use of the airport for freight handling, warehousing, and the industrial estate, and operates the financial and fiscal incentives referred to previously. Factories can be rented or purchased, and now over 4000 men are employed by 30 companies. This industrial estate produces 30 per cent of Eire's manufactured export goods. There is a wide variety of light and

Shannon Airport, with the adjoining industrial estate.

specialised products, predominantly high value in relation to weight and readily adaptable to air transport. The most important single type is electrical and electronic equipment. Shannon Industrial Estate has provided a singularly successful growth point in western Eire and population has already stabilised around Limerick and Ennis.

19

The Paris Region:
a problem of definition

What is the Paris region?

The Paris region poses an important problem, that of definition. What is the
Paris region? Is it the city of Paris, the Paris agglomeration with over 8 million
people, the Region Parisienne which includes three départements and extends up
to sixty miles away from the city, or the Paris Basin planning unit? (fig. 19.1).

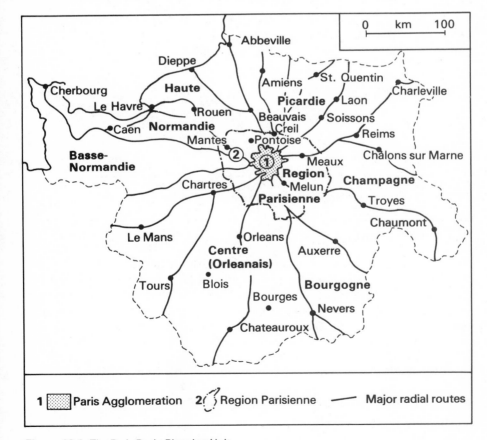

Figure 19.1 The Paris Basin Planning Unit.

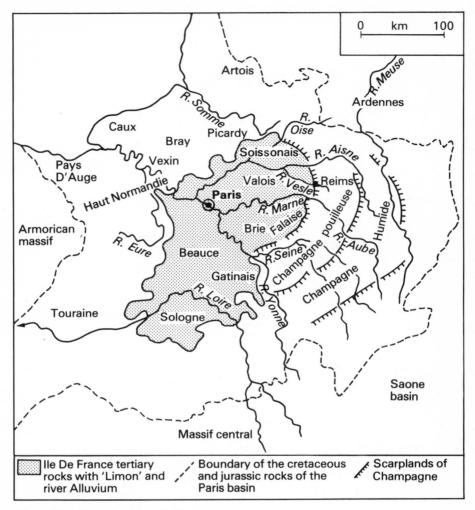

Figure 19.2 Pays of the Paris Basin.

Alternatively, is the traditional view of the Paris Basin more important, in which the convergence of the Seine and its tributaries is seen as the centre of a key agricultural lowland extending from the Loire to Normandy and from the Champagne scarplands to Picardie (fig. 19.2)? This problem of definition may be analysed in two themes which stress the economic value of the area in different ways: the scale and variety of agricultural production on the fertile 'pays' of the Paris Basin; the centralising power of the city in attracting population and resources, and the planning problems which this has involved.

Agricultural production in the pays of the Paris Basin

The land-use diversity of the Paris Basin depends essentially upon geological differences (fig. 19.2). The four essential elements are:

1. The Ile de France. This is the central area of limestones, clays and sandstones overlain by the superficial deposits of limon and alluvium and divided into separate 'pays' by the tributaries of the Seine.
2. The scarplands of Champagne and Bourgogne to the east and south-east.
3. The chalk plateau of Artois and Picardie to the north.
4. Haute Normandie. The chalk plateau and lowlands of the Lower Seine.

The Ile de France

The Ile de France is typified by the limestone *plateau of Beauce*, which has a thick covering of porous limon and a lower water-table than most other parts of northern France and, most important, is almost entirely flat. The outstanding feature is the nearly complete utilisation of the land for agriculture: in many areas cereals occupy 80 to 90 per cent of the land. Beauce is the foremost wheat-growing area of France, but barley and maize often parallel it in importance, maize in particular having grown in popularity recently because of easy mechanised harvesting, thus helping to solve labour shortages. The uniform relief has helped efficiency and mechanisation, and farms are large with consolidated holdings and large expanses of fields in a prairie-type landscape. Settlement is concentrated in large villages, because of the relative shortage of water supplies in limestone areas, and there is therefore nucleation around a few wet points.

A significant contrast is provided by *le Pays de Brie* which lies between the rivers Seine and Marne, south-east of Paris. Here the limestone contains bands of clay near the surface and lies on impervious marls, and therefore there is abundant surface water, and the water table is much higher than in Beauce. In former times, Brie was forested and marshy, and even now there is abundant woodland and a more varied land-use. Agriculture has a more mixed character, cereals comprising often a third, and permanent pasture another third of the agricultural land. Fodder crops are important, with rotation pasture and sugar beet cultivated as cash crop and fodder, as cattle and sheep provide much of the income. Brie cheese and butter are the two significant products. The smaller average size of farm and greater dispersal of settlement is more typical of dairy-farming country. Hamlets and isolated farms are common. The contrasts between these two 'pays' of the Ile de France are almost absolute.

The Champagne Scarplands

To the east and south-east of Brie lie the succession of chalk scarps and clay vales which are essentially formed by the south-east facing escarpments of the Falaise, the 'Champagne Pouilleuse' and the 'Champagne Humide'. The variety of landscape is compounded by the river gaps of the Seine, Yonne, Aube, Marne, Vesle and Aisne which cut large embayments through the scarps.

The Tertiary scarp, known as the Falaise de l'Ile de France, stretches from the Oise to the Seine but is best known in the region of Reims and Epernay for the vineyards of the Champagne wine district. There is a conjunction of physical factors. The chalk scarp has a generous covering of loam which promotes both drainage and aeration; the marginal climatic conditions are modified by the south-east facing scarp which gives maximum insolation, and the slope which provides frost drainage; chalk bedrock reflects light on to the plants and allows warmth to penetrate the soil. The survival and prosperity of viticulture in these marginal climatic conditions, however, is largely due to human factors. The medieval trade fairs, the commercial acumen of the Bishoprics of Reims and Châlons-sur-Marne, expertise in blending, and specialisation in sparkling wines, has given the wines of Champagne an international reputation. There is also considerable capital needed to sustain the blending processes, manufacturing, storage, and maturing. This was provided originally by the Benedictine Abbey of Hautvilliers, and now by the 'Maisons de Champagne', an association of manufacturing firms, including Pommery, Heidseck, Clicquot, Bollinger, in and around Reims and Epernay. It is the marginal nature of the area climatically, resulting in many poor years, which favours the large producer who can carry large stocks. This tends to maintain the system whereby 80 per cent of champagne is produced by the four large companies. The actual farm-holdings are, however, small. There are over 16 thousand small-holding vine growers, and about 90 per cent have farms of two hectares and below. The 'Maisons de Champagne' buy most of their grapes from these small tenant farmers.

La Champagne Pouilleuse (dry champagne) succeeds the Tertiary scarp, and is a landscape of thin chalk without limon, with consequently little surface vegetation. It carries a poor quality grassland with outcrops of chalk and traditionally was devoted to sheep rearing, with some cereals and large areas of fallow. The area had a history of depopulation, a low population density, and a general air of sterility, with long distances between villages. It was an almost empty land. In the last fifty years this pattern, under new attitudes and values, has become a valuable agricultural resources, as it provided a large under-used reserve of land for food production. Large-scale remembrement and a uniform open landscape has created large farms ideal for mechanised grain farming, and extensive use of fertilisers gives very profitable farming. There is a mixed farming system, with cereals, sugar beet, potatoes, fodder and root crops, and lucerne. Cattle are kept, giving dairy products for the Paris market. The landscape, still with a deserted appearance, now looks more like a prairie scene, with infrequent villages and wheatfields stretching into the distance. The N 44 road between Châlons-sur-Maine and Reims gives a typical view of this landscape.

The dry chalk country, terminated by a second scarpline, is followed by the Champagne Humide. This is lower cretaceous sand and clay, akin to the sub-scarp Wealden and Gault country of southern England, and is comparable in landscape and economy. Woodland and pasture, interspersed with orchards, produce a dairy farming economy, of which the most typical is the Marne valley from Vitry-le François to Chaumont. A 'bocage' landscape, well watered and with many villages and hamlets and isolated farms, is the norm.

The chalk plateau of Artois and Picardie

North of the river Oise, the chalk plain of Picardie, with its thick cover of limon, rises gradually across the Somme valley to the outer rim of the chalk plateau in Artois, which reaches 120 metres OD. Arable farming with cereals, sugar beet, potatoes and fodder crops is the rule. Farms of over 50 hectares, highly mechanised, rationalised by remembrement, and with open fields stretching to the horizon, repeat the picture of large-scale agriculture. Again, however, there is considerable variation with several 'pays': the Bas Boulonnais near Boulogne has jurassic clays providing good pasture for cattle and horse rearing; between Arras and Cambrai is an intensive rotation system with the highest crop yields of anywhere in Northern France; the Somme valley, often marshy, is devoted to pasture, with market gardening around Amiens.

Haute Normandie

This comprises the western side of the chalk rim of the Paris Basin, the undulating limon-covered plateau being the dominant feature, with cereal farming on medium to large, efficient farms, especially in the Pays de Caux. Further east, in Vexin, there are greater concentrations of sugar beet, barley for brewing, and other industrial crops. Near Caen is the Pays D'Auge, which is bocage country, with dairy products, including the famous Livarot and Camembert cheeses. The exposure of clays and marls in the anticline of Bray and in the valley of the Eure have led to a major development of dairy farming and orchards producing cider apples and Norman Calvados.

The preceding description of the principal 'Pays' is intended to illustrate the traditional picture of the Paris Basin as the 'Granary of Europe', with the dominance of cereals and other arable crops directly attributable to vast tracts of fertile sediments overlain by limon. It is the most advanced agricultural province in France, favoured by the physical environment and also by proximity to the industrial and urban populations of Paris and Northern France. This has stimulated food production. Movement off the land towards the urban centres has also stimulated an early and greater mechanisation, making the area one of the most efficient farming regions in France. Thus the Paris Basin has a much lower density of population and larger farms than other parts of France, providing a marked contrast to the French peasant of the 'Midi' or Brittany on his smaller and fragmented farm holding. There is a concentration of croplands, particularly cereals, north of the Loire. This is the 'intensive grain core' extending from Beauce to Artois. At the same time the widely different 'Pays' landscapes have provided a great range of farm products. The Paris Basin has both scale and variety.

The growth of the Paris agglomeration

Figures 19.1 and 19.3 illustrate the central position of Paris as the centre of French communications, and the relatively small size of cities in close proximity and within the traditionally defined Paris Basin. Paris has always been very much the undisputed capital city of France, the administrative, service, industrial, and cultural centre of the country. The reason for this has largely been the traditional administrative centralisation of French life, both under the monarchy and the republic. In 1970 there were 8·7 million people in Greater Paris, over eight times as great as Lyon, Marseilles, or Lille, its greatest rivals. There is continuing and increasing movement of population into Paris, and this may be analysed in two ways, firstly, the components of the region in terms of population migration, and secondly, the employment characteristics of the city.

Regional centre	Population (approximations 1972)
Rouen	370000
Le Havre	250000
Tours	202000
Reims	168000
Orleans	168000
Le Mans	166000
Caen	152000
Amiens	137000
Troyes	114000
Cherbourg	79000
Bourges	76000
St. Quentin	70000
Charleville	64000
Chartres	59000
Châlons-sur-Marne	56000
Chateauroux	55000
Nevers	55000
Beauvais	50000

Figure 19.3 Populations of regional centres in the Paris Basin. (From I. B. Thompson)

Area	Population change due to migration (%)
Paris City	−10·2
Inner suburbs	
north	+ 3·3
east	+ 1·7
south	+ 4·1
west	− 1·5
Outer suburban ring (Banlieu)	
Seine et Marne	+10·7
Yvelines	+17·3
Essonne	+33·5
Val De Oise	+19·7
Outlying towns (Region Parisienne)	
Mantes	+28·5
Creil	+29·2
Melun	+19·8

Figure 19.4 Population change in Paris and its Region due to migration (1962–1968). (From I. B. Thompson)

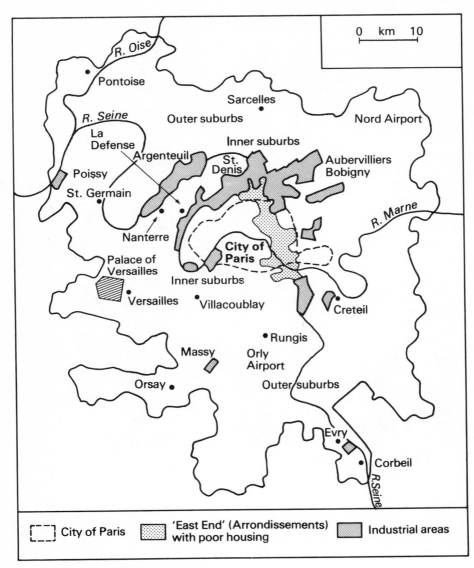

Figure 19.5 The Paris agglomeration (Banlieu). (From I. B. Thompson)

The inner city and suburbs

The Paris agglomeration consists of the city and its inner and outer suburbs. Here are most of the industrial zones (fig. 19.5) including St. Denis and Aubervilliers–Bobigny in the north, and the banks of the Seine around Argenteuil, which together constitute the northern arc of nineteenth century industrialisation. Figure 19.4 illustrates population migration, and the fact that the inner, older and more continuously built-up suburbs are losing population at a con-

Paris, showing the northern inner industrial suburbs along the Seine, and looking south- wards towards the redevelopment complex of Nanterre.

siderable rate. The outer suburbs are experiencing dramatic rates of increase. These outer suburbs constitute the residential zone which is less continuously built up. They also include high density apartment complexes such as Sarcelles (fig. 19.5), decentralised industry in new estates such as Poissy and near Orly airport at Massy, Rungis and Creteil, and the development of public service areas such as the Rungis Food Market, Orly airport and the new Paris Nord airport. Finally, there is expansion along the major routeways, which has incorporated many previously independent settlements such as Versailles, Pontoise, St. Germain and Evry-Corbeil. Population growth in these outer suburbs known as 'Paris Banlieue' has been phenomenal, but exists in a world-wide context. This is the withdrawal of population from city centres (the volcano effect) and the problem of the lower density sprawl which takes up valuable land on the edge of the city.

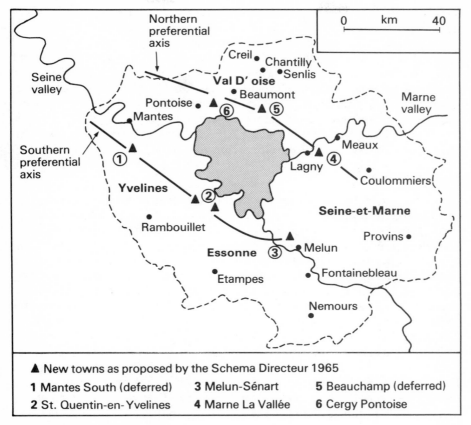

▲ New towns as proposed by the Schema Directeur 1965

1 Mantes South (deferred) **3** Melun-Sénart **5** Beauchamp (deferred)
2 St. Quentin-en-Yvelines **4** Marne La Vallée **6** Cergy Pontoise

Figure 19.6 Region Parisiènne, with outlying towns and new towns along the preferential axes.

The Region Parisienne

The Region Parisienne (fig. 19.6) includes a number of départements adjacent to Paris which are closely linked to the life of the city in terms of employment and pressure upon land. There are still separate, but fast-expanding, medium-sized towns surrounded by agricultural land and large areas of woodland, forest, and protected areas, particularly the Forest of Fontainebleau to the south, Rambouillet on the south-west and Chantilly to the north. The area acts as an open lung for the city, a safety valve, where expansion will be directed along carefully planned lines and channels. The migration and growth rates of Mantes, Creil and Melun (fig. 19.4) are indicative of the dramatic growth of this commuter zone or 'home region'.

The Paris Basin planning unit

This is related to the traditional physical and agricultural unit comprising principally the historic provinces of Champagne, Picardie, Normandy and

Orleans (fig. 19.1). From the nineteenth century onwards the effect of Paris has been felt in an adverse way in the small farming communities and villages of these provinces and the drainage of manpower and resources to the capital from what has been termed the 'Desert Français' has continued to the present day. The urban centres in the Paris Basin such as Reims and Orleans are medium-sized cities and towns which act as natural centres for the agricultural 'pays', but they are considerably smaller than would normally be expected. They have existed under the shadow of Paris for a very long period. There is therefore, a lack of equilibrium within the Paris Basin Planning Unit between the city of Paris and the major regional centres.

Paris as a node

The economic and social consequences of this polarity is shown by the employment characteristics. The Paris agglomeration had over eight million people in 1968 (18 per cent of the French population) and employed 21 per cent of the French labour force, with over four million workers. Its near monopoly in specialised functions and skilled labour is even more significant: it has 72 per cent of French research workers; 48 per cent of the total of qualified engineers; and 40 per cent of all professional and managerial grades. Paris produced 56 per cent of the output of the aircraft industry, 80 per cent of French cars, and about 70 per cent of all precision, electronic, radio and television products. The service sector is even more significant, the city having a virtual monopoly of banking, insurance and company head offices. The large consumer market, pool of skilled labour, and commercial and financial institutions have given Paris technologically advanced industries with a high growth potential, and income levels well above the national average. This economic strength is matched by an equivalent concentration of educational provision, artistic and cultural activity, which gives the city a power and relative importance in French life which is unequalled anywhere else in Europe.

Congestion

The cost to Paris is congestion. The transport system has to cope with three million daily commuters, of which only about 35 per cent travel by private car, and for these the main problem is parking. This seems strange when considering the famous wide boulevards of Haussmann (1853–70) but these have to cope with dense traffic flows, and kerbside parking is therefore banned where possible. Some 15 per cent of the commuters travel short distances by foot, and about 50 per cent rely upon public transport. The major problem here is that the Metro, the underground system, is not as extensive as that of London, and only goes as far as the inner suburban ring, at which point commuters travelling to the Seine–Banlieue area have to transfer to the municipal bus service, thus throwing extra strain on the system.

Housing problems

Housing in inner Paris is badly overcrowded. The eleventh arrondissement, as late as 1961, had 29 per cent of its houses without water, 67 per cent without personal toilet facilities, and 90 per cent without bath or shower. The problem is worse in the east end arc of the city, from Montmartre in the north through Temple, Le Marais, Popincourt and Bastille to the Gare De Lyon. The problem is one of redevelopment of the inner areas maintaining adequate residential facilities and planned expansion of the surburban zone with new residential foci, balanced industrial employment and recreation facilities, and adequate road systems.

Planning for Paris and its Region

The long-term strategy for planning was begun by the PADOG proposals in 1961, followed by the master plan, the Schema Directeur in 1965. The essentials of the plan are to reinvigorate the central areas of the city, to create planned growth in the lower Seine valley from Paris to Le Havre, and to plan for balanced development in the Paris Basin as a whole with the strengthening of the regional centres such as Orleans and Reims. The main aspects of the plan are as follows:

(a) The 'La Defense' redevelopment scheme will create a new inner suburban node with commercial, cultural, administrative and public buildings, adjacent to the University of Nanterre. The purpose of this is to establish a centre

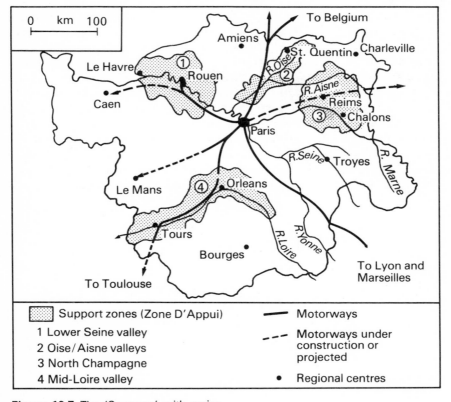

Figure 19.7 The 'Couronne' with major cities and support zones.

to the west of the existing central area of Paris. There are similar plans for Villacoublay, Rungis and Creteil to the south, and St. Denis and Bobigny to the north (fig. 19.4). The strategy here is to reinvigorate the inner suburban zones and to counterbalance the magnetism of the city centre.

(b) In addition to the Metro system, a new fast suburban railway 'The Reseau Express Regional' will link a major east–west line with two north–south lines (connecting Orly with Paris Nord Airport); and three ring motorways— the Boulevard Periphique, the Rocade De Banlieue at 15 kilometres out, and the Autoroute Interurbaine De Seine at Oise at 20 kilometres—will link with the radiating motorways out of the city.

(c) On the assumption of continued growth, the scheme estimated that the future population of Paris would rise to 14 million people, and must be decentralised, not as in the case of London. with a green belt and new towns beyond, but along two preferred axis, north and south of the river Seine (fig. 19.6). This axial pattern of growth will preserve the open land along the Seine, and provides for six new towns with populations of up to 130 000 along the lines of movement at Mantes, St. Quentin, and Melun-Senart on the south; Cergy-Pontoise, Beauchamp, and Marne La Vallée on the northern axis.

(d) The 'Couronne' is a ring of historic towns and cities at up to 200 km distance from Paris (fig. 19.7). These cities such as Amiens, Chartres, and Reims lie on the major radial routeways and at key points in the agricultural 'Pays'. In future planning, four areas have been designated as 'support zones' (zones d'appui), major new revitalised centres, with the nine regional centres of over 100 000 people expanded where necessary.

(e) The most important single area with tremendous growth possibilities is the Lower Seine (Rouen–Le Havre) axis. This is a major line of movement of railways, waterways, pipelines and motorways. There are deep water access and port facilities at Le Havre including oil refineries and terminals, and the area also includes the two largest existing urban centres outside Paris itself— Le Havre (250 000), the second port of France, and Rouen (370 000). This axis is to be developed as a strategic growth corridor from Paris to the coast.

20

Conclusion:
1945 to 1977

In Western Europe since 1945 there have been three distinct phases of development, all of which indicate a close relationship between economic geography and political factors. Immediately after 1945 there occurred the period of post-war reconstruction during which industry was revived in devastated areas such as the Ruhr, and whole transport systems, for example French railways, were completely rebuilt. This was a period of general economic recovery, and with the help of massive loans from the United States such as Marshall Aid, the basic industrial wealth of Western Europe was rebuilt. This was carried out in the presence of a general feeling by both governments and population, that there was a need for political and social, as well as economic, reconstruction. With the threat of Russian domination, there was a movement to unite into larger groups, more powerful and protective than the traditional nation state. In the sphere of defence, NATO was a reflection of this need.

The 1950s and 1960 were a period of fruition. Economic growth was widespread, substantial and sustained, with many countries achieving an average yearly rate of over 4 per cent. Europe's raw materials, particularly oil, were cheap, and the terms of trade lay heavily in favour of the industrialised countries. Agricultural production grew so that food supplies were more than adequate, leading eventually to the periodic food surpluses which have been such a feature of the contemporary scene. This widespread economic wealth and confidence was accompanied by rapid progress towards the formation of political institutions and policies which were to lead to a measure of integration in continental Western Europe. The European Community of the 'Six', later enlarged to nine member states, was formed by the fusion of the three institutions, the ECSC, Euratom and the EEC. The customs union and the removal of trade barriers has been accompanied by substantial levels of harmonisation of the economies of the member states. These include the integration of the iron and steel industries of the Rhinelands, regulation and adaptation of the declining coal industries, the operation of common agricultural policy, the construction of the Euro-route system, regulations for fair industrial competition, and investment aid from such agencies as the European Investment Bank.

During the 1970s the position has changed dramatically. The oil price rises of 1973–4 and the boom in other commodity prices have completely altered the terms of trade, and have been major causes of the inflation, loss of confidence and industrial recession of the mid-1970s. Economic growth in West Germany has been severely curtailed, and in Great Britain and Italy it has been completely eliminated. The British Steel Corporation is an example of an industry which has been working at 20 per cent below capacity for a number of years.

The cost of energy has become a major problem. The decline in the coal industries during the 1960s was largely due to imported supplies of relatively cheap oil. Now that coal is more or less competitive with oil, the EEC is faced with a number of alternatives: to end its dependence upon imported oil from politically unstable sources; to enter a period of energy conservation; greater utilisation of home energy resources; research into new non-fossil sources of energy. Great Britain is probably in the best long-term position, having large coal reserves as well as oil and natural gas. West Germany has large reserves of coal and The Netherlands of natural gas. French negotiations for reciprocal trade agreements with the Arab nations, and her nuclear and solar energy projects, are a reflection of her difficult position with few indigenous energy sources of any size. The recurrent crises in Italy during the early 1970s have been a direct result of the enormous financial burden imposed by imported oil, 85 per cent of her total energy requirement. The Community has a long-term project for producing energy by nuclear fusion (Joint European Torus or JET), but the project is not yet established because of national differences of opinion over its site. The lack of a coherent energy policy probably reflects the very divergent positions, requirements and priorities of the member states.

Another serious problem is economic divergence both at a national and regional level. Not only has West Germany become the most economically powerful state in the Community, whilst Italy and the United Kingdom have faced successive economic crises, but on a European scale the central regions of the Community have grown at the expense of the periphery. In a sense this is the result of the free market policies of fair competition pursued during the early years of the EEC. In conditions of normal competition, the natural advantages of the Rhineland axis, with its dense population, economic resources and high levels of mobility, would have emerged in any case. The success of the EEC in lowering tariff barriers, the ECSC in restructuring the coal and steel industry of the Heavy Industrial Triangle, the effect of the CAP in favouring the efficient food producers of the Paris Basin and the Netherlands, and the construction of motorway linkages between Belgium, the Netherlands, north-eastern France and the Rhinelands, have all accentuated these advantages. The very success of the Common Market has been to create a natural economic core region which is in stark contrast to some of the peripheral regions such as the Mezzogiorno, south-western France, Eire and northern Britain.

Community policy-making has gradually changed to take account of this fact. Sectoral policies such as the ECSC and the CAP have increasingly been supplemented by policies and funds which have as their aim the strengthening of the peripheral regions. The EIB is intended to aid underdeveloped regions, and by 1971 the proportion of its funds devoted to regional development schemes had reached 91 per cent of the total. The European Social Fund in 1976 devoted some three-quarters of its total aid quotas to the regions, with Italy receiving 50 per cent of the overall amount. The Regional Development Fund is specifically designed to aid regions to regain competitiveness. The imbalance between the interdependent core areas and those regions needing development or restructuring must be corrected if further progress towards economic and monetary union is to be made.

The economic problems of the 1970s have been a considerable factor in the reorientation of the Community towards other avenues of integration. In many ways the change of direction dates from the accession in 1973 of the three new member states—Great Britain, Eire and Denmark. The enlargement of the Community to nine has given encouragement to other potential members like Greece, and possibly Spain and Portugal. If the accession of these three southern European states were to take place, the centre of gravity of the Community might alter from its present position in north-west Europe towards the Mediterranean area.

However, the Community needs a period of internal improvement and structural consolidation rather than territorial expansion. Quite apart from the need to radically change the CAP and to make effective the Regional Policy, there are many other economic aspects requiring positive policies. These include energy, research and technology, aerospace and telecommunications, transport and the environment. A major structural improvement which is likely to occupy the Community during the late 1970s is the change in the composition of the European Parliament. The direct elections planned for 1978 will give the Community a new democratic base and political impetus. The parliamentarians will have a more effective mandate from the population and will be able to exercise greater control over the budget funds and economic policies, thus playing a large part in the political consolidation of the Community.

Meanwhile, the Community has already made a significant change of direction from internal policies to external affairs. The rapid growth in trade and aid to developing countries is reflected in the Lomé Convention signed with forty-seven developing countries. Trade agreements have also been concluded with many Mediterranean and North African countries, including Israel and the 'Maghreb' countries of Algeria, Tunisia and Morocco. The Mediterranean is rapidly becoming part of the Community's economic sphere of interest. It is a major supplier of primary products and, lying as it does on the southern flank of the Community, is clearly an area of strategic interest to Western Europe. The intense activity during 1976–7 on fishing limits and the hurried construction, largely at the insistence of Great Britain and Eire, of a common fisheries policy with 200-mile limits, has effectively given the Community *de facto* jurisdiction over a territorial waters zone which covers much of the continental shelf. The Community is beginning to speak with one voice in many fields of external policy. The negotiations with the Russians and Iceland over fishing rights, the energy conferences, the Conference on International Economic Co-operation (the North–South dialogue), the Law of the Sea Conference and the World Food Council are examples of the first tentative steps by which the European Community is emerging as a political entity on the international scene.

Appendix

Key dates in European integration

1946

September 19 Winston Churchill, in Zurich, urges Franco-German re-
conciliation within 'a kind of United States of Europe'.

1947

October 29 Creation of Benelux—economic union of Belgium, Luxembourg and the Netherlands.

1951

April 18 The Treaty setting up the European Coal and Steel Community (ECSC) is signed in Paris.

1953

February 10 ECSC common market for coal, iron-ore, and scrap is
opened.

May 1 Opening of the ECSC common market for steel.

1957

March 25 Signature of the Rome Treaties setting up the Common
Market and Euratom.

1959

January 1 First tariff reductions and quota enlargements in the Common Market.

1961

July 18 The six Community countries issue Bonn Declaration aiming at political union.

November 8 Negotiations with Britain open in Brussels.

1962

January 14	Community fixes basic features of common agricultural policy.

1963

January 14	President de Gaulle declares that Britain is not ready for Community membership. British negotiations broken off.
January 22	Franco-German Treaty of Cooperation signed in Paris.

1964

June 1	Yaoundé Convention with 18 African countries (ex-colonies) as associated states, comes into operation.

1965

March 31	Commission proposes that, as from 1st July 1967, all Community countries' import duties and levies be paid into Community budget and that powers of European Parliament be increased.
July 1	Council fails to reach agreement by deadline fixed on financing common farm policy; French boycott of Community Institutions begins seven-month crisis.

1966

January	Crisis resolved by the Luxembourg Accords.
May 11	Council agrees that on 1st July, all tariffs on trade between the member states shall be removed and that the common external tariff shall come into effect, thus completing the Community's customs union.

1967

May 10–11	Britain, Ireland and Denmark submit formal applications for membership of the Community.
July 1	Merger of Community executives—ECSC High Authority and EEC and Euratom Commissions.
November 27	General de Gaulle, in a press conference, objects to UK entry.

1968

July 1	Customs union completed 18 months ahead of schedule; Common Agricultural Policy also complete.
July 18–19	Six adopt basic regulations for common transport policy.
July 28	Single market introduced for dairy and beef products.
July 29	Six decide to remove last remaining restrictions on free movement of workers.

December 10	Commission Vice-President Sicco Mansholt announces 'Agriculture 1980', Commissions radical ten-year plan to reform farming in the Six.

1969

April 28	President de Gaulle resigns; succeeded in July by Georges Pompidou.
December 1–2	Heads of government of the Six, meeting at the Hague, agree to complete, enlarge and strengthen the Community.
December 19–22	Marathon Council session agrees on permanent arrangements for financing the common farm policy, providing the Community with its own resources from 1978 and strengthening the European Parliament's budgetary powers.

1970

March 4	Commission submits a three-stage plan for full monetary and economic union by 1980.
June 30	Membership negotiations open in Luxembourg between the Six and Britain, Denmark, Ireland and Norway.
November 19	Foreign ministers of the Six meet for the first time in Munich to concert their views on foreign policy.

1971

February 1	Common fisheries policy takes effect.
March 24	Six take first steps to carry out Mansholt Plan to modernise farming.
July 8	United Kingdom Government white paper recommending EEC entry issued upon successful completion of negotiations.

1972

January 22	The Treaty of Accession signed by the United Kingdom, Eire, Norway and Denmark (Norway later withdraws).
March	The 'Snake' (alignment of member states currencies) introduced.
October 19	First Summit meeting of heads of state in Paris. The summit meetings become part of the Community structure and are known as the 'European Council'.

1973

January 1	The EEC is formally enlarged to nine members.
December	Copenhagen Summit meeting.

1974

January	Oil crisis. Oil price quadrupled in three months.
December	Paris summit. Agreement to set up a Regional Development Fund.

1975

March	Regional Development Fund in operation.
March	European 'Unit of account' (UA), to be used in the 'Snake' to relate each national currency to the others.
May	Lomé Convention signed by the EEC with 47 developing countries.
June 5	Referendum in the United Kingdom shows a two-thirds majority of remaining a member of the EEC.

1976

January	Tindemans Report on Economic and Political Union.
February	The Council of Ministers recommends that Greece be admitted to the Community over a phased period.

1977

January	The 'new' EEC Commission takes office for a four-year period, headed by Mr Roy Jenkins of the United Kingdom.

Glossary

1. **Federalism.** A more rapid approach to integration by which supra-national political institutions are superimposed over national authorities.

2. **Footloose Industry.** Manufacturing industry which is not based upon resource constraints such as coalfields, but which has the ability to choose a wide range of locations.

3. **Functionalism.** The step-by-step approach to integration, through agreements in economic sectors such as agriculture, tariffs, transport, etc.

4. **Geographical inertia.** The tendency of older industrial regions to survive by the contraction and adaptation of old, heavy industries, and by the development of new light industry.

5. **Gross Domestic Product (GDP).** The total value of goods and services produced inside the country.

6. **Kennedy Round.** A major agreement in 1967 on tariff reductions amongst the industrial nations.

7. **Marshall Aid.** The aid and investment programme for the recovery of Europe provided by the United States after 1945 and named after its initiator, General Marshall.

8. **The 'Original Six' or 'EEC Six'.** Belgium, The Netherlands, Luxembourg, West Germany, France and Italy.

9. **PADOG.** Plan d'Aménagement et d'Organisation Générale.

10. **Remembrement.** The French policy of rationalisation and enlargement of land-holdings to create a more efficient farming system.

11. **Unit of Account (UA).** The monetary unit of account used in pricing agricultural commodities and in the Community budget.

12. **'Von Thunen Landscape'.** An idealised series of concentric agricultural zones around a city in which the most specialised farming is nearest the city market followed by less intensive farming types farther out.

References

General references and chapter 1

Atlas of Europe. Bartholomew-Warne, 1974.

Broad, R. and Jarrett, R. H. *Community Europe Today*. O. Wolff, 1972.

Burtenshaw, D. *Economic Geography of West Germany*. Macmillan, 1974.

Charnley, A. H. *The E.E.C. A Study in Applied Economics*. Ginn, 1973.

Clout, H. D. *The Geography of Post-War France*. Pergamon, 1972.

De La Mahotiere, S. *Towards One Europe*. Pelican, 1970.

Dickinson, R. E. *Germany*. Methuen, 1953.

Dury, G. H. *The British Isles*, 5th Ed. Heinemann, 1973.

Elkins, T. H. *Germany*, 2nd Ed. Chatto and Windus, 1968.

Farr, W. (Editor). *Guide to the Common Market*. Collins, 1972.

Harrison Church, R. J. *et al*. *Advanced Geography of Northern and Western Europe*. Hulton, 1973.

Hene, D. H. *Decision on Europe*. Jordan, 1970.

Monkhouse, F. J. *The Countries of North-West Europe*. Longmans, 1974.

Monkhouse, F. J. *A Regional Geography of Western Europe*. Longmans, 1974.

Open University Course Team. *The European Economic Community*. Open University Press, 1974.

> Unit 1–2   History and Institutions
> Unit 3–4   National and International Impact
> Unit 5–6   Economics and Agriculture
> Unit 7–8   Work and Home

Oxford Regional Economic Atlas. Western Europe. Oxford University Press, 1971.

Parker, G. *The Logic of Unity*, 2nd Ed. Longmans, 1975.

Pounds, N. J. G. *The Economic Pattern of Modern Germany*, 2nd Ed. Murray, 1966.

Scargill, D. I. *Economic Geography of France*. Macmillan, 1972.

Shackleton, M. R. *Europe*, 7th Ed. Longmans, 1974.

Statistical Office of the Communities. *Basic Statistics of the Community*. 1971–72; 1973–74; 1975–6.

Swann, D. *The Economics of the Common Market*, 3rd Ed. Penguin, 1975.

Thompson, I. B. *Modern France*. Butterworth, 1970.

Walker. D. S. *A Geography of Italy*, 2nd Ed. Methuen, 1967.

Walsh, A. E. and Paxton, J. *The Structure and Development of the Common Market*. Hutchinson, 1968.

Wreford Watson, J. and Sissons, J. B. (Editors). *The British Isles*. Nelson, 1964.

Chapter 2—Energy

Ball, N. R. Oil and natural gas prospects in the Celtic Sea. *Geography*. January 1973.

Clout, H. Nord coal miners prepare for 1983. *Geographical Magazine*. March 1972.

Economist Intelligence Unit. *Prospects for Energy in the Seventies and Beyond*. February 1973.

ECSC High Authority. *Europe and Energy*. Luxembourg. 1967.

EEC Commission. *Energy and Europe*. November 1972.

EEC Commission. *Medium-term Guidelines for Coal 1975–1985*. November 1974.

Energy in the EEC. *European Studies*, No. **5**. 1969; No. **18**. 1974.

Gas Council. *Natural Gas from the North Sea*. August 1967.

Manners, G. 1970s Power Game. *Geographical Magazine*. March 1970.

Neilson, J. Europe's Energy. *European Community*. March 1973.

Odell, P. Europe sits on its own energy. *Geographical Magazine*. March 1974.

Odell, P. New economic map of Europe. *Geographical Magazine*. September 1975.

Perry, N. Recent developments in the West German oil industry. *Geography*. November 1967.

Riley, R. C. Recent developments in the Belgian Borinage. *Geography*. July 1965.

Rowe and Pitman. *Oil in the Main: The North Sea '72*. August 1972.

Scargill, D. I. Energy in France. *Geography*. April 1973.

Sinclair, D. J. Coal in Europe. *Geographical Magazine*. June 1969.

Sinclair, D. J. Integration with the Six. *Geographical Magazine*. October 1971.

Statistical Office of the European Communities. *Energy Statistics*. 1969–72.

Chapter 3—Industry: Location and Structure

Carter, H. The location of industry in the city, in *The Study of Urban Geography*, 2nd Ed. Arnold, 1975.

Clout, H. Nord coal-miners prepare for 1983. *Geographical Magazine*. March 1972.

Clout, H. Economic change in Belgian Limburg. *Geography*. April 1974.

De La Mahotiere, S. *Towards One Europe*. Pelican, 1970.

Industrial policy and the EEC. *European Community*. April 1972.

Keeble, D. The proper place for industry. *Geographical Magazine*. August 1969.

Martin, J. E. *Greater London: An Industrial Geography*. Bell, 1966.

Martin, J. E. Industrial employment and investment in a frontier region: The Franco-German example. *Geography*. January 1973.

Paterson, J. H. *Land, Work and Resources*. Arnold, 1973.

Public enterprises in Britain and the European Community. *European Studies*, No. **12**. 1971.

Statistical Office of the European Communities. *Industrial Statistics*. 1973.

Thompson, I. B. A geographical appraisal of recent trends in the Coal Basin of Northern France. *Geography*. July 1965.

The Times Review of Industry. *Times 1000*. 1973.

Tuppen, J. N. Fos—Europoort of the South? *Geography*. July 1975.

Varying technical standards. *European Community*. June 1969.

Chapter 4—The Steel Industry

Bolter, H. The future of steel in England. *British Steel*. Autumn 1975.

Burtenshaw, D. *Economic Geography of West Germany* (Chapter 5). Macmillan, 1974.

Ferry, J. French steel enters a new phase. *British Steel*. June 1971.

Fleming, D. K. Coastal steelworks in the Common Market countries. *Geographical Review*. January 1967.

Lambert, A. M. Dutch steelmaking. *Geography*. July 1971.

Pounds, N. J. G. *The Geography of Iron and Steel*, 5th Ed. Hutchinson, 1971.

Sinclair, D. J. Steel in Europe. *Geographical Magazine*. May 1969.

Statistical Office of the European Communities. *Iron and Steel Statistics*. 1973–4.

Steel in the Nine. *Supplement to British Steel*. 1973.

Warren, K. The changing steel industry of the European Common Market. *Economic Geography*. October 1967.

Chapter 5—Vehicles, Textiles and Chemicals

Charnley, P. H. *The EEC: A Study in Applied Economics* (Chapter 3). Ginn, 1973.

The chemical industry in the European Community and the United Kingdom. *European Studies*, No. **5**. 1969.

The motor industry in the European Community and Britain. *European Studies*, No. **3**. 1969.

The textile industry in Britain and the EEC. *European Studies*, No. **11**. 1971.

Chapter 6—Agriculture

Agriculture in France. French Embassy Information Service.

Berendt, M. Soaring food prices: is Brussels to blame? *European Community*. May 1973.

Clout, H. *European Agriculture since 1945*. Macmillan, 1971.

EEC Commission. *The Agricultural Situation in the European Economic Community*. 1972/3/4 Report. EEC Commission Publications, Luxembourg.

EEC Commission. *The Common Agricultural Policy*. June 1973.

FAO. *World Review of Agriculture*. 1970 et seq.

Farming in the Common Market. *European Studies*, No. **5**. 1969.

Farming Facts: The New Common Market. Barclays Bank Ltd., Autumn 1972.

Franklin, G. H. *The European Peasantry: the Final Phase*. Methuen. 1969.
The future of European agriculture. *European Community*. October 1973.
Lambert, A. M. Farm consolidation in Western Europe. *Geography*. January 1963.
Sinclair, D. J. Danish bacon in the balance. *Geographical Magazine*. July 1971.
Statistical Office of the European Communities. *Yearbook of Agricultural Statistics*. 1973.
Trow-Smith, R. *Life from the Land: The Growth of Farming in Western Europe*. Longmans, 1967.
Van Valkenburg, S. Land-use within the European Common Market. *Economic Geography*. January 1959.
UK, Ireland, Denmark apply Common Food Policy. *European Community*. March 1973.

Chapter 7—Trade

The Associated Countries and their Development. *European Studies*, **13**. 1972.
The European Community and the Developing Countries. *European Studies*, **5**. 1969.
The European Economic Community. *Barclays Bank Economic Review*. March 1972.
External Trade Statistics. 1967/73. *Monthly Bulletin of Statistics. Department of Trade and Industry*.
Foreign Trade of the European Community 1958–1971. *European Studies*, **1**. 1968.
The Kennedy Round. *European Studies*, **3**. 1969.
Statistical Office of the European Communities. *Foreign Trade: Analytical Tables*. 1960–1973.
Statistical Office of the European Communities. *Basic Statistics of the Community*. 1973–74.

Chapter 8—Transport

Bird, J. H. Seaports and the European Economic Community. *Geographical Journal*. September 1967.
Birley, T. M. Nürnberg to become a port. *Geographical Magazine*. April 1970.
Despicht, N. S. *The Common Transport Policy of the European Communities*. PEP. London 1969.
French Embassy Information Service. *Development of the Rhône*.
French Embassy Information Service. *Transport in France*.
French Embassy Information Service. *Inland Navigation in France*.
Highways to the Sun. *European Community*. July 1967.
Jones, I. E. The development of the Rhône. *Geography*. November 1969.
North Sea ports of the European Community and Britain. *European Studies*, No. **3**. 1969.
The Rhine and the EEC. *European Studies*, No. **2**. 1968.
Rotterdam: changing tides. *Tanker and Bulk Carrier*. April 1974.
Schofield, G. The canalisation of the Moselle. *Geography*. April 1965.

Sinclair, D. J. Trade patterns on the Rhine Waterway. *Geographical Magazine.* August 1970.
Statistical Office of the European Communities. *Transport Yearbook.* 1971 *et seq.*
Transport in Europe. *Times/Le Monde Special Supplement.* 25 October 1972.
Transport in the Six and Britain. *European Studies*, No. 7. 1970.

Chapter 9—Population

Clarke, J. I. Demographic revival in France. *Geography.* July 1963.
Clout, H. French population growth 1962–68. *Geography*, No. **56**. 1971.
Clout, H. *The Massif Central.* Oxford University Press, 1973.
Elkins, T. H. *The Urban Explosion.* Macmillan, 1973.
The European Community, the United Kingdom and World Population trends. *European Studies*, **11**. 1971.
Kosinski, L. *The Population of Europe.* Longmans, 1970.
The Population of the European Community. *European Studies*, 1, 1969.
Statistical Office of the European Communities. *Basic Statistics of the Community.* 1973/74.
The Urban Phenomenon in Europe (1). *European Studies*, **10**. 1970.
The Urban Phenomenon in Europe (2). *European Studies*, **12**. 1971.

Chapter 10—Regional Disparities

Allen, K. and McClennan, M. C. *Regional Problems and Policies in Italy and France.* Allen and Unwin, 1970.
Annual Reports of the European Investment Bank. Luxembourg.
Borschette, A. A fair share for all regions: flexible approach to Regional Policy. *European Community.* October 1971.
Clark, C., Wilson, F. and Bradley, J. Industrial locations and economic potential in Western Europe. *Regional Studies.* No. **3**. 1969.
Clout, H. Industrial relocation in France. *Geography.* January 1970.
EEC Commission. *Regional Development in the Community (Analytical Survey).* Luxembourg. 1971.
EEC Commission. *Report on the Regional Problems in the Enlarged Community. COM (73) 550.* Brussels, May 1973.
EEC Commission. *First Annual Report on the European Regional Development Fund.* June 1976.
The European Investment Bank. *European Communities Commentary.* October 1973.
Europe's peripheral regions. *European Studies.* **13**. 1972.
Kormoss, I. B. F. *Les Communautés Européenes: Essai d'une Carte de Densité de Population.* Les Cahiers De Bruges, 1959.
Regional policy in the European Community. *European Studies*, **10**. 1970.
Robinson, K. W. Three nations in search of Utopia. *Geographical Magazine.* November 1971.
Sinclair, D. J. European twilight zones. *Geographical Magazine.* April 1970.

Sinclair. D. J. The EEC plans to feed her poor. *Geographical Magazine*. September 1973.
Statistical Office of the European Communities. *Basic Statistics of the Community*. 1973/74.
Statistical Office of the European Communities. *Regional Statistics*. 1972, 1974.

Chapter 11 — North-Rhine Westphalia

Barr, J. Planning for the Ruhr. *Geographical Magazine*. January 1970.
Burtenshaw, D. Regional Planning in the Ruhr. *Town and Country Planning*. May 1974.
Elkins, T. H. Life on the European Growth Axis. *Geographical Magazine*. March 1972.
Hall, P. *World Cities* (Chapter 5 Rhine–Ruhr). Weidenfield and Nicholson, 1966.
Hellen, J. A. *North-Rhine Westphalia*. Oxford University Press, 1975.
Perry, N. Planning problems and structural change in the Ruhr. *Regional Studies, Association Conference*. March 1968.
Pounds, N. J. G. *The Ruhr*. Faber, 1952.
Retraining workers in the Ruhr. *European Community*. May 1970.

Chapter 12 — Three City Regions

Dickinson, R. E. *Germany* (Chapter 21). Methuen, 1961.
Elkins, T. H. *Germany*. Chatto and Windus, 1968.
Gutkind, E. A. *Urban Development in Central Europe*, Vol. 1. Collier Macmillan, 1964.
Knowles, R. and Stowe, P. *Europe in Maps*, Book II, No. **14**. Longmans, 1971.
Mutton, A. F. *Central Europe*, 2nd Ed. Longmans, 1968.
West Germany. *Times Supplement*. 10 June 1974.
Yates, E. M. The development of the Rhine. *Transactions of the Institute of British Geographers*, June 1963.

Chapter 13 — Belgium

Clout, H. *The Franco-Belgian Border Region*. Oxford University Press, 1975.
Dark and light in the Borinage. *European Community*. September 1973.
Economic Problems in Belgium's Wallonia. *European Studies*, **11**. 1971.
Elkins. T. H. Liège and the problems of southern Belgium. *Geography*, April 1956.
Knowles, R. and Stowe, P. *Europe in Maps*, Book II (No. **6**, Liège). Longman, 1971.
Riley, R. C. Recent developments in the Belgian Borinage. *Geography*. July 1965.
Stevenson, G. Cultural regionalism and the Unitary State idea in Belgium. *Geographical Review*. October 1972.

Chapter 14—Randstad Holland

Burke, L. *Greenheart Metropolis*. Macmillan, 1966.

Coghill, I. G. *Western Europe*, Chapter 2. F. Warne, 1970.

Hall, P. *The World Cities* (Chapter 4). Weidenfeld and Nicholson, 1972.

Information Service, The Hague. *The Randstad: the Urbanised Zone of the Netherlands*. March 1970.

Lawrence, G. R. P. *Randstad Holland*. Oxford University Press, 1973.

Vandenberg, M. *Monument of an era:* Rotterdam, Europe's oil port. *Architects Journal*. March 1974.

Ministry of Housing and Physical Planning. *Summary of the Report on Urbanisation in Netherlands*. February 1976.

Rotterdam, changing tides. *Tanker and Bulk Carrier*. April 1974.

Chapter 15—Denmark

Bunting, B. T. The present reorganisation of agriculture in Denmark. *Geography*. April 1968.

Collected papers: Denmark. *Twentieth International Geographical Union Congress (Copenhagen University, Geographical Institute)*. 1964.

Guidebook to Denmark. *Nineteenth International Geographical Union Congress (Copenhagen University, Geographical Institute)*. 1964.

Knowles, R. and Stowe, P. *Europe in Maps*, Book I. (No. **4**). Longmans, 1969.

Sinclair, D. J. Danish bacon in the balance. *Geographical Magazine*. July 1971.

Somme, A. (Editor) *A Geography of Norden*. Heinemann, 1961.

Chapter 16—Piedmont, Lombardy and Liguria

Cole, J. P. *Italy*. Chatto and Windus, 1964.

Italy. *Economist*. 14 March 1967.

Lutz, V. *Italy, A Study in Economic Development*. Oxford University Press, 1962.

Rodgers, A. The industrial geography of the port of Genoa. *University of Chicago. Research Paper*, No. **66**. 1960.

Walker, D. *A Geography of Italy*. Methuen, 1967.

Chapter 17—The Mezzogiorno

Coghill, I. G. *Western Europe* (Chapter 7). F. Warne, 1970.

The Mezzogiorno. *Town and Country Planning*. June 1974.

Mountjoy, A. B. Planning and industrial developments in Apulia. *Geography*. November 1966.

Mountjoy, A. B. Planning and industrial developments in eastern Sicily. *Geography*. November 1970.

Mountjoy, A. B. Pressures and progress in southern Italy. *Geographical Magazine*. November 1970.

Mountjoy, A. B. *The Mezzogiorno*. Oxford University Press, 1973.

Smith, C. D. Mezzogiorno in perspective. *Geographical Magazine*. July 1970.

Chapter 18—Eire

Buchanan, C. *Irish Regional Studies*. Dublin, 1968.
Europe's Peripheral Regions. *European Studies*. No. **13**. 1972.
Offshore Ireland. *The Economist*. 25 January 1975.
Recent industrial development in Ireland. *Geography*. November 1967.
D.342. Regional Imbalance (p. 12, Southern Ireland). Open University Press,
Sinclair, D. J. Europe's developing country. *Geographical Magazine*. May 1971.

Chapter 19—The Paris Region

Abraham, L. Changing face of Paris. *Geographical Magazine*. February 1968.
Coghill, I. G. *Western Europe* (Chapter 6). F. Warne, 1970.
French Embassy Information Service. *Planning and Development of the Paris
    Region*.
Hall, P. *The World Cities* (Chapter 3). Weidenfeld and Nicolson, 1966.
Knowles R. and Stowe, P. *Europe in Maps*, Book II. No. **8**. Longmans, 1971.
Thompson, I. B. *The Paris Basin*. Oxford University Press, 1973.

Index